Milton among the
Philosophers

Milton among the Philosophers

Poetry and Materialism in Seventeenth-Century England

Stephen M. Fallon

Cornell University Press
Ithaca and London

Copyright © 1991 by Cornell University

All rights reserved. Except for brief quotations in a review, this book, or
parts thereof, must not be reproduced in any form without permission in
writing from the publisher. For information, address Cornell University
Press, 124 Roberts Place, Ithaca, New York 14850.

International Standard Book Number 0–8014–2495–X
Library of Congress Catalog Card Number 90–55729
Printed in the United States of America
*Librarians: Library of Congress cataloging information
appears on the last page of the book.*

First Published 1991 by Cornell University Press
First printing, Cornell paperbacks, 2007
ISBN 978-0-8014-7367-8 (paperback)

For
Nancy Hungarland Fallon,
Associate Sole

Stranger: So much, then, for those who give an exact account of what is real or unreal. We have not gone through them all, but let this suffice. Now we must turn to look at those who put the matter in a different way, so that, from a complete review of all, we may see that reality is just as hard to define as unreality.

Theaetetus: We had better go on, then, to their position.

Stranger: What we shall see is something like a battle of gods and giants going on between them over their quarrel about reality.

Theaetetus: How so?

Stranger: One party is trying to drag everything down to earth out of heaven and the unseen, literally grasping rocks and trees in their hands, for they lay hold upon every stock and stone and strenuously affirm that real existence belongs only to that which can be handled and offers resistance to the touch. They define reality as the same thing as body, and as soon as one of the opposite party asserts that anything without a body is real, they are utterly contemptuous and will not listen to another word.

Theaetetus: The people you describe are certainly a formidable crew. I have met quite a number of them before now.

Stranger: Yes, and accordingly their adversaries are very wary in defending their position somewhere in the heights of the unseen, maintaining with all their force that true reality consists in certain intelligible and bodiless forms. In the clash of argument they shatter and pulverize those bodies which their opponents wield, and what those others allege to be true reality they call, not real being, but a sort of moving process of becoming. On this issue an interminable battle is always going on between the two camps.

—Plato, *Sophist* 245e–246c

Contents

Acknowledgments   *ix*

Introduction   *1*

1. Mechanical Life: Descartes, Hobbes,
   and the Implications of Mechanism   *19*

2. The Life of the Soul: The
   Cambridge Reaction   *50*

3. Material Life: Milton's
   Animist Materialism   *79*

4. Milton and Anne Conway   *111*

5. Milton's True Poem and the
   Substance of Epic Angels   *137*

6. Sin and Death: The Substance of
   Allegory   *168*

7. To Shadowy Types from Truth:
   Satan's Mechanist Descent   *194*

8. "After Another Method": Sacred
   War as Philosophical Battle   *223*

Epilogue   *244*

Index   *257*

Acknowledgments

"Say muse, . . . who first, who last." Robert J. Wickenheiser, my first Milton teacher, inspired a love for the poet that shows no signs of flagging. My greatest intellectual debt is to my last Milton teacher, William Kerrigan, who has watched over and guided my passage from student to colleague. Between first and last, Gordon Braden, Alastair Fowler, James Nohrnberg, and Thomas P. Roche, Jr., bountifully fed my appetite for news of the Renaissance and the seventeenth century.

My formal teachers are outnumbered by my informal ones. From our meeting in 1984 until his untimely death, Phillip Gallagher and I shared ideas, criticism, and friendship. Phil's characteristically stringent comments on my work in progress have made this a better book. For lively debate and invaluable criticism, I thank the members of the Newberry Milton Seminar, especially Achsah Guibbory, Norman Herstein, Helen Marlborough, Janel Mueller, and Stella Revard. It was my good fortune to meet John W. Yolton at a crucial juncture and to benefit from his constructive questions, sage advice, and moral support. I am grateful for the advice and encouragement of Owen Barfield and Craig Davis. David Loewenstein, Christia Mercer, Lynn Sumida Joy, and James Turner read and improved parts of the book. It is hard to measure the salutary effect of John Rumrich's critical response to the entire manuscript; many arguments are sharper thanks to his perceptive eye and his deep knowledge of Milton. The book has had the advantage of thoughtful and penetrating comments from the readers for the Press, Michael Lieb and Gordon Teskey.

For their contributions to my thinking and writing, I am grateful to many colleagues at Notre Dame, and in particular to Christopher Fox, Theresa Krier, Clark Power, and Phillip Sloan. I learn best by teaching, and my perceptive and demanding students have made sure that I have learned a lot. I owe a particular debt to my diligent and resourceful research assistants, Gerard Schiela, Christine Dombrowski, and John Ryan.

It has been a great pleasure working with everyone at Cornell University Press. One could not ask for a finer editor than the efficient and witty Bernhard Kendler. Managing Editor Kay Scheuer and copy editor Janice Feldstein showed me how to improve what I thought was a finished product.

The earliest version of this work was supported by a Charlotte Newcombe fellowship for 1984–85. Two summers of reading funded by Notre Dame's Institute for Scholarship in the Liberal Arts allowed me to expand and deepen my study. I completed my research and wrote the final version with the aid of a 1988–89 research fellowship from the National Endowment for the Humanities.

A version of Chapter 6 appeared in *English Literary Renaissance* 17 (1987): 329–50. A section of Chapter 3 is condensed from "The Metaphysics of Milton's Divorce Tracts," in *Politics, Poetics, and Hermeneutics in Milton's Prose*, ed. David A. Loewenstein and James Grantham Turner (Cambridge: Cambridge University Press, 1990). I am indebted to the editors for permission to reprint. I thank Cambridge University Press for permission to quote from *The Philosophical Writings of Descartes*, translated by John Cottingham, Robert Stoothoff, and Dugald Murdoch and published in two volumes in 1984 and 1985. Passages of Milton's poetry from *John Milton: Complete Poems and Major Prose*, ed. Merritt Y. Hughes, are reprinted with the permission of Macmillan Publishing Company. Copyright © 1985 by Macmillan Publishing Company. Copyright 1957 by The Odyssey Press, Inc. If not otherwise noted, passages are taken from *Paradise Lost.* Milton's prose is cited from *The Complete Prose Works of John Milton,* ed. Don M. Wolfe et al., 8 vols. (New Haven: Yale University Press, 1953–82), with the Latin text further located in *The Works of John Milton,* ed. F. A. Patterson et al., 20 vols. (New York: Columbia University Press, 1931–40). The Yale edition is cited in the text as *CP;* the Columbia edition is cited as *Works.*

My in-laws, Robert and Marilyn Hungarland, have been an appreciative, if partial, audience for my writing. My parents, William and Margaret Fallon, a partial audience if ever there was one, have taught me the value of hard work and the greater value of family. My greatest debt is acknowledged in the dedication; Nancy, who writes for general audiences, has been clarity's partisan in the war against jargon. Finally, our children, Sam, Claire, and Dan, have taught me the wonder and resilience of life.

STEPHEN M. FALLON

Notre Dame, Indiana

Milton among the Philosophers

Introduction

"Think only what concerns thee and thy being"—so Raphael admonishes Adam shortly before the fall in *Paradise Lost* (8.174). But what does concern Adam and his being? The immediate context of Raphael's charge, the lecture on "lowly wisdom" occasioned by Adam's speculative cosmological questions, suggests one answer: Adam is to keep his eyes on the ground, tend the plants rooted there, and not eat the apple with its fallacious promise of ascent. But in the epic's larger context, the command takes on a meaning unintended by the angel; while the epic deftly skirts cosmology, it directly confronts ontology—Adam is to look to the "ground" or substance of his being. Adam's "know thyself" involves an effort of metaphysical understanding as well as of will. It was into the mouth of Raphael, the apparent obscurantist of Book 8, that Milton put the most concise and beautiful expression of his animist materialism three books earlier (5.469–500). All that exists, from angels to earth, is composed of one living, corporeal substance. An understanding of this monism is necessary for Adam if he is to grasp his place in Milton's universe; the same understanding is necessary for us if we are to grasp much of the action of *Paradise Lost* as well as the poem's participation in a seminal debate in early modern thought.

This book will raise several questions about the philosophy incorporated in *Paradise Lost*. What led Milton to his unusual version of animist materialism? How does it relate to other metaphysical models in the mid-seventeenth century, a period fertile in such models? Why did Milton feel compelled to introduce his philosophy into his poetry? Are poetry and philosophy happily combined or "unhappily perplexed" in *Paradise Lost*?[1]

There is an initial improbability about asserting metaphysical concerns as central to Milton's career and to the genesis of *Paradise Lost*. Milton participated heartily in the seventeenth-century game of metaphysician-baiting.[2] As a student he referred to metaphysics as "this monkish disease" and "not an Art at all, but a sinister rock, a Lernian bog of fallacies" (*CP* 1:301). In 1642 he wrote with contempt of "metaphysical gargarisms" choking hapless students and in 1659 called for a system of divinity "without schoole terms and metaphysical notions" (*CP* 1:854; 7:304). Scattered throughout Milton's own system of divinity are attacks on metaphysical language.[3] Adam seems to be falling in with this attack on metaphysics in his response to Raphael's exhortation to lowly wisdom:

> apt the Mind or Fancy is to rove
> Uncheckt, and of her roving is no end;
> Till warn'd, or by experience taught, she learn
> That not to know at large of things remote
> From use, obscure and subtle, but to know
> That which before us lies in daily life,
> Is the prime Wisdom; what is more, is fume,
> Or emptiness, or fond impertinence.
>
> (8.188–95)

Metaphysics had come to be synonymous with the "obscure and subtle." Adam's final words echo Milton's evocative phrase

---

[1] The phrase is from Samuel Johnson's "Life of Milton," in *Johnson's Lives of the Poets: A Selection*, ed. J. P. Hardy (Oxford: Clarendon Press, 1971), p. 107.
[2] Tarred by association with scholastic wrangling, the term "metaphysical" became a byword for obscurity and meaningless speech. Bacon saves the term but assigns it to the study of the "forms," redefined as the mechanical laws governing the interaction of bodies (*New Organon* II, ii and ix). Hobbes repeatedly derided the tendency of metaphysicians to use "insignificant speech."
[3] See *CP* 6:262, 421, 580.

in *An Apology against a Pamphlet* (1642), "the pride of a *metaphysi-call* fume" (*CP* 1:933). But one must distinguish between the term "metaphysics" as a club to beat scholasticism and metaphysics as the inquiry into the nature of things. If Adam's "fume" echoes Milton's early condemnation of metaphysical language, his "prime Wisdom" echoes the "first philosophy" and "wisdom" of Aristotle's *Metaphysics*. Under its alternate name of "first philosophy," metaphysics concerned itself in the seventeenth century, as before, with the nature and existence of God, mind, and body and with the relationships between mind and body.[4] Milton's own idiosyncratic metaphysical model, developed most explicitly in his *Christian Doctrine*, and the rigorous adherence of narrative to that model in *Paradise Lost* are the clearest indications that the poet shared one of the central preoccupations of seventeenth-century philosophy: the question of substance.[5]

The theological and ethical stakes of the philosophical debates were so high that it would be surprising had Milton not followed them with interest. The new philosophies of the seventeenth century were feared by many as threats to the incorporeal soul and, by extension, to theism. Many observers thought that the sort of mechanism proposed by Descartes and others would lead to materialism and eventually to atheism. Hobbesian materialism and Spinoza's identification of God with nature were proof for many that the new philosophy was dangerous.[6] The philosophical foundations of freedom of the

---

[4]Descartes's original title for the *Meditations on First Philosophy* was the *Metaphysics*. That he did change the title illustrates the pejorative force of "metaphysics"; that he could change the title illustrates the interchangeability of these terms.

[5]For the centrality of the question of substance, see Louis E. Loeb, *From Descartes to Hume: Continental Metaphysics and the Development of Modern Philosophy* (Ithaca: Cornell University Press, 1981), pp. 76–110.

[6]Leibniz writes in 1669 that Bacon "has rightly said that casually sampled philosophy leads away from God but that drunk more deeply, it leads back to him. This is confirmed in our own century, which is fruitful alike of science and impiety. . . . It has become apparent that mechanical explanations . . . can be given for most of the things which the ancients referred only to the Creator or to some kind (I know not what) of incorporeal forms. The result was that truly capable men for the first time began to try to save or to explain natural phe-

will in particular were threatened by the growing authority of mechanist explanations of phenomena.[7] If, as Hobbes argued, all is matter in motion—even thought—then our choices are determined by antecedent physical motions, and freedom of the will is an illusion. Thus defenders of free will had to meet the challenge of the necessitarians on the ground of metaphysics. If certain metaphysical models obviated freedom of the will, then those models had to be refuted.

The threat to Christian conceptions of freedom and moral responsibility was clear to literary figures in the age immediately after Milton's, notably Swift and Pope.[8] We have reason to expect, then, that a strongly libertarian poet who developed an unusual metaphysical model in the mid-seventeenth century did so partly in response to contemporary philosophical debate. But Milton scholarship offers a chaotic list of sources and analogues for Milton's materialism. Marjorie Nicolson's articles linking Milton to Henry More and contrasting him with Hobbes offer only a half-truth, for in some ways Milton's metaphysics is closer to Hobbes's than More's. Denis Saurat traces Milton's monism to the *Zohar* and relates it to the theories of the cabbalist Robert Fludd, an older contemporary of Milton, but ignores less occult philosophers; while recent scholars have credited Saurat with recognizing Milton's monism, they have rejected most of the particulars of his argument. Otherwise, scholars have pointed to ancient and patristic sources. William Hunter suggests that Milton finds authority for his opinion in

---

nomena . . . without assuming God or taking him into their reasoning. . . . Unfortunately there are others who have gone even further and who now doubt the authority of the sacred scriptures . . . , thus bringing an unconcealed atheism into the world" (*The Confession of Nature against Atheists*, in *Leibniz: Philosophical Papers and Letters*, ed. Leroy E. Loemker [Dordrecht: Reidel, 1976], pp. 109–10).

[7]For the growing authority of mechanist philosophies in the seventeenth century, see E. J. Dijksterhuis, *The Mechanization of the World Picture* (Oxford: Clarendon Press, 1961).

[8]See Swift's "Mechanical Operation of the Spirit," which satirizes the mechanistic thrust of the new philosophies by associating it paradoxically with the *spirit* of the enthusiastic preachers, presented here as a gas. See also the *Dunciad*, in which Pope presents mechanism as leading to atheism and the discrediting of morality (4.469–76, 645–50).

Gregory of Nyssa. A.S.P. Woodhouse traces the exposition of Milton's monist ontology in the *Christian Doctrine* and for possible influences offers Eusebius, the Stoics, and, once again, Fludd. Harry F. Robins argues that Milton's ontology is influenced by Origen. J. H. Adamson points to the family resemblance between Milton's monism and the Christian *ex Deo* tradition, derived from Plotinus's cosmogony and finding expression in Gregory of Nyssa, pseudo-Dionysius, Scotus Erigena, Meister Eckhart, Nicholas of Cusa, and Jacob Boehme. Of recent attempts to trace early analogues to Milton's monism, the most interesting is that of John Peter Rumrich, who points to crucial similarities with the thought of Duns Scotus.[9]

I want to redirect attention to the contemporary context of Milton's monism. Whatever the parallels between Milton's thought and ancient and patristic texts, the contemporary metaphysical debate is the indispensable context of Milton's materialism.[10] Following Christopher Hill's advice that we consider the possibility that "Milton got his ideas not only from books but also by talking to his contemporaries," I am suggest-

---

[9]Marjorie Nicolson, "The Spirit World of Milton and More," *Studies in Philology* 22 (1925): 433–52, "Milton and Hobbes," *Studies in Philology* 23 (1926): 405–33, and "Milton and the Conjectura Cabbalistica," *Philological Quarterly* 6 (1927): 1–18; Denis Saurat, *Milton: Man and Thinker* (New York: Dial Press, 1925); William Hunter, "Milton's Materialistic Life Principle," *Journal of English and Germanic Philology* 45 (1946): 68–76 (in another article, "Eve's Demonic Dream," *ELH* 13 [1946]: 255–65, Hunter does draw parallels between Milton and the Cambridge Platonists, but in doing so he seems to disagree with the first article and ascribe to Milton a belief in separate incorporeal substance); A.S.P. Woodhouse, "Notes on Milton's Views on the Creation: The Initial Phases," *Philological Quarterly* 28 (1949): 211–36; Harry F. Robins, *If This Be Heresy: A Study of Milton and Origen*, Illinois Studies in Language and Literature, no. 51 (Urbana: University of Illinois Press, 1963); J. H. Adamson, "The Creation," in William B. Hunter, C. A. Patrides, and J. H. Adamson, *Bright Essence: Studies in Milton's Theology* (Salt Lake City: University of Utah Press, 1971), pp. 81–102; John Peter Rumrich, *Matter of Glory: A New Preface to "Paradise Lost"* (Pittsburgh: University of Pittsburgh Press, 1987), pp. 147–66.

[10]Maurice Mandelbaum has pointed to the "role . . . played in the thought of a person or of a period by a dominant philosophic issue which serves to incite and in large measure to control that thought," in "The History of Ideas, Intellectual History, and the History of Philosophy," *History and Theory: Studies in the Philosophy of History*, vol. 5: "The Historiography of Philosophy" (1965), p. 37.

ing that Milton came to view whatever he borrowed from the ancient philosophers and church fathers through the prism of contemporary debate.[11] Accordingly, the early chapters of this book reconstruct the philosophical context of Milton's materialism. My interest centers on the debate precipitated by the radical new philosophies of Descartes and Hobbes. This debate consumed the Cambridge Platonists Ralph Cudworth and Henry More and played a decisive role in the development of Milton's materialism.

Chapter 1 examines competing mechanist metaphysical models that would have been known to Milton, focusing on the mind-body problem. Here I present in some detail the views of Descartes, Hobbes, and Gassendi and trace the volatility of the debate over incorporeal substance to its implications for belief in God, immutable morality, the immortality of the soul, and the freedom of the will. In Chapter 2 I examine the reaction of the Cambridge Platonists. Although Milton has been compared with these thinkers, and particularly with Henry More, I demonstrate that the dualist response of the Cambridge Platonists to the challenge of mechanism differs essentially from Milton's. Chapter 3 explores Milton's monism. I highlight the materialism that sets Milton apart from the Cambridge Platonists and the vitalism that sets him apart from mechanists as widely divergent as Descartes and Hobbes. An analysis of Milton's prose points to the development of that monism during crucial years of metaphysical debate in England. Chapter 4 locates in the brilliant and quirky thought of Anne Conway, a student of Henry More who diverged radically from her teacher, the closest analogue to Milton's animist materialism. The relation of Milton's system to those of Descartes, Hobbes, Spinoza, and

[11]Christopher Hill, *Milton and the English Revolution* (New York: Viking, 1977), p. 5. In his illuminating discussion of Milton's monism, William Kerrigan recognizes the importance of the contemporary context of Milton's philosophy, noting that Milton "favored a marriage between the old humanism and the new empiricism, not a divorce" (*The Sacred Complex: On the Psychogenesis of "Paradise Lost"* [Cambridge: Harvard University Press, 1983], p. 195). Milton's use of ancient sources reflects seventeenth-century philosophical convention; most thinkers took ideas from several sources and traditions.

More can be extrapolated from Conway's discussion of these philosophers.

Chapter 5 tests the coherence between the sensuous poetry of angels in *Paradise Lost* and Milton's conception of spirit and matter. The rigorous ontological consistency of the spirit world of *Paradise Lost* is demonstrated by contrast with the confusion and ontological looseness of several contemporary long poems, including ones by the Fletchers, Peyton, Beaumont, Heywood, Benlowes, More, and Cowley. Thanks to Milton's materialism, angels, men, and devils share the stage in *Paradise Lost* without contradiction. Chapter 6 demonstrates that an apparent exception to the ontological integrity of Milton's epic, the allegory of Sin and Death, actually preserves it. With Augustine and Aquinas (and Descartes), Milton viewed evil as the privation of entity. He employs allegory to divide the ontologically deficient realm of evil from the realm of substantial creatures in his poem.

The final chapters explore ways in which *Paradise Lost* responds to the contemporary philosophical debate. Milton's strategy is to give Cartesian and above all Hobbesian ideas to the devils. The devils' sin finds a correlative in their descent toward the condition of Cartesian and Hobbesian man, as viewed by the philosophers' contemporary enemies. The devils take refuge from Milton's monism alternately in Cartesian and Hobbesian ontologies. Cartesian dualism fails them because it jars with the observable facts of Milton's monist universe. Hobbesian materialism is a more viable alternative; the devils can exist as Hobbesian materialists by migrating away from God toward the lower end of Milton's unbrokenly material continuum of being. There is an irony here, as my early chapters highlight connections between Milton and Hobbes. But it is precisely shared materialist assumptions that make possible the Hobbesian descent of the devils in Milton's universe. Chapter 8 interprets the War in Heaven as a battle between Milton's vitalist and Hobbes's mechanist monisms, a battle in which Milton grants his monism the victory it would never achieve outside the poem.

A fact and a prejudice have obscured the contemporary philosophical context of Milton's materialism. The obstacle of fact is easily removed. Nowhere in his works does Milton mention the philosophers with whom my study is concerned. But Milton was hesitant to mention any of his contemporaries, whether philosophical or not. Johnson traced this reticence to the poet's arrogance or egotism: Milton "considered his mention of a name as a security against the waste of time and a certain preservative from oblivion."[12] Moreover, Milton's failure to mention contemporary philosophers by name itself reflects the rhetorical practice of philosophers in the mid-seventeenth century, a practice traceable in part to the new philosophies' pretensions to originality. Cudworth's failure to name Hobbes in the course of a massive folio volume attacking Hobbes by implication and epithet ("a besotted atheistical philosopher") is a variation of this convention.

It is unimaginable that Milton was not familiar in general terms with the thought of the most notorious intellectual celebrity of his day, and the poet's widow in fact left testimony of his knowledge of Hobbes. According to John Aubrey, "His widow assures me that Mr. Hobbs was not one of his acquaintance; yet her husband did not like him at all: but he would grant him to be a man of great parts, a learned man. Their interests and tenets did run counter to each other. v. Mr Hobbes Behemoth."[13]

---

[12]Johnson, "Life of Milton," pp. 55–56. Milton mentions contemporary public figures and political writers in his polemical prose, but in the works in which he articulates his materialism, the *Christian Doctrine* and *Paradise Lost*, the case is different. The theological treatise, reflecting its genre, cites church fathers and theologians; the epic names only one contemporary, Galileo. One might think that traces of Milton's readings in contemporary philosophy would have been left in the Commonplace Book, but this document is a topically arranged record of Milton's reading in history, ethics, economics, and politics. As James Holly Hanford notes, it is "a rough guide to one large department of Milton's reading. It is to be observed that Milton does not record in the volume notes from works to which he must constantly have been referring" ("The Chronology of Milton's Private Studies," in Hanford's *John Milton: Poet and Humanist* [Cleveland: The Press of Western Reserve University, 1966], pp. 80–81).

[13]John Aubrey, "Minutes of the Life of Mr. John Milton," in *The Early Lives of Milton*, ed. Helen Darbishire (London: Constable, 1932), p. 7. Because Aubrey mentions *Behemoth*, Hobbes's work on the Civil War, it might appear that he has

And if we lack more direct testimony, Milton's silence on the philosophers should be set against his close friendship with several men keenly interested in philosophical questions. In the library of Dr. Nathan Paget, Milton could have read works by several authors to be discussed in this book, including Descartes, Hobbes, Gassendi, Kenelm Digby, and Walter Charleton.[14] John Dury, a friend of Milton from the 1640s on, apparently met and conversed with Descartes before 1635, well before the publication of Descartes's first book, *The Discourse on the Method*, in 1638. Samuel Hartlib, a mutual friend of Dury and Milton, relates a charming story of Dury valiantly and naïvely trying to help Descartes out of his foundational doubt: "Hee [Descartes] discoursed with Mr. Dury complaining of the uncertainties of all things, which Dur. refuteth by the truths and certainties of those reports in the Scripture and an infallible way of interpreting them which hee denied."[15] Given Dury's misapprehension of the nature and purpose of Descartes's doubt, it is difficult to credit the following story, but Hartlib in 1642 commended Dury for having set down a work on first

in mind only political differences. But the notes date from 1681, before the publication in 1682 of *Behemoth*; "behemoth" and "leviathan" are synonymous, and it is likely that Aubrey has *Leviathan* in mind.

[14]Milton was a close friend of Paget certainly by 1660 and probably as early as the 1640s. For Milton and Paget's library, see "Nathan Paget and His Library," in Hill, *Milton and the English Revolution*, pp. 492–95. A copy of the printed auction catalog of Paget's library can be found in the Library of the U. S. Surgeon General's Office (*Bibliotheca Medica Viri Clarissimi Nathanis Paget, M.D.* [London, 1681]). Among the books of interest for this study are Descartes's *Principles of Philosophy* and Hobbes's *De Homine* and *De Corpore*. As for the Cambridge Platonists, it is impossible that Milton could have read with his own eyes More's middle and late prose, and this late prose and Ralph Cudworth's *True Intellectual System of the Universe* were published too late to influence him. But the temporal discrepancies are negligible. Cudworth's ideas were worked out and current among his circle decades before they were published, and More's later works elaborate ideas developed by the early 1650s. Moreover, while it is likely that Milton followed the career of Henry More, whose stay at Christ's College overlapped with his own, I present More and Cudworth not as sources of Milton's thought, but as thinkers who, like Milton, responded to Hobbes's threat to free will with metaphysical systems of their own.

[15]Hartlib's *Ephemerides*, quoted in G. H. Turnbull, *Hartlib, Dury and Comenius: Gleanings from Hartlib's Papers* (Liverpool: University Press of Liverpool, 1947), p. 167.

principles in which Hartlib found all Descartes's principles, set out more clearly than by Descartes himself.[16] The widely traveled Dury was in London and thus available to Milton from 1646 to 1652. Hartlib, who persuaded Milton to write *Of Education*, persuaded Henry More to initiate his correspondence with Descartes.

Another friend of Milton's from the 1650s on to maintain an active interest in Continental metaphysics was Henry Oldenburg, a tireless worker whose voluminous correspondence served, like Mersenne's before his, as a clearinghouse of philosophical and scientific thought. In a famous letter to Oldenburg of September 1661, Spinoza lays out his position "first, that in the universe there cannot exist two substances without their differing entirely in essence; secondly, a substance cannot be produced, since to exist is of its essence; thirdly, every substance must be infinite, or supremely perfect in its kind."[17] We have no way of knowing whether or not Oldenburg showed Milton this letter, or if he did whether it influenced the final formulation of Milton's own monism, but such a letter from Spinoza to Milton's close friend at a time when Milton was moving toward the mature expression of his monism suggests that lines of indirect intercourse between Milton and philosophers were open.[18] In any event, it is far more probable that a person of Milton's learning and interests followed the contemporary debate over substance (at least in its general lines) through conversation and perhaps through having relevant texts read to him, than that he remained oblivious to it, especially as his own idiosyncratic materialism directly addresses the debate's central issues.

Even if Milton's silence on contemporary philosophy is ex-

---

[16]Ibid., p. 231.

[17]Baruch Spinoza, *The Ethics and Selected Letters*, trans. Samuel Shirley and ed. Seymour Feldman (Indianapolis: Hackett, 1982), p. 228.

[18]Richard Popkin has pointed recently to an indirect biographical link between Milton and Leibniz involving Oldenburg and Dury. Oldenburg seems to have been the one to give Milton his copy of Bodin's *Heptaplomeres*; Milton apparently sent his copy to Dury, from whose hands it made its way into Leibniz's. See "The Dispersion of Bodin's Dialogues in England, Holland, and Germany," *Journal of the History of Ideas* 49 (1988): 157–60.

plained and his friendship with men active in philosophical circles is pointed out, what of the widely shared prejudice that Milton is no philosopher? The author of the standard biography argues that "unlike Hobbes and Locke and others of his century, he developed no philosophical system to influence society in ages to come. . . . Let me say it plainly: Milton was simply not a profound or an original thinker."[19] Milton might not be a Descartes or Leibniz, but his decision to lay aside his plans for an epic of Great Britain and to write instead a creation epic addressing "the way things are" testifies to his interest in philosophy, if only as an inspired amateur. And the bold metaphysical speculation in *Paradise Lost* and the *Christian Doctrine* becomes more compelling and less quixotic when set in its contemporary context.

The impression that Milton's philosophy is negligible can be traced to the influence of the history of ideas method in Milton studies. It is time to exorcize the ghost of A. O. Lovejoy. Lovejoy is largely responsible for overcoming the disciplinary compartmentalization that obscured the connections between Milton and his nonliterary contemporaries, and his conception of "unit ideas" into which systems of thought can be analyzed has proved a powerful tool for uncovering significant parallels in otherwise disparate systems of thought.[20] But Lovejoy's belief that an individual thinker's originality lies in his or her selection from a slowly changing stock of unit ideas rather than in the invention of new ideas virtually ensures that he will focus on what is least original in the authors under study.[21] A related problem with Lovejoy's practice is the implicit assertion that recurrent ideas are in fact continuing ideas, that a manifestation of a unit-idea can be traced genetically to earlier manifestations of the same idea. Earlier manifestations of later

[19]William Riley Parker, *Milton: A Biography*, 2 vols. (Oxford: Clarendon Press, 1968), 1:641.
[20]For Lovejoy's important theoretical statements, see *The Great Chain of Being: A Study in the History of an Idea* (Cambridge: Harvard University Press, 1936), pp. 3–23; and "The Historiography of Ideas," in *Essays in the History of Ideas* (Baltimore: The Johns Hopkins University Press, 1948), pp. 1–13.
[21]See Mandelbaum, "History of Ideas, Intellectual History, and the History of Philosophy," p. 37.

ideas become, in Lovejoy's practice, *causes* of those ideas. We can be grateful for Lovejoy's warnings against the illusion that major figures continually reinvented the wheel, but we should be wary of an alternative danger, the illusion of a determinism of ideas guiding passive writers as they formulate their systems.

Another troublesome aspect of Lovejoy's theory, carried out with a vengeance in his practice, is the explicit subordination of literature to the history of philosophy; according to Lovejoy, "the ideas in serious reflective literature are, of course, in great part philosophical ideas in dilution—to change the figure, growths from seed scattered by great philosophic systems which themselves, perhaps, have ceased to be."[22] It is hard to say which is less defensible here: the assumption of a clear divide between literary and philosophical writing (begin with Plato and choose your own list of hybrids), or the assumption that the ideas of fictional texts are in every case derivative from the ideas of academic philosophy. Lovejoy's approach does not bode well for the poets. They are praiseworthy only to the extent that they body forth accepted philosophical systems and refrain from complicating matters with their own whimsies.

This view of the role of poets might explain Lovejoy's preoccupation and exasperation with Milton. He wrote an influential essay on the fortunate fall in *Paradise Lost*, peppered *The Great Chain of Being* with discussions of and allusions to Milton, and, revealingly, chose Milton studies as his prime disciplinary example in his essay "The Historiography of Ideas." Lovejoy's fascination with Milton mixes respect for his poetic powers with contempt for his thought. Milton, as a poet trying to be a philosopher, becomes "an interesting example of a mind beset by cross-currents"; Lovejoy can speak matter-of-factly of "the amazing superficiality of Milton's theodicy." Milton earns these harsh and unwarranted criticisms not only for his refusal to accept poetry's role as subservient to academic philosophy, but also for his getting things badly wrong from Lovejoy's perspective: Milton is "antipathetic to the principle of plenitude [and]

[22]Lovejoy, *Great Chain of Being*, pp. 16–17.

to that of sufficient reason," the two principles anchoring the great chain.[23]

Exasperated with Milton, Lovejoy turns to Alexander Pope as the model of a poet who knows his place. The phrase "great chain of being" itself is adapted from the "Vast chain of being" in Pope's *Essay on Man* (1.237), and quotations from that poem punctuate Lovejoy's discussion of the chain of being in the eighteenth century. Lovejoy's Pope decorously mouths the ideas of others ("Pope puts the same disparagement of man into four pungent lines . . . "; "Pope . . . translated these reflections into verse").[24] Lovejoy condescends to both Pope and Milton, but differently. If the idea of the chain of being was to become more than "merely the occasion for poetic rhapsodies such as [Pope's]," at least Pope had gotten the idea straight.[25] Pope makes no explicit or implicit claims for originality and thus does not complicate Lovejoy's conception of the "philo-

[23]Ibid., pp. 160, 212, 164. Marjorie Nicolson, who wrote her doctoral dissertation on plenitude and sufficient reason in Henry More under Lovejoy, imported Lovejoy's prejudices into the heart of Milton studies. Nicolson is more sympathetic to Milton than is her teacher, but the sympathy comes at a price: the domestication of Milton as a quasi-Cambridge Platonist. Nicolson's articles on Milton's relationship to Hobbes and More are skewed by the failure to emphasize Milton's crucial differences with More and intriguing similarities with Hobbes, and also by the Lovejoyan tendency to make the poet derivative from the philosopher. Despite intermittent rumblings of disagreement, Nicolson's articles are still influential over half a century after they appeared. Robert West associates Milton's thought with the Cambridge Platonists, whom he condescendingly titles "philosophasters" ("Milton as a Philosophical Poet," in *Th'Upright Heart and Pure*, ed. Amadeus P. Fiore, O. F. M. [Pittsburgh: Duquesne University Press, 1967], p. 139), and Samuel Mintz repeats the formula "All that Hobbes upheld, Milton opposed" ("The Motion of Thought: Intellectual and Philosophical Backgrounds," in *The Age of Milton: Backgrounds to Seventeenth-Century Literature*, ed. C. A. Patrides and Raymond B. Waddington [Manchester: Manchester University Press, 1980], p. 165). For counterclaims of parallels between Milton and Hobbes, see George Williamson, "Milton and the Mortalist Heresy" (1935), reprinted in *Seventeenth Century Contexts* (London: Faber and Faber, 1960), pp. 148–77, and Harold Fisch's introduction to his edition of Richard Overton's 1644 *Mans Mortalitie* (Liverpool: Liverpool University Press, 1968), p. xxiii.
[24]Lovejoy, *Great Chain of Being*, pp. 192, 196; in each example, the thinker behind the poem is Bolingbroke.
[25]Ibid., p. 61.

sophical" poet's role in the history of ideas: the packaging and popularization of the ideas of the philosopher.

This conception of the philosophical poet is itself rooted in seventeenth-century philosophical debate. Reacting against "metaphysical" language, many philosophers clamored for a language stripped of deceptive figures and metaphors. Hobbes argued that loose and metaphorical ways of speaking had fostered the illusion of incorporeal beings and insubstantial faculties. Thomas Sprat, in a celebrated passage in his *History of the Royal Society* (1667), objected to "specious *Tropes* and *Figures*" and "this vicious abundance of *Phrase*, this trick of *Metaphors*, this volubility of *Tongue*, which makes so great a noise in the world" and obscures the truth it is meant to reveal. The only cure for the disease of philosophic language is a turn away from the figurative and poetic, "a constant Resolution to reject all amplifications, digressions, and swellings of style; to return back to the primitive purity and shortness, when men deliver'd so many *things* almost in an equal number of *words*."[26] Two decades later Locke would join the chorus calling for the reformation of language in his *Essay concerning Human Understanding* (1689).[27]

The rhetoric of Hobbes, Sprat, and Locke suggests a stripping down of the language of philosophy to naked essentials, which would clear the way for poets to reclothe the truths revealed by philosophy in metaphors and figures. But the perceived need for this rhetoric points to the connections between poetry and philosophy in Milton's time. Pierre Bayle at the end of the seventeenth century illustrates the intercourse between poetry and philosophy in his article on the Greek poet Simonides, who was asked by Hiero, tyrant of Syracuse, for a definition of God. Like Milton's over two thousand years later, Simonides' search for an answer led him into speculation on

[26]Thomas Sprat, *The History of the Royal Society of London* (II, xxx), in *Critical Essays of the Seventeenth Century*, ed. J. E. Springarn, 3 vols. (Oxford: Clarendon, 1908–9), 2:117–18.
[27]See especially Book III, chaps. ix–xi: "Of the Imperfection of Words," "Of the Abuse of Words," and "Of the Remedies of the Foregoing Imperfections and Abuses."

corporeal and incorporeal substance and on the materiality and extension of God.[28] In the seventeenth century, philosophers employed in their writings not only incidental metaphors and figures, but also fictional modes of presentation. René Descartes claims the poet's prerogative to make a world in the *Discourse on the Method* and the *World*; when presenting his physical and cosmological views, he "decided to leave our world wholly for [the learned] to argue about, and to speak solely of what would happen in a new world. I therefore supposed that God now created, somewhere in imaginary spaces, enough matter to compose such a world."[29] Descartes is motivated by a desire to avoid the censure of the orthodox, for his mechanistic conception of the origin and working of the universe clashed with Genesis. But even as the fictional frame protects the author, the "clear and distinct" nature of the framed discussion tips his hand; the fiction is Descartes's truth. Descartes's strategy is located between the conventions of philosophical epic and familiar "nonfictional" philosophical discourse. Philosophy's counterfactual and poetry's fictional meet in the middle and authorize speculation.

Descartes illustrates the permeability of the border between philosophy and poetry (broadly conceived) in the seventeenth century. Working in the other direction, Milton, in setting out to write an epic of heaven, the world, and hell, committed himself to an expansion of Genesis and an exploration, in the tradition of Lucretius, of the way things are.[30] In the seventeenth century it was nearly impossible to separate consideration of Genesis from the questions raised by natural philoso-

---

[28]Pierre Bayle, *Historical and Critical Dictionary: Selections*, trans. Richard H. Popkin (Indianapolis: Bobbs-Merrill, 1965), pp. 272–87.

[29]René Descartes, *The Discourse on the Method*, V, in *The Philosophical Writings of Descartes*, trans. John Cottingham, Robert Stoothoff, and Dugald Murdoch, 2 vols. (Cambridge: Cambridge University Press, 1984–85), 1:132. This edition, cited hereafter as Cottingham, contains a running marginal notation to the standard original-language Adam and Tannery edition, against which all quotations from Descartes have been checked.

[30]In *De rerum natura* Lucretius adapts and rearticulates the atomistic philosophy of Epicurus, but he seems also to have expanded upon his Epicurean inheritance and included in his poem his own original speculations.

phy, and there is no reason to suppose that Milton wished to effect such a separation.[31] Milton's theological epic thus inevitably became a philosophical epic.

Coleridge testifies to the success of Milton's merging of art and thought when he says that in the "combination of poetry with doctrines" Milton surpassed Dante.[32] But this judgment brings us back to the question of originality. Lovejoy believed that poets combine poetry with doctrines, but was skeptical about poets' ability to be coherently original. That Milton's philosophical speculations are coherent and original is the argument of the middle chapters of this book. The theology of *Christian Doctrine* is indebted to many thinkers, ancient and modern, but Milton's synthesis is unique and uniquely heretical. It is hardly plausible that Milton, who argued that accepting religious doctrine on the testimony of others makes one "a heretick in the truth," would accept another man's natural philosophy, particularly as the natural philosophy of *Paradise Lost* is part and parcel of its theodicy (*CP* 2:543).

To appreciate the degree to which Milton's philosophical epic represents an original contribution to seventeenth-century debate, one must turn from the history of ideas to intellectual history and the history of philosophy. Richard Rorty offers a down-to-earth definition of intellectual history as "descriptions of what the intellectuals were up to at a given time, and of their interaction with the rest of society." With J. B. Schneewind and Quentin Skinner, Rorty acknowledges the immensity of the enterprise in a metaphor of a hypothetical thousand-volume *Intellectual History of Europe*.[33] The small section of the impossible, hypothetical project staked out in this book is a description

[31]For the interpenetration of theology and natural philosophy in Milton's time, see Richard S. Westfall, *Science and Religion in Seventeenth-Century England* (New Haven: Yale University Press, 1958), and Michael Hunter, *Science and Society in Restoration England* (Cambridge: Cambridge University Press, 1981). For the reciprocal implications of Genesis and natural philosophy, see Don Cameron Allen, *The Legend of Noah: Renaissance Rationalism in Art, Science, and Letters* (Urbana: University of Illinois Press, 1963).

[32]From his 1818 lecture "Donne, Dante, and Milton," excerpted in *The Romantics on Milton*, ed. Joseph Wittreich, Jr. (Cleveland: The Press of Case Western Reserve University, 1970), p. 234.

[33]Rorty, "The Historiography of Philosophy: Four Genres," in *Philosophy in History: Essays on the Historiography of Philosophy*, ed. Richard Rorty, J. B.

of what Milton and other intellectuals in the middle third of the seventeenth century were thinking about the nature of substance and what has come to be called the mind-body problem. While the book will touch on the relations between metaphysics and politics, it will not attempt to explore the interaction of its subjects "with the rest of society."[34] Dominick LaCapra suggests that "there is at present an excessive tendency to give priority to social or sociocultural approaches and to downgrade the importance of reading and interpreting complex texts." He also warns of a problem inherent in an intellectual history too dependent on social history: emphasis on ideas that have had a significant impact on their own time can lead us to ignore "aspects of the past that may have 'lost out.'"[35] Milton's monist contribution to the seventeenth-century metaphysical debate is a shining example of an idea that has "lost out." By the next century, Milton's animist materialism could appear to Samuel Johnson as a private preoccupation that should have been left out of an epic concerned with sacred truths, rather than an essential part of a Lucretian epic of creation.

If we want to understand Milton's monism, we must look beyond Johnson's eighteenth-century stone-kicking certainty. The more one looks at the unfolding of the seventeenth-century metaphysical debate, the less fantastic and quirky Milton's monism appears. Charles Taylor writes, "The idea that the only two viable alternatives might be Hobbes or Descartes is espoused by many, and is a perfectly comprehensible thesis even to those who passionately reject it. They feel its power, and the need to refute it. Such was not the situation in the 1640s."[36] Milton's monism was a solution to a question for which Hobbes's and Descartes's answers were not yet seen as

Schneewind, and Quentin Skinner (Cambridge: Cambridge University Press, 1984), p. 68; Rorty, Schneewind, and Skinner, "Introduction" to *Philosophy in History*, pp. 1–14.

[34]For an argument relating Milton's monism to the commodification of the subject associated with emergent capitalism, see Christopher Kendrick, *Milton: A Study in Ideology and Form* (New York: Methuen, 1986).

[35]Dominick LaCapra, *Rethinking Intellectual History: Texts, Contexts, Language* (Ithaca: Cornell University Press, 1983), pp. 66, 35.

[36]Charles Taylor, "Philosophy and Its History," in *Philosophy in History*, ed. Rorty et al., p. 21.

exhaustive. Milton himself is valuable to historians of philosophy as a vivid example of the applicability of Taylor's statement to metaphysical debate in Milton's England. Without an awareness of that debate we are left with a Milton whose monism is a product of isolated communion with dusty books, when in fact it is a response to an urgent philosophical debate, with free will hanging in the balance.

～1

Mechanical Life: Descartes, Hobbes, and the Implications of Mechanism

"From the concept of freedom, then, all idea of necessity must be removed" (*CP* 6.161). This sentence from the *Christian Doctrine* defines the central challenge facing Milton as he wrote his epic theodicy, *Paradise Lost*. Philosophical developments in the mid-seventeenth century were making that removal increasingly difficult. To make good on a program to remove necessity from will, one had to leave the confines of theology and engage the discourse of natural philosophy.

This observation, necessary in an era of specialization, would not have surprised Milton. For his contemporaries had a healthy disregard for what we think of as the boundaries between the disciplines. In this last age of the polymath and universal system builder, writers took for granted the interpenetration of philosophy and theology, science and politics. Science, or natural philosophy, was only then in the process of separating itself from what we call philosophy. And with the rise of mechanism in natural philosophy, questions we regard as the province of ethics and theology inevitably arose, questions concerning freedom of the will, moral responsibility, and the immortality of the soul. While some have looked to technological innovation as the chief social consequence of the scientific revolution of the seventeenth century, Michael Hunter finds this approach anachronistic: "For many, the most important social corollary of intellectual life was the way it informed conduct. It was widely believed that the fabric of society depended on a philosophical and theological consensus, and hence unorthodox viewpoints which seemed to undermine this and to encourage immoral attitudes were regarded with alarm."[1]

One such unorthodox viewpoint viewed with alarm was the revival of Epicurean atomism. The popular and incorrect picture of Epicurus as a libertine and hedonist owes nothing to what is known of Epicurus's life and everything to what were considered the implications of his teachings. Not only did Epicurus's doctrine of the origin of the universe in chance collision of atoms threaten theism, but his materialism precluded the immortality of the soul and thus called into question the eschatological supports of morality. Epicurus's belief in free will notwithstanding, many viewed his extension of atomist first principles to psychology and epistemology as destructive of free will.

Despite the stigma of libertine atheism attached to Epicurean atomism, many sixteenth- and seventeenth-century thinkers were attracted to the explanatory power of the atomist model. Although Aristotelian natural philosophers well into the seventeenth century continued to find explanations for the observed facts of nature in the intermixing of the four elements, in substantial forms, and in final causation, these explanations began to lack persuasive power in comparison with mechanical explanations among experimental scientists, who found Aristotelian substantial forms and the polarity of act-potency to be merely verbal.[2] Epicurus held out the possibility that underlying the visible phenomena of nature were smaller versions of the same thing. People could observe the effects of physical collision on the bowling green or the firing range—what if the invisible substratum operated in the same way? If so, then the laws of physics promised to be rationalizable and calculable. Moreover,

---

[1]Michael Hunter, *Science and Society in Restoration England* (Cambridge: Cambridge University Press, 1981), p. 162.
[2]For a healthy reminder that Renaissance Aristotelianism was far from univocal, see Charles B. Schmitt, *Aristotle and the Renaissance* (Cambridge: Harvard University Press, 1983).

the atomist theory was not empirically falsifiable—by definition, the atoms were too small to be seen. This combination of
factors made atomism nearly irresistible to scientists.[3] Pierre
Gassendi takes advantage of this latitude to speculate, not entirely facetiously, on the nature of the soul. The human soul
"not only gives life, feels, and moves, but also understands,
reasons, wonders, probes abstruse questions, speaks, laughs,
makes laws, discovers skills, and so forth. The nature of the
soul is located in these qualities. But if you wish to know in
addition to this what its color, texture, and substance are, you
must wait until you have eyes and a microscope up to such a
task."[4] The tension between the potentially great explanatory
value of the atomist model and its stigma of libertine atheism
led to an impasse in early-seventeenth-century England. To the
extent that one accepted Epicurean atoms as a metaphysical
first principle, one was brought into conflict with orthodox
beliefs in the incorporeality of the rational soul, freedom of the
will, and Genesis creation. It is not surprising that an atomist
group gathered at the beginning of the century around Henry
Percy, ninth earl of Northumberland, was dogged by accusa-
tions of atheism.[5]

René Descartes

The extraordinarily enthusiastic response to René Descartes
in England, and particularly among the Cambridge Platonists,

---

[3]For an overview of the topic of this paragraph, see Robert Kargon, *Atomism in
England from Hariot to Newton* (Oxford: Clarendon Press, 1966), chap. 1,
"Atomism and Aristotelianism." Kargon concisely expresses the strides made
by atomism in the seventeenth century: "In 1600, atomism was a 'radical'
philosophy, destructive of the still prevailing scholastic world-picture. By 1700,
atomism as a mechanical philosophy was, in England, the conservative view"
(p. 133).
[4]*The Selected Works of Pierre Gassendi*, ed. and trans. Craig B. Brush (New York:
Johnson Reprint Corporation, 1972), pp. 337–38 (*Syntagma philosophicum*, pt. I,
bk. 2, chap. 5).
[5]Kargon, *Atomism*, pp. 5–17. In his riveting account of the Galileo affair, Pietro
Redondi has argued persuasively that Galileo's condemnation by the Holy
Office derived more from his atomism than from his Copernicanism. See
Galileo Heretic, trans. Raymond Rosenthal (Princeton: Princeton University
Press, 1987).

owed much to the perception that he pointed a way beyond this impasse. Descartes offered a way to reconcile mechanist physics with Christian orthodoxy through a radical new dualism. While Descartes's division of spirit and matter recalls Platonist discussions of the opposition of soul and body, of forms and recalcitrant matter, the resemblance is superficial. Descartes rejects both the ontological dependence of the visible world upon the ideas dear to the Platonists and the teleological relationship of form and matter central to the Aristotelians. Instead, he asserts the coexistence of two independent substances, thinking and extended. Mechanical causation is a sufficient explanation for phenomena in *res extensa*, but it does not invade the preserve of reason and will, *res cogitans*. The price Descartes pays for this solution is the problem of puzzling out how mental events can affect physical events and vice versa.

Descartes enters ontology through epistemology. In casting about for that which can be known indubitably, he lights on the cogito—one can doubt the existence of anything except the mind that experiences the doubt. The "I" that is known to exist is identified with mind and is set in contradistinction to body, the common perception of which arrives through the notoriously unreliable physical senses. When Descartes adds that the essence of mind is thought and the essence of body is extension, an epistemological observation becomes an ontological principle.

Having established to his satisfaction the existence of *res cogitans*, Descartes turns to the ontological status of *res extensa* by way of a proof of the existence of God. To the datum that we possess the idea of a God "eternal, infinite, immutable, omniscient, omnipotent," Descartes applies the scholastic assumption that "it is manifest by the natural light that there must be at least as much reality in the efficient and total cause as in the effect of that cause" and concludes that the cause of the idea of God cannot lie in man who is neither eternal, infinite, immutable, nor omnipotent, and therefore that there must be a God actually existent who causes the idea of himself in our minds.[6]

[6]Cottingham 2:28 (*Meditations on First Philosophy* III). The Cartesian argument outlined here has affinities with Aquinas's Henological Argument (*Summa theologiae* I, Q.2, art.3).

From here, the step to *res extensa* is quick. A good God would not let us be deceived by appearances into a belief in a material universe that does not exist. Thus, after careful scrutiny by reason, the material world can be shown to exist, but no reliable knowledge of it can be acquired through the senses. In his physical writings, Descartes makes clear that the material world is governed by mechanical laws and not by final or formal causes.

Descartes's contemporaries challenged this route from the cogito to the assertion of a dualism of unextended, thinking mind and extended, unthinking body. Gassendi pointed out that it is not self-evident that the "I" that thinks is unextended and incorporeal; thought could be a property of subtle matter. Gassendi claimed, moreover, that Descartes's definition of mind was not in fact a definition at all. After all, we know without Descartes that the mind thinks: "What we are unclear about, what we are looking for, is that inner substance of yours [*intima tua substantia*] whose property is to think. Your conclusion should be related to this inquiry, and should tell us not that you are a thinking thing, but what sort of thing this 'you' who thinks really is."[7] Marin Mersenne and Antoine Arnauld ("Second and Fourth Sets of Objections to the *Meditations*") pointed to the Cartesian circle: God guarantees the validity of clear and distinct ideas, but his existence is derived from the clear and distinct idea of God.

Despite these challenges, Descartes's dualism was immediately and immensely influential (winning over even the atomist Gassendi), not least because it was attractive to both the atomists and their theological enemies. In maintaining the existence and mental activity of incorporeal substance while at the same time elaborating a mechanical model of causation in corporeal substance, Descartes was seen to be opening a conceptual space for God that many feared had been closed, explicitly or implicitly, by the ancient and modern atomists and by Hobbes. Atomist models of the chance construction of the universe seemed to leave God little to do; atomist insistence on the

[7]"Fifth Set of Objections to the *Meditations*," in Cottingham 2:192–93, and in the *Oeuvres de Descartes*, ed. Charles Adam and Paul Tannery, 12 vols. (rev. ed., Paris: Vrin/C.N.R.S., 1964–76), 7:276.

corporeality of all substance seemed to lead in two atheistic directions: either there is no God or he is corporeal. *Res cogitans* provided an incorporeal God with a habitation and thus made him less of an anomaly.

Res cogitans also provided a haven for conceptions foreign to a mechanist such as Hobbes: personal immortality, the rational soul, and freedom of the will. Descartes writes that "the first and most important prerequisite for knowledge of the immortality of the soul is for us to form a concept of the soul which is as clear as possible and is also quite distinct from every concept of body."[8] Descartes was willing to assign all events in the realm of *res extensa* to the concatenation of material and efficient cause, but in the realm of *res cogitans* he left the will free: "It is only the will, or freedom of choice, which I experience within me to be so great that the idea of any greater faculty is beyond my grasp; so much so that it is above all in virtue of the will that I understand myself to bear in some way the image and likeness of God."[9] Error arises from the disparity between the godlike, unlimited will and the limited understanding. To avoid error we turn to innate ideas, which do not come through the deceptive senses, but through the "power of thinking" within one.[10] The familiar linking of immortality, freedom of the will, and innate ideas to incorporeal substance allied Descartes with perennial Christian attacks on materialism.

If the attributes of *res cogitans* appealed to contemporary incorporealists, Descartes's handling of *res extensa* encouraged the atomists. Robert Kargon has documented the favorable reception of Descartes by the atomists of the Newcastle Circle, a

[8]Cottingham 2:9 (*Meditations*, Synopsis).
[9]Cottingham 2:40 (*Meditations* IV).
[10]Cottingham 1:303 ("Comments on a Certain Broadsheet"). See also Cottingham 2:26, 47 (*Meditations* III, V). Descartes's treatment of will and intellect reverses Sidney's famous formula in *An Apology for Poetry*: "our erected wit maketh us know what perfection is, and yet our infected will keepeth us from reaching unto it" (*Critical Theory since Plato*, ed. Hazard Adams [New York: Harcourt Brace Jovanovich, 1971], p. 158). Curiously, Descartes seems to back away from this position in the *Principles of Philosophy* (I, 41), where he advocates both absolute freedom of the will and a Hobbesian reconciliation of freedom with necessity, defending the contradiction by pointing to the incomprehensibility of God's order.

group including Hobbes.[11] While Descartes is not technically an atomist (he denied the vacuum and the indivisibility of corpuscles), his physics shares salient features with Epicurean and Gassendian atomism: both explain natural phenomena by the collision of corporeal particles, and both explain celestial motions through rectilinear motion and collision.[12] In *The World* and *The Principles of Philosophy* Descartes develops his mechanist theory of vortices to explain the emergence of the cosmos from original confusion in a model reminiscent of the chance creation of Epicurus.

Having used God to validate the existence of the physical universe, Descartes carefully circumscribes God's role in natural philosophy. Surpassing Francis Bacon in the separation of science and religion, Descartes banishes formal and final causation from science (*Principles of Philosophy* I, 28). While he insists that the world was created and is preserved by God, it is regulated by "the laws of mechanics, which are identical with the laws of nature."[13] Descartes's insistence that God continues to "preserve" the universe (as orthodox theology would have it) begins to look less orthodox when pushed. This preservation is creation under another name, for an immutable God creates immutably; special intervention in the cosmos would point to a change in God, who established the laws of nature at creation. Descartes writes in his suppressed *The World* (1629–1633, pub. 1664) that "it follows of necessity, from the mere fact that [God] continues to preserve [the world], that there must be many changes in its parts which cannot, it seems to me, properly be attributed to the action of God (because that action never changes), and which therefore I attribute to nature. The rules by which these changes take place I call the 'laws of nature.'"[14]

---

[11]Kargon, *Atomism*, pp. 63–76.

[12]For a comparison of Cartesian and atomist physics, see ibid., p. 68. For Descartes on celestial motion see the *Principles of Philosophy* II, 37–42.

[13]Cottingham 1:139 (*Discourse on the Method* V).

[14]Cottingham 1:92–93 (*The World*, chap. 7). Cottingham prints selections from this fascinating work (1664). For a facsimile of the first edition (in French, with facing translation), see *Le monde, ou traité de la lumière*, trans. Michael Sean Mahoney (New York: Abaris, 1979).

In effect, God's continuing preservation of the world is equivalent to the immutability of mechanical laws of nature. Mechanism entered into Descartes's biology and anthropology as well as his cosmology. His claim that animals are unconscious machines is familiar from the *Discourse on the Method* V. In the *Treatise on Man* (1629–33, pub. 1664), the *Passions of the Soul* (1646, pub. 1649), and the *Description of the Human Body* (1647–48, pub. 1664), Descartes argues that the human body is a machine as well. Breaking decisively with tradition, he maintains that the principle of life is not the soul, which as *res cogitans* has the sole function of thinking, but "the appropriate disposition of the bodily organs which are required for making the movement."[15] Descartes's analogy for this point resonates with later characterizations of mechanist materialism:

> Death never occurs through the absence of the soul, but only because one of the principal parts of the body decays. And let us recognize that the difference between the body of a living man and that of a dead man is just like the difference between, on the one hand, a watch or other automaton (that is, a self-moving machine) when it is wound up and contains in itself the corporeal principle of the movements for which it is designed . . . ; and, on the other hand, the same watch or machine when it is broken and the principle of its movement ceases to be active.[16]

Descartes pressed his exploration of this machine by experiment and observation, and the image of "rationalist" Descartes inserting his finger into the opened end of the heart of a live dog is a graphic reminder of the deceptiveness of labels.[17]

The human body is equivalent in Descartes's scheme to an animal, a complex machine. Man is set apart from the animal by the presence of the mind or soul, the *res cogitans*. The soul's

[15]Cottingham 1:315 (*Description of the Human Body* I).
[16]Cottingham 1:329–30 (*Passions of the Soul* I, 6). For the line connecting Descartes's animal automata or beast-machines with the man-machine of the materialists of the next age, see Leonora C. Rosenfeld, *From Beast-Machine to Man-Machine: The Theme of Animal Soul in French Letters from Descartes to La Mettrie* (New York: Oxford University Press, 1940).
[17]Cottingham 1:317 (*Description of the Human Body* II).

or mind's province of thought is in one sense broadly conceived; it is not reasoning alone. The mind or soul "understands, wills, imagines, remembers and has sensory perceptions; for all these functions are kinds of thought [*pensées*]."[18]
But in another sense the province of the mind is conceived
more narrowly. There is a strong dose of mechanistic psychology in *The Passions of the Soul*. Whether one responds with courage or terror to the sight of a dangerous animal depends, for
example, "upon the particular temperament of the body *or* the
strength of the soul" (my emphasis). A moment later, Descartes
leans toward the former, mechanist term of the either/or: "The
reason for this is that brains are not all constituted in the same
way."[19]

Descartes's equivocation seems inevitable given the ontological distance he inserts between mind and matter. If the mind is
not extended, how can the motions of the body impress and
move it? How can the mind in turn move the extended body;
where does the push begin? The degree to which Descartes
allows mechanism into his discussion of the soul's passions indicates the severity of his problem. As early as 1633, Descartes
had devised a response to the central question raised by his
dualism. Despite its attribute of nonextension, the soul has its
"principal seat [*siège principal*]" in the pineal gland, which is the
focus of a kind of hydraulic system of animal spirits refined
from the blood.[20] Sensory impressions force spirits through
the hollow nerves, causing the pineal gland, located at the con-
fluence of all the nerves, to pivot; conversely, the pivoting of
the gland forces the animal spirits through the nerves to the
muscles to make them move. The soul, seated in the gland, is
the ultimate recipient of incoming messages and the source of
outgoing commands. The elaborate discussion of this hydraulic

[18]Cottingham 1:314 (*Description of the Human Body* I).
[19]Cottingham 1:342–43 (*Passions of the Soul* I, 36 and 39).
[20]Cottingham 1:340 and Adam and Tannery 11:352 (*Passions of the Soul* I, 32).
Exposition of the pineal-gland theory can be found in the *Treatise on Man*
(Cottingham 1:100–108) and *The Passions of the Soul* (Cottingham 1:340–48).
Descartes chooses the pineal gland as the site of the soul because it is single,
whereas the other cerebral structures and the external sense organs are double
(*Passions* I, 32).

system diverts our attention (and Descartes's) from the fact that the question of mind-body interaction has been miniaturized rather than resolved.

The intractability of the problem of mind-body interaction, illustrated in the inadequacy of the pineal-gland argument, echoes the incompatibility between Descartes's mechanist cosmology and his insistence on his belief in biblical creation. The incorporeal God of Christian orthodoxy seems as marginalized in Cartesian creation as the soul is in the Cartesian body. As in his discussion of the man-machine in the *Treatise on Man*, Descartes takes pains in the *World* to present his mechanist picture of the origin of the universe as a heuristic fiction. In order to avoid disputes in cosmology with the learned, he will set aside our world, created as described in Genesis, and speak of what *could* happen if God were to create another:

> Even if in the beginning God had given the world only the form of a chaos, provided that he established the laws of nature and then lent his concurrence to enable nature to operate as it normally does, we may believe without impugning the miracle of creation that by this means all purely material things could in the course of time have come to be just as we now see them. And their nature is much easier to conceive if we see them develop gradually in this way than if we consider them only in their completed form.[21]

The clarity offered by the mechanical as opposed to the Genesis model of creation could be said by Descartes's own criterion (clear and distinct ideas are true ideas) to lead us to question what Descartes means when he labels the mechanist creation a "false hypothesis" employed "to provide an explanation of the true natures of things."[22] With Hobbes and Gassendi, and against the Baconian insistence on certainty, Descartes acknowledged the validity of hypotheses in sciences in which

[21]Cottingham 1:133–34 (*Discourse on the Method* V); see cognate passages in the *World*, chap. 6, where Descartes writes of a chaos "as confused and muddled as any the poets could describe," and the *Principles of Philosophy* III, 45 (Cottingham 1:91, 256).
[22]Cottingham 1:267 (*Principles of Philosophy* IV, 1).

geometrical proof is impossible.[23] Granted that Descartes offers his mechanist picture of the origin of the world as hypothesis rather than fact, it remains true that in cosmological physics hypothesis is as close to fact as we come—closer, the implication is clear, than Genesis. Descartes's description of his mechanist model of creation in the *Discourse on the Method* and the *Principles of Philosophy* as a fiction, fable, or false hypothesis is itself a fiction. Descartes reveals the motive for this fiction when explaining to Mersenne his decision in 1634 to suppress the *World* in response to the church's condemnation of Galileo's cosmology.[24] Descartes's ostensible subordination of the heuristic fiction of mechanist creation to the truth of the Genesis creation account is a strategic evasion; the explicit statements of orthodoxy are covers behind which Descartes can retreat if challenged on his implicit challenge to the literal truth of Genesis.[25] This reading is supported by the report of a conversation Descartes had with a Mlle de Schurman of Utrecht, whom he observed studying the Hebrew Bible in 1640. Descartes was "astonished that a person of such merit would give so much time to a thing of such little importance." Having read the first chapter of Genesis in Hebrew, "he had found in it nothing clear and distinct, nothing that one could comprehend *clearly and distinctly.* . . . He was not able to understand what Moses wished to say, and instead of bringing him new light, all that he read served only to confuse and muddle him more; he therefore has renounced that study."[26]

In sum, Descartes cuts two figures in the mechanist debate of the mid-seventeenth century. The foundational role of God and the strong arguments for the incorporeality of the soul

[23]See Descartes's letter to Mersenne of May 17, 1638 in *Descartes: Philosophical Letters*, ed. and trans. Anthony Kenny (Oxford: Oxford University Press, 1970), pp. 55–56; see also Kargon, *Atomism*, pp. 107–8.

[24]Letter of April 1634, in Kenny, *Descartes*, pp. 25–26.

[25]Descartes's familiarity with this strategy is attested to by his ascription to his erstwhile disciple Regius in 1647 of the "aim of satisfying in some way his more simple-minded readers and fellow theologians by citing the authority of Scripture, while the more sharp-witted of his readers would recognize that he is speaking ironically" (Cottingham 1:302 ["Comments on a Certain Broadsheet"]).

[26]I have translated the exchange reported in Adam and Tannery 4:700–701.

and reason in the *Discourse on the Method* and the *Meditations* were perceived as bulwarks against mechanist explanations of metaphysics and anthropology. But Descartes's strong implicit challenge to Genesis in the shape of an atomist random creation and also the wide latitude given to mechanism not only in physiology but also in psychology raised fears among incorporealists that he was a wolf in sheep's clothing.

Thomas Hobbes

As we shall see in the next chapter, Descartes's early English admirers began to think that Descartes had prepared the way for Thomas Hobbes, the "monster of Malmesbury."[27] This fear seems odd to us—we are used to viewing Descartes as the founder of modern mind-body dualism and Hobbes as an important influence on modern mechanist, materialist monism. The fear, we can safely say, would have struck Descartes and Hobbes themselves as odd. Each philosopher was aware of the work of the other. Sir Kenelm Digby sent Hobbes a copy of the *Discourse on the Method* in 1637, the year of its publication.[28] The two men were acquainted through their mutual friend Mersenne, the tireless correspondent whose monk's cell in Paris was a magnet for the chief philosophers and scientists of mid-seventeenth-century Europe and a clearinghouse for their ideas.[29] At Mersenne's prodding, Hobbes composed his "Ob-

---

[27]The line from Descartes to Hobbes is logical rather than temporal or causal. They developed their distinctive metaphysical systems simultaneously (as did Pierre Gassendi) in the 1630s. Hobbes's 1641 "Objections" to Descartes's *Meditations* grow out of an already completed vision of the mechanist materialism informing the *Leviathan* of a decade later. In fact, most English philosophers were aware of Hobbes before Descartes, who was perceived initially as answering the challenge of Hobbes.

[28]See Marjorie Nicolson, "The Early Stages of Cartesianism in England," *Studies in Philology* 26 (1929): 358.

[29]There is even a story that Hobbes once dined with Descartes, along with Pierre Gassendi. See Sterling P. Lamprecht, "The Role of Descartes in Seventeenth-Century England," in *Studies in the History of Ideas*, vol. 3, ed. Columbia University Department of Philosophy (New York: Columbia University Press, 1935), pp. 190–91; for the possible dinner meeting Lamprecht cites Aubrey's *Brief Lives*.

jections" to Descartes's *Meditations*, in which the great differences between Descartes and Hobbes become obvious and their debate heated. Hobbes vigorously attacks Descartes's incorporealism and innatism. Given the sharpness of the exchanges in the "Objections" and Descartes's "Replies" and their mutual refusal to allow each other's working definitions of "mind," "idea," "will," etc., it is not surprising that Descartes asked Mersenne to trouble him no more with Hobbes's writings.[30]

Nevertheless, in several important ways Hobbes and Descartes were kindred spirits. Both saw in geometry a foundation for natural philosophy, banished formal and final cause from the practice of science, and argued for a mechanistic universe driven by material and efficient causation alone.[31] Both denied the existence of atoms and the possibility of a vacuum (against emerging scientific orthodoxy) while advancing corpuscular theories that allied them with more thoroughgoing Epicurean atomists such as Gassendi and Charleton. Robert Boyle's comparison of Descartes and the Greek atomists can be applied to Hobbes as well: "I considered that the atomical and the Cartesian hypotheses, though they differed in some material points from each other, yet in opposition to the Peripatetic and the other vulgar doctrines they might be looked upon as one philosophy. For they agree with each other and differ from the schools in this grand and fundamental point, . . . both the Cartesians and the atomists explicate the same phenomena by little bodies variously figured and moved."[32]

---

[30]Lamprecht, "Role of Descartes," p. 191; Samuel I. Mintz points to a more humanly frail reason for their mutual animosity: each claimed priority for the discovery that secondary qualities are subjective—as Mintz notes, Galileo was actually the first, in his *Il Saggiatore* (1623). See *The Hunting of Leviathan: Seventeenth-Century Reactions to the Materialism and Moral Philosophy of Thomas Hobbes* (Cambridge: Cambridge University Press, 1962), p. 10; this book is the best account of the reaction against Hobbes.

[31]For Hobbes's collapsing of formal and final cause into material cause, see Hobbes, *De Corpore: The Elements of Philosophy concerning Body* II, x, 7, in *The English Works of Thomas Hobbes*, ed. Sir William Molesworth, 11 vols. (London: John Bohn, 1839–45), 1:131–32. References to all of Hobbes's works except for *Leviathan* will be from this standard edition, cited as Molesworth. For Hobbes's complete eradication of final cause as opposed to Descartes's maintaining of final cause in *res cogitans*, see Mintz, *Hunting of Leviathan*, p. 66.

[32]Quoted in Charles T. Harrison, "Bacon, Boyle, Hobbes, and the Ancient Atomists," *Harvard Studies and Notes in Philology and Literature* 15 (1933): 210.

Hobbes and Descartes resemble each other in violating Bacon's prescriptions and starting from a priori first principles; Hobbes's first principle, however, *is* opposed to Descartes's. Every element in Hobbes's philosophy rests on his certainty that the universe contains nothing other than matter in motion, which can be analyzed mathematically. From the moment at age forty that he discovered geometry, "the ways of motion simply," he was convinced that this science could be used to understand everything, including ethics and politics.[33] In his dedication to *De Corpore* (1655) he praises Galileo for opening "the gate of natural philosophy universal, which is the knowledge of the nature of *motion*."[34] Motion causes everything:

> But the causes of universal things . . . are manifest of themselves, or (as they say commonly) known to nature; . . . for they have all but one universal cause, which is motion.
>
> For Nature worketh by Motion; the Wayes and Degrees whereof cannot be known, without the knowledge of the Proportions and Properties of Lines, and Figures.
>
> Nature does nothing but by motion.[35]

Hobbes's matter differs from Descartes's *res extensa* in being characterized primarily by motion rather than by extension; he glances at Descartes when he argues that to say that "*extension* is *body*" exemplifies the absurdity of "the giving of names of *bodies*, to *accidents*."[36] In assigning motion to matter Hobbes violates the traditional notion that matter by itself is inert and

[33]Hobbes, *De Corpore* I, vi, 6, in Molesworth 1:73. The depth of Hobbes's geometric certainty is evidenced by the coherence of his writings over his productive life. The mature metaphysical and political system laid out in the *Leviathan* is already present in the *Elements of Law* of 1640 and the *De Cive* of 1641. David Johnston argues persuasively that the main contribution of *Leviathan* to Hobbes's oeuvre is not its new ideas but its metaphorical power and rhetorical brilliance. See *The Rhetoric of Leviathan: Thomas Hobbes and the Politics of Cultural Transformation* (Princeton: Princeton University Press, 1986).
[34]Molesworth 1:viii.
[35]Molesworth 1:69 (*De Corpore* I, vi, 5); *Leviathan*, ed. C. B. Macpherson (Harmondsworth: Penguin, 1968), p. 686 (chap. 46); Molesworth 4:437 (*Considerations upon the Reputation . . . of Thomas Hobbes*).
[36]*Leviathan*, p. 114 (chap. 5).

that spirit (or form) is the principle of both motion and life. Hobbes argues that life is not the principle of motion but rather a special case of motion.

Hobbes's redefinition of life confronts the reader on the first page of *Leviathan*: "For seeing life is but a motion of Limbs, the begining whereof is in some principall part within; why may we not say, that all *Automata* . . . have an artificiall life?"[37] Hobbes is not drawing the familiar seventeenth-century distinction between the life of an organic body with its intrinsic principle of motion and the machine put in motion by an external efficient cause; living bodies and machines differ only because nature makes one and man another. The term "artificial" means not that the life of machines is "ersatz," but only that it has man as its efficient cause. One of the distinctive marks of Hobbes's brilliant rhetorical style is the couching of his most controversial arguments in the simplest and most direct language; when he says that "life is but a motion of Limbs," that is just what he means.

To this point, Hobbes echoes Descartes's assertions that the life of the body is mechanical and that living and dead bodies differ as do working and broken watches. Hobbes differs in unambiguously extending the mechanism to mind and thought. The same mechanical laws that govern the motions of a clock govern mental motions. The term "incorporeal substance" cannot be summoned to provide a foundation for thought, because it is absurd. To put together the words "incorporeal" and "substance" is an abuse of speech, a forgetting of the proper definitions of words, equivalent to speaking of round quadrangles.[38] To speak of incorporeal or immaterial substances violates the foundation of Hobbes's metaphysics: "The World . . . is Corporeall, that is to say, Body; and hath the dimensions of Magnitude, namely, Length, Bredth, and Depth: also every part of Body, is likewise Body, and hath the like dimensions; and consequently every part of the Universe,

---

[37] *Leviathan*, p. 81 (Introduction).
[38] For the absurdity of the term "incorporeal substance" and its exemplification of the "abuse of speech," see *Leviathan*, pp. 108, 113, and 171 (chaps. 4, 5, and 12) and Molesworth 4:398 (*An Historical Narrative concerning Heresy*).

is Body, and that which is not Body, is no part of the Universe: And because the Universe is All, that which is no part of it is *Nothing*; and consequently *no where.*"³⁹ No conceptual space is left for incorporeal substance. Mistaken belief in such substance arises from ignorance of the nature of perception: what we "see" is not the external object but the motion occasioned by the object, motions that can be duplicated by dreams or, in the case of bright light, by pressing a finger to the eyelid.⁴⁰ A mistaken idea of the directness of perception misled superstitious Greeks, from whom we inherited our philosophical language, into a belief that the imaginations attendant upon dreams arise from external objects; because these objects were not tangibly present, they were taken to be incorporeal: "It was hard for men to conceive of those Images in the Fancy, and in the Sense, otherwise, than of things really without us: Which some (because they vanish away, they know not whither nor how,) will have to be absolutely Incorporeall, that is to say Immateriall, or Formes without Matter."⁴¹ In this passage Plato's supramundane Ideas, Aristotle's substantial forms, and Descartes's *res cogitans* are tarred with the same brush of superstitious demonism.

The invocation of incorporeal substance, Hobbes insists, is not only absurd and superstitious, it is unnecessary and unparsimonious. To Hobbes it is self-evident that because thought is found only in bodies, the body must be the subject of thought. He argues that it is illogical to assume that that which thinks is thought and accuses Descartes of confusing the activity with the subject. In *De Homine* Hobbes voices the radical conclusion to which his fundamental assumptions lead him: "*Conceptions* and *apparitions* are nothing *really*, but *motion* in some internal substance of the *head*."⁴² Descartes faced the problem of finding the link between motion in the brain and thought: Hobbes

³⁹*Leviathan*, p. 689 (chap. 46).
⁴⁰For a cogent discussion of Hobbes on perception, see John W. Yolton, *Perceptual Acquaintance from Descartes to Reid* (Minneapolis: University of Minnesota Press, 1984), pp. 130–32.
⁴¹*Leviathan*, p. 658 (chap. 45).
⁴²Molesworth 4:31 (*De Homine* VII, 1).

simply identifies them—thought equals motion. In a favorite phrase, thought is a corporeal "tumult in the mind." For Hobbes the "motions of the mind" are corporeal motions; the term "metaphorical motion" is "absurd speech: for though Words may be called metaphoricall, Bodies, and Motions cannot."[43]

With incorporeal substance goes the rational soul, that entity separating man from animal. Hobbes argues:

> The Imagination [for Hobbes another name for "idea"] that is raysed in man (or any other creature indued with the faculty of imagining) by words, or other voluntary signes, is that we generally call *Understanding*; and *is common to Man and Beast* [my emphasis]. For a dogge by custome will understand the call . . . of his Master; and so will many other Beasts. That Understanding which is peculiar to man, is the Understanding not onely his will; but his conceptions and thoughts, by the sequell and contexture of the names of things.[44]

The essential difference between man and beast is *artificial*: "Besides Sense, and Thoughts, and the Trayne of thoughts [all common to beasts], the mind of man has no other motion; though by the help of Speech, and Method, the same Facultyes may be improved to such a height, as to distinguish men from all other living Creatures."[45] Speech is the "invention" by which man distinguishes himself from the animals. This artificiality should recall the passage on artificiality quoted earlier from *Leviathan*'s first page:

> Nature (the Art whereby God hath made and governes the World) is by the *Art* of man, as in many other things, so in this also imitated, that it can make an Artificial Animal. For seeing life is but a motion of Limbs, the beginning whereof is in some principall part within; why may we not say, that all *Automata* (Engines that move themselves by springs and wheeles as doth a watch) have an artificiall life? For what is the *Heart*, but a *Spring*; and the

---

[43]*Leviathan*, p. 119 (chap. 6).
[44]*Leviathan*, pp. 93–94 (chap. 2).
[45]*Leviathan*, p. 99 (chap. 3).

Nerves, but so many *Strings*; and the *Joynts*, but so many *Wheeles*, giving motion to the whole body, such as was intended by the Artificer? *Art* goes yet further, imitating that Rationall and most excellent worke of Nature, *Man*. For by Art is created that great LEVIATHAN called a COMMON-WEALTH, OR STATE, (in Latin CIVITAS) which is but an Artificiall Man.

Readers have been puzzled as to why the enemy of metaphor in philosophy opens his major work with a metaphor, but in one sense this is not metaphor at all. The principle of life in watch, man, and state is motion. Moreover, man as distinct from beast is already artificial. The mental motions of man, particularly deliberation, are common to the state's corporate body. The continuity of the principle of life and action precludes the need for metaphor.

In collapsing the boundaries between human, animal, and mechanical life, Hobbes denies the distinction between the spontaneous actions of man and the passive reactions of animals and machines. The entire apparatus of Renaissance faculty psychology, with the will as semi-autonomous entity responding to the direction of the reason and the prompting of the passions, is rejected. Hobbes replaces it with a model of sensory input translated mechanically into behavioral output. We are inevitably inclined to follow what gives us pleasure and avoid what gives us pain. What we call "deliberation" is the arithmetical summing up or "reckoning" of corporeal, sensory signals. What we call "will" is not a faculty but *"the last Appetite in Deliberating."*[46] Like any other mental phenomenon it is a corporeal motion in the brain determined by antecedent corporeal motions. Hobbes sardonically dispatches freedom of the will: "If a man should talk to me of a *round Quadrangle*; or *accidents of Bread in Cheese*; or *Immaterial Substances*; or of *A free Subject*; *A free-Will*; or any *Free*, but free from being hindred by opposition, I should not say he were in an Errour; but that his words were without meaning; that is to say, Absurd."[47] For Hobbes the only freedom is that compatible with necessity.

---

[46]*Leviathan*, p. 128 (chap. 6).
[47]*Leviathan*, p. 113 (chap. 5).

Man necessarily chooses what he chooses; liberty lies in the absence of external impediment in acting on the necessary choices.

Here we find one of the main reasons for the violent reaction to Hobbes. Hobbes's determinism constricts the moral sphere. If our actions are the inevitable consequence of prior corporeal motions, then how are we to be held responsible for them? And if the chain of corporeal motions originates, as Hobbes suggests, in the will of God, then how is God to be free of the guilt for our sins? These questions were particularly important for libertarian thinkers such as Milton. Hobbes's determinism can be read as a secularization of Calvinism:

> Every act of mans will, and every desire, and inclination proceedeth from some cause, and that from another cause, which causes in a continuall chaine (whose first link in the hand of God the first of all causes) proceed from *necessity*. . . . And therefore God, that seeth, and disposeth all things, seeth also that the *liberty* of man in doing what he will, is accompanied with the *necessity* of doing that which God will, & no more, nor lesse. For though men may do many things, which God does not command, or is therefore Author of them; yet they can have no passion, nor appetite to any thing, of which appetite Gods will is not the cause. And did not his will assure the *necessity* of mans will, and consequently of all that on mans will dependeth, the *liberty* of men would be a contradiction, and impediment to the omnipotence and *liberty* of God.[48]

Hobbes's distinction between God as the immediate author of our actions and God as the first cause of our actions holds little comfort for those concerned about the justice of God's damning sinners, but Hobbes, a thoroughgoing voluntarist, does not share this worry: the damnation of sinners who act by necessity is

---

[48]*Leviathan*, p. 263 (chap. 21). Hobbes cites Luther and Calvin in support of his determinism against Bishop Bramhall in *The Questions concerning Liberty, Necessity, and Chance* (Molesworth 5:1–2). For a discussion of differences between Hobbes and Calvin, see Leopold Damrosch, Jr., "Hobbes as Reformation Theologian: Implications of the Free-Will Controversy," *Journal of the History of Ideas* 40 (1979): 339–52.

just because God so ordains it. Unlike Calvin, whom he resembles, Hobbes ascribes God's dominion over our wills to what he describes as God's ordinary as opposed to his immediate work.[49] That is to say, our wills are moved by nature, not by God's immediate intervention. Hobbes does not bother himself with arguments about original sin or the universal meriting of damnation—his interests are metaphysical, physical, and political rather than theological. Hobbes retains, in a rare turning aside from the implications of his principles, the categories of praise and blame seemingly rendered meaningless by his model of will. But praise and blame are conceived as added links in the universal causal chain, as devices to influence behavior inaugurated by men themselves acting even in this under the impulsion of prior determining causes.

If Hobbes's determinism erodes the meaning of moral choice, his nominalism erodes the sense of the good itself. All is body, all knowledge comes from the sensations caused in our bodies by other bodies, and words (including "universals") are merely ways we have of talking about bodies. Such a conception leaves no room for the transmission or even existence of the immutable moral principles. Good and evil, like other abstract words, are terms of convenience rooted in corporeal experience: "Whatsoever is the object of any mans Appetite or Desire; that is it, which he for his part calleth *Good*: And the object of his Hate, and Aversion, *Evill*. . . . For these words of Good [and] Evill . . . are ever used with relation to the person that useth them: There being nothing simply and absolutely so; nor any common Rule of Good and Evill, to be taken from the nature of the objects themselves."[50] Good and evil, right and wrong, follow not from immutable principles but from contracts. Sin is a violation of the law, and in the state of nature before the contract of law there is no sin. In order to avoid sin, one should follow the command of God's earthly representative, that is to say one's civil government, a prescription that also assures civil tranquillity.

---

[49]See *Leviathan*, p. 471 (chap. 37).
[50]*Leviathan*, p. 120 (chap. 6).

Politics, metaphysics, and ethics converge here; it is no accident that Hobbes's great political masterpiece begins with a discussion of metaphysics. The illusion of autonomy fostered by the notion of free will, located in an incorporeal mind exempt from the chain of physical causation, can disturb the docility of the political subject. No abstract or transcendent notions of right and wrong should intervene between the authority of the civil government and the obedience of the governed. In fact, Hobbes argues that "there can therefore be no contradiction between the Laws of God, and the Laws of a Christian Common-wealth."[51] Accordingly, the interpretation of Scripture is authorized by the civil sovereign: "The Scripture, therefore, what it is, and how to be interpreted, is made known unto us here, by no other way than the authority of our sovereign lord both in temporals and spirituals, the King's Majesty."[52] Conscience is a dangerous conception and merely the stubborn and unwarranted conviction of right in those whose business it is to obey. Steven Shapin and Simon Schaffer argue persuasively that the roots of Hobbes's materialist ontology are political; Hobbes saw belief in incorporeal substance as the fountain of claims of inspiration and conscience that unsettled civil order.[53]

Hobbes's masterstroke in countering the politically disruptive religious enthusiasm of his time is his domestication of God. Because God is beyond the reach of our senses, from which we receive *all* of our knowledge, we have no reason to

---

[51]*Leviathan*, p. 625 (chap. 43).

[52]Molesworth 4:363–64 (*An Answer to a Book Published by Dr. Bramhall, . . . Called the "Catching of the Leviathan"*).

[53]Shapin and Schaffer connect Hobbes's denial of a vacuum to his sense that it provided an illusory home for incorporeal substance: "In Hobbes's view the elimination of vacuum was a contribution to the avoidance of civil war. The dualist ontology deployed by priests spoke of existents which were not matter: this made men 'see double' and resulted in the fragmentation of authority which led inexorably to chaos and civil war. Aristotelians spoke of separated essences which were poured into corporeal entities; vacuists populated the spaces they prohibited to matter with immaterial spirits. These were the ontological resources of the enemies of order" (*Leviathan and the Air-Pump: Hobbes, Boyle, and the Experimental Life* [Princeton: Princeton University Press, 1985], pp. 108–9).

worship God other than as the civil authorities command. This project of domestication follows from Hobbes's materialist metaphysics and mechanical psychology. Infinity, for example, is a conception with no place in a philosophy that derives all knowledge from sense: "Whatsoever we imagine, is *Finite*. Therefore there is no Idea, or conception of anything we call *Infinite.*"[54] Hobbes for similar reasons denies validity to all of the traditional attributes of God. Because God is incomprehensible, it is presumptuous to treat his infinity, omnipresence, eternity, etc., as philosophical truths available to reason: "When men out of the Principles of naturall Reason, dispute of the Attributes of God, they but dishonour him: For in the Attributes which we give to God, we are not to consider the signification of the Philosophicall Truth; but the signification of Pious Intention, to do him the greatest Honour we are able."[55]

Hobbes's attacks on the language of the perfections of God were disturbing; the implication of his materialism for theology did not escape Bishop Bramhall, despite the conventional gestures toward the incomprehensibility of God. In *The Catching of Leviathan* (1658) Bramhall asked shrewdly: "When they have taken away all incorporeal spirits, what do they leave God himself to be? . . . And what real being can God have among bodies and accidents? For they have left nothing else in the universe." His hand forced, Hobbes acknowledges his belief in the materiality of God: "To his Lordship's question here: *What I leave God to be?* I answer, I leave him to be a most pure, simple, invisible spirit corporeal."[56] This radical conclusion was the specter that haunted orthodox thinkers in the seventeenth century, who were alarmed by the growing currency of materialist thinking. It is enough to explain Hobbes's contemporaries' yoking him with Spinoza, despite their very different ideas of God and matter. The implications explode what was left of Chris-

[54]*Leviathan*, p. 99 (chap. 3); Hobbes accordingly denies the conception of infinite space.

[55]*Leviathan*, p. 404 (chap. 31).

[56]Molesworth 4:312–13 (*An Answer to a Book Published by Dr. Bramhall, . . . Called the "Catching of the Leviathan"*). I quote Bramhall from Hobbes's *Answer*; Hobbes quotes accurately the work Bramhall appended to his *Castigations of Mr. Hobbs* (London, 1658), pp. 471–72.

tian orthodoxy after the assault on will and moral responsibility. The final demolition of the notions of liberty, responsibility, and orthodox Christian theism, along with the final usurpation or victory of mechanism, can be witnessed in Hobbes's speculative critique of the conception of the unmoved mover in *De Corpore*:

> Though from this, that nothing can move itself, it may rightly be inferred that there was some first eternal movent; yet it can never be inferred, though some used to make such inference, that that movent was eternally immoveable, but rather eternally moved. For as it is true, that nothing is moved by itself; so it is true also that nothing is moved but by that which is already moved. The questions therefore about the magnitude and beginning of the world, are not to be determined by philosophers, but by those that are lawfully authorized to order the worship of God.[57]

If even the voluntarist deity of Hobbes is a first moved, then the coils of mechanism surround the supernatural as well as the natural. This comment concerning God seems to crown the frontal assault launched by Hobbes against orthodox philosophy and theology, the pious bow to the authority of the theologians notwithstanding.[58] Many of the best minds of the seventeenth century directed their efforts to fending off this assault.

Pierre Gassendi

It cannot be said of Gassendi, as it can of Descartes and Hobbes, that English intellectuals of mid-century must have been aware of his philosophy; it would thus be unwarranted to suppose Milton's knowledge of Gassendi (although he is represented, along with his English popularizer, Walter Charleton, in the library of Milton's friend Nathan Paget). But because Gassendi illustrates so clearly the role of ethical and religious

[57]Molesworth 1:412.
[58]In Hobbes's works, this passage remains an isolated speculation. Normally he writes of a God free from external causation.

imperatives in metaphysical debate in the mid-seventeenth century, I have included him here. Orthodox imperatives exerted great pressure on his revival of Epicurean atomism.

Gassendi was the chief propagandist for Epicurean natural philosophy in the seventeenth century. He explicated and defended Epicurus's atomist and mechanist physics and biology, and he shared with the ancient philosopher a belief in freedom of the will and moral responsibility.[59] But Gassendi, a Catholic priest, was from the beginning careful to distance himself from Epicurus's conceptions of the origin of the world and the foundation of free will, and as his project of historical recovery progressed he found increasing room in his metaphysics for a non-Epicurean incorporeal soul.

Epicurus argued that atoms in motion form the substrate of all phenomena. Initially and from eternity, all atoms fell through space in straight and parallel lines. This condition would still hold to this moment were it not for the "swerve" of the atoms, a tendency toward random, undetermined deviation from this parallel movement. The collisions resulting from the swerve of atoms allowed for the formation of clusters of atoms; the universe as we know it took shape according to the operation of mechanical laws on the randomly swerving atoms. The same swerve was invoked to account for freedom of the will. The "swerve" is by definition a random, uncaused physical event that begins an atomic chain of causation.

The problems with Epicurus's swerve from a Christian perspective are obvious. Christian orthodoxy would hardly be satisfied with eternally existing atoms as material cause, and random "swerve" as efficient cause, of creation. The atomist view undermines not only literal Genesis creation but any meaningful notion of final cause. The universe is not planned by God; it happens. And if "swerve" leads to heresy in the case of creation, it leads to nonsense in the case of will. A random, corporeal anomaly such as the atomic swerve is no more compat-

---

[59]For Gassendi's skillful use of the genre of the history of philosophy as a vehicle for his own philosophical concerns, see Lynn Sumida Joy, *Gassendi the Atomist: Advocate of History in an Age of Science* (Cambridge: Cambridge University Press, 1987).

ible with a libertarian conception of the will than is mechanist determinism. Hobbes might be willing to see randomness as the sole alternative to necessity, but libertarians were not.[60]

Gassendi, like Walter Charleton after him, purified his version of Epicureanism by removing what he saw as atheistic elements. He repudiated the eternity of the atoms (called "this faeculent Doctrine of Epicurus" by Charleton)[61] and insisted that God created the atoms and set them in motion. The providential plan, he suggested, is wrapped up in God's initial imparting of motions to the newly created atoms. The threat of atomist physics to human will was less easily circumvented. If Hobbes could find Calvinist support for his determinism of the will, Gassendi's Catholicism like Milton's Arminianism pointed toward freedom of the will. Gassendi wrote that "if [our souls] do everything unavoidably and inevitably, the reason of human life perishes."[62] But the value of Gassendi's hypothetical atomist model was the simple explanatory power of its mechanism, applied to all corporeal phenomena, an explanatory power that Hobbes easily transferred to the will. Gassendi felt the difficulty keenly.

Gassendi worked himself out of this impasse of mechanism with two apparently conflicting strategies: hylozoism and incorporealism. The hylozoist Gassendi argued for a nonmechanical principle of causation in matter, ultimately traceable to the motion given to atoms at their creation but not limited to rectilinear motion. He dismisses both the Platonists, who argue that the cause of motion is incorporeal, and the Aristotelians, whose language of matter and form "escapes our comprehension" and aligns himself with the Stoics and Epicurus, who argued for nonmechanical but corporeal causes. The atomists "insisted . . . that the efficient principle was to be distinguished

---

[60]See my "'To Act or Not': Milton's Conception of Divine Freedom," *Journal of the History of Ideas* 49 (1988): 425–49.
[61]*Physiologia Epicuro-Gassendo-Charltoniana: or A Fabrick of Science Natural, upon the Hypothesis of Atoms* (1654), reprinted in facsimile with an introduction by Robert Kargon (New York: Johnson Reprint Corporation, 1966), p. 125.
[62]"Ethics," *Opera Omnia*, 6 vols. (Lyons, 1558), 2:831, quoted in Lisa T. Sarasohn, "Motion and Morality: Pierre Gassendi, Thomas Hobbes and the Mechanical World-View," *Journal of the History of Ideas* 46 (1985): 369.

from the material principle as different in thought, but not in fact and substance. . . . They did not consider atoms, which they said are the matter of all things, as inert or motionless, but rather as most active and mobile, so much so that they held them to be the first principle from which things take their motion."[63] Gassendi describes the intrinsic motion of atoms in terms normally reserved for the incorporeal spirit, language foreshadowing Milton's own on the material spirit:

> Since the principle of action and motion in each object is the most mobile and active of its parts, *a sort of bloom of every material thing and which is the same thing that used to be called form*, and may be thought of as a kind of rarefied tissue (*contextura*) of the most subtle and mobile atoms—it may therefore be said that the prime cause of motion in natural things is the atoms, for they provide motion for all things when they move themselves through their own agency and in accord with the power they received from their author in the beginning; and they are consequently the origin, the principle, and cause of all motion that exists in nature.[64]

Unlike Descartes and Hobbes, Gassendi never banished final cause from physics, and when writing the *Syntagma* he had diverged so far from pure mechanism as to impute a form of mental activity to inanimate objects, a teleological notion for which the mechanists derided Aristotle: "Each natural agent [including "inanimate" ones] tends to a certain end. . . . You say, therefore, must a certain cognition be attributed to the seeds, not only of animals, but also of plants, stones, and other things? But if you wish me to deny this, explain therefore how they finish their own operations so exquisitely."[65] This princi-

---

[63]*Syntagma philosophicum*, "The Physics," bk. 4, in *The Selected Works of Pierre Gassendi*, ed. and trans. Craig B. Brush (New York: Johnson Reprint Corporation, 1972), pp. 411–12. This text is cited hereafter as Brush.

[64]"Physics," bk. 4, in Brush, p. 422; my emphasis.

[65]"Physics," quoted in Sarasohn, "Motion and Morality," p. 372. Sarasohn suggests incorrectly that here Gassendi imputes to this minimal cognition "the freedom to act without being determined to a certain end," despite having quoted Gassendi's point that what separates human from other cognition is that the latter "has been determined to its own operations, so that it can run to nothing else."

ple of cognition separates Gassendi's mature atomism from the
collision mechanics of Descartes and Hobbes and provides a
middle term between mechanism and Neoplatonist notions of
a world soul.

The dangers of materialist mechanism moved Gassendi not
only toward Stoic hylozoism but also toward an incorporealism
that he considered dictated by Christian doctrine. In the 1641
"Objections" to Descartes's *Meditations*, he had insisted on at
least the possibility of the corporeality of that which thinks: "It
remains for you to prove that the power of thought is something so far beyond the nature of a body that neither a vapour
nor any other mobile, pure and rarefied body can be organized
in such a way as would make it capable of thought. . . . You say
'I am not a vapour or anything of this kind.' But if the entire
soul is something of this kind, why should you, who may be
thought of as the noblest part of the soul, not be regarded as
being, so to speak, the flower, or the most refined and pure and
active part of it?"[66] But by the time he came to write the *Syntagma*, Gassendi acknowledged as self-evident the necessity of incorporeal substance for intellectual actions: "As for the fact
that the human soul acts upon its own body and moves it despite the fact that the soul is incorporeal, we shall say in its place
that the human soul, insofar as it is the intellect, or mind, and
so incorporeal, does not stimulate actions except for intellectual, or mental, and incorporeal ones, and insofar as it is sentient, animate, and endowed with the power of moving bodies,
and so is corporeal, does stimulate corporeal actions and moves
its own body."[67] This position is remarkably close to Descartes's:
life has a corporeal rather than an incorporeal cause, but incorporeal substance is required for thinking. Significant differences remain, however. Gassendi maintained the mechanist
principle that incorporeal substance, being unextended, cannot "push" corporeal substance and thus account for corporeal
motions. Whereas Descartes displaces the problem of dualism

[66]"Fifth Set of Objections to the *Meditations*," Cottingham 2:183, 185. Gassendi
addresses Descartes satirically throughout with the tag "O Mind"; Descartes in
turn sprinkles his response with the salutation "O Flesh."
[67]"Physics," bk. 4, in Brush, p. 413.

in his conception of the pineal gland, Gassendi displaces the problem into the soul, which now is both corporeal and incorporeal. But the very objection that leads Gassendi to reject the pineal-gland theory precludes an answer to the problem of the communication of the corporeal and incorporeal soul.[68]

The strains placed upon familiar conceptions of incorporeal substance appear in bolder relief in the work of Gassendi's English popularizer, Walter Charleton. Charleton was a friend of Hobbes and a fellow member of the group of Royalists and atomists gathered around the duke and duchess of Newcastle.[69] Attracted earlier to the occultist teachings of Paracelsus and van Helmont, Charleton was led to atomist mechanism through Hobbes's recommendation of the works of Gassendi.[70] Charleton's *Physiologia Epicuro-Gassendo-Charltoniana: or A Fabrick of Science Natural, upon the Hypothesis of Atoms* (1654) is based closely on Gassendi's *Epicuri Physiologia*, a section of the *Animadversiones in Decimum Librum Diogenis Laertii.* Among Charleton's most interesting additions are his responses to Descartes's writings, a tactic foreign to Gassendi's historical method in the *Animadversiones.*

The vacillation on the place of incorporeal substance in an atomist metaphysic is if anything more pronounced in Charleton than it is in Gassendi. Charleton writes that "the *Faculties* of an Animal (we exclude the Rational Faculty of man, from the sphere of our assertion) are *Identical* with the *Spirits* of it, i.e. the most subtile, most free, and most moveable or active part of its materials. . . . To those Worthies, who have with impartial and profound scrutiny searched into the mystery, hath it appeared . . . consentaneous, that the spirits are of the same nature with the Faculty, and not only movent, but Instrument."[71]

---

[68]This dilemma would call forth later in the century Spinoza's double-aspect theory and Leibniz's preestablished harmony.

[69]For Charleton's relation to this group, see Kargon, *Atomism,* pp. 77–92.

[70]Historians have argued that the royalist Charleton repudiated Paracelsan thought because he considered it tainted by association with sectarian "enthusiasm." See P. M. Rattansi, "Paracelsus and the Puritan Revolution," *Ambix* 11 (1963): 24–32; N. R. Gelbart, "The Intellectual Development of Walter Charleton," *Ambix* 18 (1971) 149–68; Hunter, *Science and Society in Restoration England,* pp. 28–29.

[71]*Physiologia,* p. 272.

The faculties and spirits are related, Charleton continues, as fountain and rivulets. Charleton's position here echoes Hobbes's denial to faculties of ontological status apart from bodily mechanism. Unlike Hobbes, however, he suggests that the matter, in the form of the spirits, can generate as well as communicate motion. The spirits are simultaneously the faculty and the instruments of the faculty. The word "movent" equivocates nicely—it means both that which moves and that which is moved; it is the same word Hobbes uses for God in his skeptical analysis of the conception of the prime mover.[72] The active power of the spirits lessens the need for the incorporeal soul as principle of the faculties in man, despite Charleton's exemption of the rational faculty in this passage. Significantly, both the equivocal language of "movents" and the exemption of the rational faculty are absent from the passage in Gassendi behind Charleton's.[73] Charleton has one eye on extending Gassendi's attempt to purify atomism by ascribing thought to incorporeal substance and another eye on extending the role of the corporeal spirits. Milton, as we shall see, did not shy away from explicitly identifying the spirits even with the rational faculty.

Charleton's sanitizing of Epicurean atomism had the intended effect of making it available to scientists in a culture quick to penalize teachings perceived to be non-Christian, but the mixture of atomism with incorporealism was unstable. Two dualisms, the Epicurean dualism of matter and void and the firmly entrenched dualism of body and incorporeal soul, clash and threaten the argument of the *Physiologia*. Charleton uses the word "incorporeal" in two ways, to denote both the "negation of corporeity" and "also a true and germane *Substance*, to which certain *Faculties* and *Operations* essentially belong; and in that sense it is adscriptive properly to God, Angels, the Souls of

---

[72]See above at note 57 (Molesworth 1:412).
[73]"Ex hoc est certè, cur Facultates nihil esse distinctum videantur ab ipsismet spiritibus; hoc est à subtilissima, liberrima, actuosissima principiorum parte. Tametsi enim spiritus videantur esse nihil aliud, quàm organum quoddam primarium, quod Facultas in vna parte residens, transmittit in aliam; nihilominùs ij non sunt alterius naturæ, quàm ipsa facultas, vt neque aqua in riuulis, alterius naturæ ab ea, quae in fonte." *Animadversiones in Decimum Librum Diogenis Laertii*, 3 vols. (1649; facs. rpt. New York: Garland, 1987), 1:311.

men, &c. spiritual Essences."[74] The void, being nothing, cannot be a part of anything in the manner that the soul is a part of man. But it is not surprising that Charleton must often remind readers of this distinction, for he speaks of the atoms and void in the language usually employed for discussions of body and spirit. When Charleton speaks of the corporeal and the incorporeal, one must be careful to sort out whether he means the bodily and the spiritual or the atoms and the void. The equivocation can be disorienting, as when Charleton asserts "that the INCORPOREAL, and therefore Invisible part of the Universe, the *Inane Space*, may bear the name of the DARK, and the CORPOREAL and visible part of the LUMINOUS side of Nature."[75]

Descartes's dualism brought the "mind-body problem" to the center of mid-seventeenth-century intellectual life. The status of the soul became at once more exalted and more precarious when it was conceived as an anomaly in an otherwise material and mechanical world. If the soul was formerly taken as the form of the body, what happened when the reality of Aristotelian forms was challenged, or when the forms were redefined following Bacon as mechanical laws? And again, how does the Cartesian soul, so alien from *res extensa*, communicate with the body? Descartes's admission of corporeal, mechanical causation into the domain of what we call psychology highlights the vulnerability of soul within a mechanical theory of nature. The mechanical philosophies placed a strain on traditional Christian beliefs in creation, the immortality and incorporeality of the soul, the immutability of moral standards, and the creature's moral responsibility. Hobbes dispatched the problems of the compatibility of mechanism and Christian doctrine not by circumscribing the former, as did Gassendi, but by radically redefining the latter. The corporeal, mortal soul follows the same laws as grosser corporeal entities. God's role in creation is asserted, but the logic of that role of unmoved mover is questioned. In a philosophy of motion in which irresistible motions

[74]*Physiologia*, p. 68.
[75]Ibid., p. 84.

take the place of immutable moral principles, God acts and establishes laws arbitrarily. Despite the distance on key points between Hobbes and the dualist Descartes, we can recognize why nervous contemporaries viewed Hobbes's impieties as the inevitable successors of Descartes's mechanism. In the next chapter I will examine the response of the Cambridge Platonists to the metaphysical and moral challenge.

~ 2

The Life of the Soul:
The Cambridge Reaction

"I act, therefore I am."[1] Benjamin Whichcote's revision of Descartes's cogito signals the opposition of the Cambridge Platonists to the mechanical philosophies of their time. A group of liberal divines centered at Milton's own college, Christ's, the Cambridge Platonists preached the virtues of toleration, the responsibility of free choice guided by immutable moral principles, and the pervasive and activating presence of spirit in the world of incorporeal substance. Whichcote's substitution of action for thought is doubly expressive. First, Whichcote shares the Cambridge emphasis on morality; while Descartes accepts a provisional morality so that he can be free to pursue philosophical and scientific truth, the Cambridge Platonists place the recognition of and adherence to immutable moral principles at the center of the intellectual life. At the same time, the Cambridge Platonists substitute activity for thought as the essential attribute of incorporeal substance. They did not see how matter could think, initiate motion, or organize itself. Matter was for them by definition passive and inert, requiring spirit to form, shape, and move it. More dispatches Hobbes's central

[1]Benjamin Whichcote, *Discourses*, quoted in *The Cambridge Platonists*, ed. C. A. Patrides (Cambridge: Cambridge University Press, 1969), p. 15.

assumption in two lines of *Democritus Platonissans*: "For matter pure is a pure nullitie; / What nought can act is nothing, I am sure."[2] Pure matter can only be Aristotelian *prima materia*, unformed and lacking qualities. (For Hobbes, who assumes differently, *materia prima* is "a mere name."[3])

The Platonists grouped Descartes, Gassendi, and Hobbes, despite these thinkers' sometimes acrimonious differences, under the single rubric of mechanism. Hobbes is the major target of Cambridge Platonist polemic; the school's familiar irenic tone is tested by their outrage at Hobbes's extension of mechanism into the mind. Descartes is treated sometimes with admiration for his defense of incorporeal substance and his arguments for the existence of God, but at other times as a fellow traveler of the materialists, whose mechanical physiology and cosmology lead one down a slippery slope to Hobbes's materialism.

While Cudworth and especially More were conversant with current scientific thought, their main intellectual concerns were theological and ethical.[4] The Cambridge Platonists devoted themselves to defending the government of the world by a rational God, the immutability of moral laws, the incorporeality of the soul, and the freedom of the will. The threat of mechanical philosophy to these beliefs drives their writings. The im-

---

[2]*The Complete Poems of Dr. Henry More*, ed. Alexander B. Grosart (1878; facs. rpt. New York: AMS Press, 1967), *Democritus Platonissans*, canto 16; all further references to this edition, which follows the revised edition of 1647, appear in the text under the names of the individual poems: *Psychozoia, Psychathanasia, Democritus Platonissans, Antipsychopannychia, The Præexistency of the Soul, Antimonopsychia,* and *The Oracle.*

[3]*The English Works of Thomas Hobbes*, ed. Sir William Molesworth, 11 vols. (London: John Bohn, 1839–45), 1:118 (*De Corpore* II, viii, 24).

[4]Despite the disagreement on the extension of spirit and a marked difference in method (Cudworth, like Gassendi, approached philosophy through the history of philosophy), the thought of Cudworth and that of More are strikingly similar. The question of the direction of influence is unclear. More published eagerly, while Cudworth held on to his works; John Passmore argues that despite More's preceding Cudworth into print by decades, there are several good reasons to see Cudworth as the leader of the pair. See Passmore's *Ralph Cudworth: An Interpretation* (Cambridge: Cambridge University Press, 1951), pp. 16–18. In this chapter I pass over the question of priority and present their views together.

mutable moral principles championed by the Cambridge Platonists are logically but not temporally prior to the actions of
God, which unfold in accordance with those moral principles.
If the world is a product of chance or arbitrary fiat rather than
of reason, then claims for immutable, transcendent principles
of truth and morality become problematic. Cudworth explicitly
ties mechanical cosmology to ethical relativism in his posthumous *Treatise concerning Eternal and Immutable Morality* (1735).
And if mechanist cosmogony erodes the authority of immutable moral law, Hobbes's mechanist psychology threatens the
individual autonomy that gives meaning to moral choice.
Hobbes says coolly to Bishop John Bramhall, with whom he
carried out a lengthy published debate on liberty, "I have no
dominion over my will."[5] The Cambridge Platonist John Smith
comments on the insufficiency of the mechanical model of
physiology and its implications for the will:

> When we come to examine those Motions which arise from the
> Body, this stream runs so far under ground, that we know not
> how to trace it to the head of it; but we are fain to *analyse* the
> whole artifice, looking from the *Spirits* to the *Blood*, from that to
> the *Heart*, viewing all along the *Mechanical* contrivance of *Veins*
> and *Arteries*: neither know we after all our search whether there
> be any *Perpetuum mobile* in our own Bodies, or whether all the
> motions thereof be onely by the redundancy of some external
> motions without us; nor how to find the First mover in nature;
> though could we find out that, yet we know that there is a Fatal
> determination which sits in all the wheels of meer Corporeal mo-
> tion; neither can they exercise any such noble freedome as we
> constantly find in the Wills of men, which are as large and un-
> bounded in all their Elections as Reason it self can represent
> Being it self to be.[6]

[5]Molesworth 5:405 (*The Questions concerning Liberty, Necessity, and Chance* 33, k).
On Cudworth's work as a response to Hobbes's threat to free will, see Samuel I.
Mintz, *The Hunting of Leviathan: Seventeenth-Century Reactions to the Materialism
and Moral Philosophy of Thomas Hobbes* (Cambridge: Cambridge University
Press, 1962), pp. 110–33.
[6]"A Discourse Demonstrating the Immortality of the Soul," in *Select Discourses*
(1660; facs. rpt. New York: Garland, 1978), p. 90. Smith died in 1652; this
posthumous collection was prepared by John Worthington. For Descartes and
Smith, see J. E. Saveson, "Descartes' Influence on John Smith, Cambridge
Platonist," *Journal of the History of Ideas* 20 (1959): 258–63.

Like Joseph Glanvill's in his later *Vanity of Dogmatizing* (1661), Smith's skepticism here is provisional. The lack of empirical proof for a noncorporeal principle of life gives way to an a priori commitment to an incorporealist philosophy that can legitimate the subjective experience of free will. We do not know by observation whether life rises from an internal (incorporeal) principle or merely represents a continuation in the body of external particle motions, but the mechanist alternative precludes freedom and is therefore unacceptable. This a priori commitment to free will is shared by Cudworth and More. Cudworth reveals on the first page of *The True Intellectual System of the Universe* that the motivation for his massive historical treatise on metaphysics with its incorporealist polemic is a desire to defend free will:

> When I engag'd the Press, I intended onely a Discourse concerning *Liberty* and *Necessity*, or to speak out more plainly, *Against the Fatall Necessity* of all *Actions* and *Events*; which upon whatsoever *Grounds* or *Principles* maintain'd, will (as We Conceive) Serve The *Design of Atheism*, and Undermine *Christianity*, and all *Religion*; as taking away all *Guilt* and *Blame*, *Punishments* and *Rewards*, and plainly rendring a *Day of Judgment*, Ridiculous: And it is Evident that some have pursued it of late, in order to that End. But afterwards We consider'd, That this which is indeed a *Controversy*, concerning The *True Intellectual System of the Universe*, does, in the full Extent thereof, take in *Other* things.[7]

More's commitment to free will and aversion to Calvinist predestination appeared early: as a schoolboy he was threatened with the rod for questioning the reformed teaching of the inability to merit salvation by the free action of the will.[8] In his philosophy also the imperative of defending freedom of the will requires an incorporealist metaphysic: "mens actions are sometimes *free* and sometimes *not free*; but in that they are at any time

[7]Ralph Cudworth, *The True Intellectual System of the Universe* (1678; facs. rpt. Stuttgart-Bad Cannstatt: Friedrich Frommann, 1964), p. A3ʳ (Preface). Cudworth's massive work begins with Book I but never reaches Book II; in references I cite chapter and section numbers in large and small Roman numerals and subsection numbers where supplied in Arabic numerals.
[8]This story is quoted from Richard Ward's 1710 *Life of More* in Grosart's edition of More's poetry, pp. xiii–xiv.

free, is a Demonstration that there is a Faculty in us that is incompetible to [not within the capacity of] *mere Matter*."⁹

Cudworth and More countered the threats to free will and theism that they perceived in mechanist philosophy by arguing for an animate universe. Spirit, one of the two constituent parts of reality and the only self-active part, is incorporeal and not subject to mechanical laws. It pervades the universe and is ultimately responsible for every motion and change; pure mechanism can account for no organic operation, nor even for the origin of present mechanical motion. A low-level and unconscious spirit, Cudworth's "plastic nature" or More's "Spirit of Nature," guides the formation of everything from iron ore to a blade of grass to the complex human body. Spirit moves the heart, the matter of which by definition cannot move itself.

Despite their insistence on the presence of spirit behind every physical motion, it would be a mistake to view Cudworth and More as obscurantist reactionaries, bravely if foolishly doing battle with the new science and its clear appeal to the evidence of the senses. Again and again champions of the action of incorporeal phenomena invoked the evidence of the senses against "empiricist" skeptics.¹⁰ Joseph Glanvill, a member of the Royal Society with close ties to the Cambridge Platonists, writes,

> I must confess, there is *one Argument* against me, which is not to be dealt with, *viz.* a *mighty confidence* grounded upon *nothing*, that *swaggers*, and *huffs*, and swears there are no WITCHES. For such *Philosophers* as *these*, let them enjoy the *Opinion* of their own *Super-*

⁹Henry More, *The Immortality of the Soul* (1659), rpt. in *A Collection of Several Philosophical Writings*, 2 vols. (1662; facs. rpt. New York: Garland, 1978), p. 77 (II, iii, 21). The works in this folio edition (*An Antidote against Atheism*,1652; *Enthusiasmus Triumphatus*, 1656; *Epistolae Quatuor ad Renatum Des-Cartes*, 1655; *Immortality*; and *Conjectura Cabbalistica*, 1653) are paginated separately; further references to these works will be from this edition.
¹⁰In a valuable recent study, Kyungwon Shin places Cudworth and More in a native tradition that combined empiricism and idealism: "Cheyne, Hale, the Cambridge Platonists, and Shaftesbury, all search for an organic unity between the corporeal and the incorporeal worlds, necessarily adopting both empiricism and idealism" ("The English Origins of Wordsworth's Romanticism" [Ph.D. dissertation, University of Minnesota, 1988], p. 62).

lative Judgments, and enter me in the first rank of *Fools* for crediting my *Senses*, and those of all the world, before their *sworn* Dictates. If they will believe in *Scott*, *Hobbes*, and *Osborne*, and think them more infallible than the *Sacred* Oracles, the *History* of all Ages, and the *full expression* of our *own*, who can help it? They must not be *contradicted*, and they are resolved not to be perswaded.[11]

Glanvill's senses convince him that there are spirits active around him as surely as Hobbes's senses convince him that there are not. Having noted the soberness and reputations for veracity of many who have left accounts of apparitions, Cudworth echoes Glanvill in yoking spirit beliefs with responsible empiricism:

Whereas the Atheists impute the *Original* of these things, to mens Mistaking both their *Dreams*, and their *Waking Phancies*, for *Real Visions* and *Sensations*; they do hereby plainly contradict one Main Fundamental Principle of their own *Philosophy*, that *Sense* is the only *Ground of Certainty*, and the *Criterion* of all *Truth*: for if Prudent and Intelligent persons may be so frequently mistaken, in confounding their own *Dreams* and *Phancies* with *Sensations*, how can there be any Certainty of knowledge at all from Sense?[12]

Perhaps more surprising, the champions of the active presence of incorporeal substance behind corporeal motion also adopted mechanical explanations to demonstrate that presence.[13] More himself disqualifies various organs as material principles or locations of the *"the seat of Common Sense"* on mechanical grounds: the pumping of the heart, for example, would not allow us "to see things steddily or fix our sight in the

---

[11]Joseph Glanvill, *Saducismus Triumphatus* (London, 1682), sig. E8r.

[12]Cudworth, *True Intellectual System*, p. 700 (V, i). He refers chiefly to Hobbes here.

[13]Basil Willey has discussed the extent to which seventeenth-century writers on various sides of the materialism-vs.-incorporealism debate depended on the explanation of natural processes, even mental ones, "by constructing an illustrative mental picture of the process on mechanical principles" (*The Seventeenth Century Background: Studies in the Thought of the Age in Relation to Poetry and Religion* [London: Chatto & Windus, 1942], p. 176).

same place."[14] Glanvill, noting his debt to More, attacks Hobbes's conception of memory as decaying sense by pointing to the gelid constitution of the brain, which is "of such a clammy consistence, that it can no more retain it [motion] then a *Quagmire*."[15] Materialist mechanists extrapolated from the observation of corporeal motion the reduceability of mental activity to microscopic particle motion within the body. Incorporealists for their part granted the value of empirical observation, but in such observation they found confirmation of the inadequacy of corporeal motion to account for thought and other actions.

While the Cambridge Platonists were disturbed by many of the implications of the mechanist world-view, they were not obscurantist opponents of research into the nature of things. Among the most interesting chapters in the history of seventeenth-century natural philosophy is the debate between More and Robert Boyle over the metaphysical implications of Boyle's air-pump experiments. More welcomed the experiments as a weapon in his battle against atheism, interpreting the results as confirming the existence not of a relative vacuum as Boyle supposed but of incorporeal substance.[16] Boyle welcomed More's interest but disagreed with the use to which his experiments had been put.

The Cambridge Platonists' relation to atomism, like their relation to empirical science, is far from simple; both Cudworth and More subscribe to a carefully redefined atomism. In the preface to the *True System*, Cudworth declares that he "conceive[s] this *Atomick Physiology*, as to the Essentials thereof, to be

---

[14]More, *Immortality of the Soul*, p. 78 (II, iv, 4).

[15]Joseph Glanvill, *The Vanity of Dogmatizing* (London, 1661), p. 38; this work, along with the later versions, *Scepsis Scientifica* (1665) and "Against Confidence in Philosophy, and Matters of Speculation" (1676), is available in facsimile in *The Vanity of Dogmatizing: The Three Versions*, crit. introd. Stephen Medcalf (Hove, Sussex: Harvester Press, 1970).

[16]For the debate, see More, *An Antidote against Atheism*, pp. 43–46 (II, ii) and Boyle, *An Hydrostatical Discourse, Occasioned by the Objections of the Learned Dr. Henry More, against Some Explications of New Experiments Made by Mr. Boyle* (1672). See also Steven Shapin and Simon Schaffer, *Leviathan and the Air-Pump: Hobbes, Boyle, and the Experimental Life* (Princeton: Princeton University Press, 1985), pp. 207–24.

Unquestionably True."[17] Rightly understood, atomism is not a breeding ground for atheism, but rather "the most effectual Engin against Atheism that can be."[18] Cudworth's support for this statement is in part historical: Cudworth reads the ancient pre-Democritic atomists as uncompromising incorporealists and theists.

Cudworth and More's atomist gambit was shrewd if ultimately ineffective. They attempted to redefine atomism in order to bring this increasingly influential system into line with their own incorporealist convictions. They argued that true ancient atomism bore little resemblance to the bastard atomism of Democritus, Epicurus, and their seventeenth-century followers.[19] More announces that the atomic philosophy descended to Democritus through Pythagoras from its ultimate source, the Sidonian Moschus or Moses himself.[20] Cudworth contends that what we think of as atomism is actually only a half, and the inferior half, of ancient atomist doctrine. Early mechanist atomists viewed the "doctrine of Atoms" as "a Part or Member of the whole Philosophick System, and that the meanest and lowest part too, it being only used to explain that which was purely Corporeal in the World; besides which they acknowledged something else, which was not meer Bulk and Mechanism, but Life and Self Activity, that is, Immaterial or Incorporeal Substance; the Head and Summity whereof is the Deity distinct from the World."[21] The cardinal principle of early atomism was "*De Nihilo Nihil, in Nihilum Nil posse reverti,*

---

[17]Cudworth, *True Intellectual System*, p. *2ʳ (Preface). For More's declaration of an atomist conception of matter, see his *Immortality of the Soul*, p. 3 (Preface), and his *Answer to a Learned Psychopyrist concerning the True Notion of a Spirit*, appended to Joseph Glanvill's *Saducismus Triumphatus* (London, 1689), pp. 224 ff.

[18]Cudworth, *True Intellectual System*, p. 12 (I, viii).

[19]John Webster named Descartes as the reviver of Democritus in *Academiarum Examen, or the Examination of Academies* (London, 1654), p. 106.

[20]More, *Conjectura Cabbalistica*, pp. 102–3 (Appendix to the Defence of the Philosophick Cabbala i, 8). Cudworth also endorses this speculation in the *True Intellectual System*, p. 12 (I, x), and in the posthumous *Treatise concerning Eternal and Immutable Morality* (London, 1731), pp. 55–64 (II, iv).

[21]Cudworth, *True Intellectual System*, p. 18 (I, xviii).

That *Nothing can come from Nothing, nor go to Nothing*."[22] Cudworth claims (although his evidence is thin here) that this principle led the ancient atomists to an acknowledgment of incorporeal substance (and by extension theism):

> *It is impossible for a real Entity to be made or Generated from Nothing preexisting.* Now there is Nothing of Soul or Mind, Reason and Understanding, nor indeed of Cogitation and Life, contained in the Modifications and Mechanism of Bodies.

> Because there is nothing else clearly intelligible in Body, besides Magnitude, Figure, Site, and Motion, and their various Conjugations, . . . *Life, Cogitation,* and *Understanding* can be no Corporeal things, but must needs be the Attributes of another kind of Substance distinct from Body.[23]

The villains of the history of philosophy are Democritus and Leucippus, not because they introduced atomism, but because they stripped genuine atomist doctrine of its incorporeal half:

> This entire Body of Philosophy came to be *Mangled* and *Dismembred*, . . . some snatching away the Atomical Physiology, without the Pneumatology and Theology; and others, on the contrary, taking the Theology and Doctrine of Incorporeals, without the Atomical or Mechanical Physiology. The former of these were *Democritus, Leucippus,* and *Protagoras,* who took only the dead Carcase or Skeleton of the old *Moschical* [or Mosaic] *Philosophy,* namely the Atomical Physiology; the latter *Plato* and *Aristotle,* who took indeed the better Part, the *Soul, Spirit,* and *Quintessence* of it, the Theology and Doctrine of Incorporeals, but Unbodied, and Devested of its most Proper and convenient Vehicle, the Atomical

[22]Ibid., p. 30 (I, xxviii). Cudworth marshals this principle against Aristotle's substantial forms, which, he thinks, come into and leave existence with the modifications of matter.

[23]Ibid., pp. 36, 50 (I, xxix and xl). Cudworth notes also that the ancients, lacking a notion of the immediate creation of souls by God, accepted the logical consequence of the preexistence of souls. More's *Conjectura Cabbalistica,* George Rust's *Letter of Resolution concerning Origen* (1661), and Glanvill's *Lux Orientalis* (1662) are related philosophical theodicies that share the provocative and audacious claim that the preexistence of souls is necessary to acquit God of the injustice of consigning innocent souls to a fallen world. Instead, they argue that postlapsarian human souls sinned before their incarnation.

Physiology, whereby it became exposed to sundry Inconveniences.[24]

As Cudworth concludes from his exhaustive historical survey, Democritus and Leucippus stray as far from ancient atomist teachings as do Plato and Aristotle.

For all Cudworth's immense learning, there is something perverse about the history offered in the *True Intellectual System*. On the basis of scanty and often perforce second- or third-hand sources, Cudworth redefines atomism so radically that it is no longer a mechanical philosophy.[25] Little remains of atomism as a doctrine beyond the assertion that what is visible is ultimately resolvable into indivisible parts. Gassendi and Charleton attempted to make atomism compatible with theism and incorporealism; to make the more difficult argument that atomism *entails* incorporealism Cudworth must make agile use of the historical record. But as has been suggested there are strong contemporary pressures at work on Cudworth's ostensibly historical project. When Cudworth claims that the ancient atomists "would have concluded it, the greatest Impudence or Madness, for men to assert that Animals also consisted of mere Mechanism; or, that Life and Sense, Reason and Understanding, were really nothing else but Local Motion, and consequently that themselves were but Machins and *Automata*," the targets of his polemic become clear.[26] Behind the text stand Descartes and Hobbes.

---

[24]Cudworth, *True Intellectual System*, p. 51 (I, xlii).

[25]Hans Blumenberg has argued that seventeenth-century atomism reoccupied the position of medieval voluntarist nominalism: both "regard the origin of the world as an event inaccessible to human rationality" (*The Legitimacy of the Modern Age*, trans. Robert M. Wallace [Cambridge: MIT Press, 1983], p. 151). Cudworth's redefinition marks a futile attempt to link atomism with rationalism and realism.

[26]Cudworth, *True Intellectual System*, p. 50 (I, xli). The assertion that "animals consisted of mere Mechanism" is tied firmly to Descartes, who also equated local motion with life and sense, if not reason and understanding as did Hobbes. Cudworth argued against Descartes and with tradition that the presence of the soul and not mechanical motion separates the living from the dead body (I, i, 29). More picks up Descartes's watch analogy (*Passions of the Soul* I, 6) but uses it against him: "they . . . imagine, that though neither Silver, nor Steel, nor Iron, nor Lute-Strings, have any Sense apart, yet being put together

Anti-Hobbesian animus fuels the works of Cudworth and
More. More's two main philosophical works, *An Antidote against
Atheism* and *The Immortality of the Soul*, are directed explicitly
against Hobbes, and Cudworth's *True Intellectual System* is a
monumental refutation of a contemporary never mentioned by
name, but referred to repeatedly as a "sottish and impudent"
thinker and a "modern atheistical writer."[27] Hobbes attacks
cherished parts of the Cambridge system: incorporeal substance, the innate idea, rational religion, freedom of the will,
toleration, etc. Hobbes's argument that Descartes's term "'a
great light in the intellect' is metaphorical, and so has no force
in . . . argument" seems calculated to infuriate the Cambridge
Platonists, who talked of the "inner light" as a real and incorporeal phenomenon, taking as their text Proverbs 20:27: "The
spirit of man is the candle of the Lord."[28] The many differences between Hobbes and the Platonists are rooted in the
clash between their monist and dualist metaphysics. To Hobbes
it is self-evident that there is nothing in the universe but matter
in motion. To the Platonists, as to Descartes though in a different way, it is self-evident that reality is twofold. More charges
revealingly that Hobbes, in stating that "incorporeal substance"

---

in such a manner and formed as will (suppose) make a compleat *Watch*, they
may have *Sense*; that is to say, that a Watch may be a living creature, though the
several parts have neither *Life* nor *Sense*" (*Immortality of the Soul*, p. 77 [II, iv, 1]).
[27]A disjunction at one point between the text and the lengthy synoptic table of
contents offers an intriguing clue to the pervasive presence of Hobbes in Cudworth's book. Pointing to a passage in the text quoted from Plato's *Sophist* 246[b],
the table of contents paraphrases not Plato but Hobbes on body. The quotation
from Plato reads as follows: "They contend strongly, that that only really Is,
which is Tangible or Can Resist their Touch; concluding Body and Substance,
to be one and the self-same thing. And if any one should affirm, that there is
any thing Incorporeal, they will presently cry him down, and not hear a word
more from him" (768). Pointing to the last sentence in the Contents is this
sentence: "From whence it follows, that *Incorporeal Substance*, is *Incorporeal Body*,
or *Contradictious Nonsense*; and that whatsoever is not *Body*, is *Nothing*" (i2[v]). For
the source passages, see *Leviathan*, ed. C. B. Macpherson (Harmondsworth:
Penguin, 1968), pp. 108, 429, 439 (chaps. 4 and 34).
[28]See Patrides, *Cambridge Platonists*, pp. 11–18. Hobbes is quoted from "Third
Set of Objections to the *Meditations*," xiii, in *The Philosophical Writings of Descartes*, trans. John Cottingham, Robert Stoothoff, and Dugald Murdoch, 2 vols.
(Cambridge: Cambridge University Press, 1984–85), 2:134.

is a contradiction in terms, merely assumes what needs to be proved.[29]

In his refutation of materialism Cudworth quotes Hobbes extensively and argues that without the continuing presence of activating spirit the world would grind to a halt: "were there no other *Substance* in the World besides this *Magnitude* or *Extension*, there could be no *Motion* or *Action* at all in it; . . . but all would be a dead *Heap* or *Lump*."[30] The activity of spirit lies behind "mechanical" as well as mental phenomena; without spirit, there would be no engine of corporeal activity. The rarefied animal spirits, advanced by some as the principle of life and action, are subordinated to truly incorporeal substance. More insists then that "that which impresses *Spontaneous Motion* upon the *Body*, or more immediately upon the *Animal Spirits*, that which *imagines*, *remembers*, and *reasons*, is an *Immaterial Substance distinct from the Body*, which uses the *Animal Spirits* and the *Brains* for instruments in such and such Operations."[31]

The activity of incorporeal substance is crucial in the theories of perception of the Cambridge Platonists. They viewed Hobbes's argument that knowledge is derived from sense perceptions and the subsequent motions derived from these perceptions as an attempt to account for action while denying any active principle.[32] They argued that knowledge arises from the mind's active employment of innate ideas to make sense of perceptual data. Without these innate ideas, the existence of which Hobbes denied, there would be no way for our minds to order the chaos of sense impressions received passively. The world would remain forever the confusion of William James's perceiver with full sensory capacity but no knowledge or expe-

---

[29]More, *Immortality of the Soul*, p. 40 (I, x, 1).

[30]Cudworth, *True Intellectual System*, p. 829 (V, iii). For a typical, lengthy quotation of Hobbes (in this case the famous passage on there being no place for anything but body in the universe), see p. 650 (V, i).

[31]More, *Antidote against Atheism*, p. 36 (I, xi, 11).

[32]Hobbes's conception anticipates Locke's *abrasa tabula*. Henry More was familiar with the *abrasa tabula*, but he applied it only to sensation. In his annotations to Glanvill's *Lux Orientalis* he writes: "To all sensitive objects the soul is an abrasa tabula, but for moral and intellectual principles, their ideas or notions are essential to the soul" (quoted in Florence Isabel MacKinnon, *Philosophical Writings of Henry More* [New York: Oxford University Press, 1925], p. 260).

rience, as More suggests in the Spenserian verse of *Psycha-thanasia* (III.ii.45):

> Of old Gods hand did all forms write
> In humane souls, which waken at the knock
> Of *Mundane* shapes. If they were naked quite
> Of innate forms, though heaven and earth should rock
> With roring winds, they'd hear no more then senseless stock.

Cudworth contends that this "atheistic argument" leads to an absurd conclusion: "The world could not be made by *Knowledge* and *Understanding*, because there could be no *Knowledge* or *Understanding* of the world, or of anything in it, before it was made. For according to these Atheists, *Things* made *Knowledge*, and not *Knowledge Things*; they meaning by *Things* here, such only as are *Sensible* and *Corporeal*." Cudworth leaves no doubt as to whom he refers, for he immediately quotes Hobbes on knowledge and understanding as a corporeal "Tumult in the Mind."[33] This "sottish conceit" leads to another absurdity, that pools and mirrors see and understand. Cudworth immediately presents his alternative, "*Sensible* things . . . are not *Known* or *Understood* either by the *Passion*, or the *Phancy of Sense*, not by any thing meerly *Forreign* and *Adventitious*, but by *Intelligible Ideas* Exerted from the Mind it self, that is, by something *Native* and *Domestick* to it," and he quotes Boethius for confirmation: "Whatsoever is Known, is Known not by its own Force and Power, but by the Force and Power, the Vigour and Activity of that thing it self which Knows or Comprehends it." Cudworth divides the perceptive power of the soul in two: "besides Passion from Corporeal things, or the Passive Perception of the Sense, there is in the Souls of Men another more Active Principle or an *Innate Cognoscitive Power*, whereby they are enabled to Understand or Judge of what is Received from without by Sense."[34] Even the first apparently passive function of the soul is in fact active; as Cudworth explains it, the motions transmit-

---

[33]Cudworth, *True Intellectual System*, p. 730 (V, i); Cudworth quotes *Leviathan*, p. 403 (chap. 31).
[34]Cudworth, *Eternal and Immutable Morality*, p. 131 (IV, i).

ted by the senses to the brain are not direct images of external objects, but "dumb signs" of those objects, which the soul translates by providing the images for which the motions act as signs.[35] The innate notions of the mind serve not only as the key for deciphering sensory motions, but also as the basis of the rational understanding of morality and theology. Notions of good, evil, the perfections of God, etc., are not matters of convention as they are for the nominalist Hobbes, but a priori truths. To those, such as Hobbes, who argued that the innate idea of God is merely something constructed by the fancy, More was just as peremptory as was Hobbes with those who spoke of incorporeal substance: "I answer, that no man can discourse and reason of any thing without recourse to settled Notions deciphered in his own Mind."[36]

The Cambridge Platonists diametrically opposed the materialist Hobbes on every significant philosophical and theological issue. Their relation to the dualist mechanists Descartes and Gassendi is more complex. Although they knew Descartes much better, Cudworth does mention Gassendi several times in his *True Intellectual System*. While he styles himself a Christian atomist like Gassendi, Cudworth suspects Gassendi of giving too much latitude to mechanism. Cudworth finds grounds for condemnation even in Gassendi's project of Christianization of ancient atomism, a project in which his mechanist and therefore atheistic allegiances are paradoxically revealed: "We may observe the Fraud and Juggling of *Gassendus*, who . . . extol[s] and applaud[s] *Epicurus*, as one who approached nearer to Christianity than all the other Philosophers, in that he denied the *World to be an Animal*; whereas according to the Language and Notions of those times, to deny the *Worlds Animation*, and to *be an Atheist* or to deny a *God*, was one and the same thing."[37] Gassendi runs afoul of Cudworth's massive demonstration of the basic monotheism underlying the apparent polytheism of the ancient Greeks and Romans. Cudworth construes early pa-

[35]Ibid., pp. 216–17 (IV, iii). See John W. Yolton, *Perceptual Acquaintance from Descartes to Reid* (Minneapolis: University of Minnesota Press, 1984), pp. 28–29.
[36]More, *Antidote against Atheism*, p. 14 (I, iv, 1).
[37]Cudworth, *True Intellectual System*, p. 462 (IV, xxix).

gan beliefs in an animate universe as gestures toward a belief in the manifestation of one God in an animate universe. Gassendi, like Descartes, violates the Cambridge imperative of the activity of spirit behind all phenomena.

If the Cambridge Platonists were initially more favorable to Descartes, it is because his mechanist theory is prefaced by strong arguments for the existence of God and incorporeal substance. No less a mechanist than Gassendi, Descartes presented a different face. The Cambridge Platonists welcomed Descartes's arguments for the incorporeality of mind and God, and they borrowed his language and key conceptions. Cudworth, for example, accepted extension as the defining attribute of corporeal substance and endorsed the Cartesian term "*res extensa.*"[38] Even so, they had some reservations about the incorporealist Descartes; Cudworth joined the chorus criticizing the "Cartesian circle" and Descartes's use of the ontological argument.[39] And when the Cambridge Platonists turned to his physics and cosmogony, they became hostile. Their writings increasingly presented Descartes as a suspect theist or fellow traveler of the atheistic mechanists.

In Henry More's reactions to Descartes one can trace the growing ambivalence toward Descartes in Cambridge. More corresponded with Descartes in the year prior to Descartes's death, and his early reaction, though qualified with doubts, was enthusiastic. In his works through the 1650s, More celebrates Descartes; in the *Conjectura Cabbalistica* he adds him to the line of Moses, Pythagoras, and Plato.[40] As Cudworth did with the ancient atomists, More commends Descartes for demonstrating the limitations of matter in motion. When More calls in the *Immortality of the Soul* for "the reading of *Des-Cartes* in all publick Schools or Universities," he does so largely because he is convinced that readers will see in Descartes what mechanism

[38] Ibid., p. 829 (V, iii).
[39] Ibid., pp. 717, 723 (V, 1).
[40] More, *Conjectura Cabbalistica*, p. 104 (Appendix to the Defence of the Philosophick Cabbala i, 8). Compare H. Darsy's encomiastic poem printed in Glanvill's *Vanity of Dogmatizing*: "Summon *Des-Cartes, Plato, Socrates*; / Let this great *Triad* speak your praise" (sig. B5ᵛ).

can and cannot do.[41] In the late 1650s More argued that events that cannot be explained mechanically call for explanation by spirit. By the end of the next decade, in the *Divine Dialogues* of 1668, More would write that mechanism can do nothing: "there is no purely-Mechanical *Phænomenon* in the whole Universe."[42]

The Platonists came to fear that a dualist metaphysic promising to harmonize science and theology could be used as an instrument for expanding the province of the former and contracting the province of the latter. Descartes's mechanism could not be ignored after Hobbes's universal materialism threatened the existence of spirit altogether, and Descartes's corporeal principle of life fell under suspicion. Cudworth attacks Descartes's description of animals (and human bodies) as automata, and he labels Descartes's attempt to explain the beating of the heart by "a *Pulsifick Corporeal Quality*" in the heart "very Unphilosophical and Absurd."[43] While Cudworth denies that life can be derived from body, More challenges Cartesian physiology on mechanical grounds. The pineal gland, he argues, is "so

---

[41]More, *Immortality of the Soul*, p. 13 (Preface). The standard view that More discovered Descartes's unpalatable mechanism after a period of uncritical enthusiasm can be found in John Tulloch, *Rational Theology and Christian Philosophy in England in the Seventeenth Century*, 2d ed., 2 vols. (Edinburgh, 1874), 2:368–97; Sterling P. Lamprecht, "The Role of Descartes in Seventeenth-Century England," *Studies in the History of Ideas*, vol. 3, ed. Columbia University Department of Philosophy (New York: Columbia University Press, 1935), pp. 181–240; Marjorie Nicolson, "The Early Stages of Cartesianism in England," *Studies in Philology* 26 (1929): 356–74; and Ernst Cassirer, *The Platonic Renaissance in England*, trans. J. P. Pettegrove (London: Nelson, 1953), pp. 129–56. Recently, Alan Gabbey has significantly modified the received view, pointing out that all of More's later substantive objections to Descartes are contained in the correspondence of 1648–49. Gabbey suggests that it is More's polemical purpose that changes rather than his understanding of Descartes; in the 1640s and 1650s More was confident of an alliance between the new philosophy and the theology that was always his chief concern. As the 1660s progressed, More became more pessimistic and turned more exclusively to theological writings. See Gabbey, "Philosophia Cartesiana Triumphata: Henry More (1646–1671)," in *Problems of Cartesianism*, ed. Thomas M. Lennon, John M. Nicholas, and John W. Davis (Montreal: McGill-Queen's University Press, 1982), pp. 171–250.
[42]Henry More, *Divine Dialogues* (London, 1668), "The Publisher to the Reader."
[43]Cudworth, *True Intellectual System*, p. 161 (III, xxxvii, 17).

weak and so small a thing" that it "seems utterly unable to *determine* the *Spirits* with that force and violence we find they are determined in *running, striking, thrusting* and the like."[44] More is pressing not for a better mechanical explanation of movement, but for a nonmechanical one.

The Platonists were even less patient with Cartesian cosmology. According to Descartes's vortex theory (*Principles of Philosophy* III), *res extensa*, after creation by God, organized itself into the visible universe in accordance with natural forces. Final causes lose their scientific and metaphysical value. Cudworth names Descartes chief of the "mechanic Theists," with the emphasis more and more on the adjective as the treatise progresses. He charges that Descartes and his fellow "mechanic Theists" claim more for matter than even the ancient atheist materialists, who never suggested that the *"Fortuitous Motions* of Atoms" led to our ordered world without first producing *"Inept Combinations"* and *"Nonsensical Systems."*[45] Cudworth would choose Aristotle, vilified by Hobbes and criticized by Descartes, over either of these modern mechanists, because Aristotle insists on final causes in nature:

> *Aristotle's* System of Philosophy seems to be more consistent with Piety, than the Cartesian *Hypothesis* it self, which yet plainly supposeth Incorporeal Substance. For as much as this latter makes God to contribute nothing more to the Fabrick of the World, than the Turning round of a *Vortex* or Whirlpool of Matter; from the fortuitous Motion of which, according to certain General Laws of Nature, must proceed all this Frame of things that now is, . . . without the Guidance of any Mind or Wisdom. Whereas *Aristotle's* Nature is no Fortuitous Principle, but such as doth Nothing in *Vain*, but all for *Ends*, and in every thing pursues *the Best*; and therefore can be no other than a Subordinate Instrument of the Divine Wisdom.[46]

Cudworth betrays his ultimate judgment of Descartes when he substitutes "Pretended" for "mechanic" in attacking the

[44]More, *Immortality of the Soul*, p. 81 (II, v, 3).
[45]Cudworth, *True Intellectual System*, p. 683 (V, i); see a similar argument by John Ray in 1691, quoted in Lamprecht, "Role of Descartes," p. 226.
[46]Cudworth, *True Intellectual System*, p. 54 (I, xlv).

great "*Insensibility of Mind*, or *Sottishness* and *Stupidity* in *Pretended Theists*" for their denial of the value of final cause and teleology in science.[47] "Sottishness and stupidity" are terms linked to Hobbes throughout the treatise, and clearly "mechanic theism" is one short step from atheistic materialism in Cudworth's mind. Cudworth and More, despite their sympathy with Descartes, both suggest that Hobbesian materialism is the logical conclusion of Cartesian mechanism.[48] They were alarmed also by the voluntarism that Descartes shared with Hobbes. In his response to the sixth set of objections to his *Meditations*, Descartes asserts the same indifference of God's will that More and Cudworth attack as evidence of atheism in Hobbes. God establishes the good and the just, and even the laws of the triangle, by his free choice, which is logically prior to innate truth or morality.[49] Cudworth handles this "error" with only slightly less vehemence than he reserves for Hobbes: by allowing God's will to "*Devour* and *Swallow* up" God's wisdom, Descartes reveals that he, "notwithstanding all his pretences to Demonstrate a Deity, was indeed but an *Hypocritical Theist*, or *Personated* and *Disguised Atheist*."[50] By 1671, increasingly alarmed at the threat of mechanism to incorporealism and theism, More was distancing himself actively from his former ally, who is now styled as

> that pleasant Wit *Renatus des Cartes*, who by his jocular *Metaphysical Meditations*, has so luxated and distorted the rational Faculties of some otherwise sober and quick-witted Persons, but in this point by their over-great admiration of *Des Cartes* not sufficiently cautious, that deceived partly by his counterfeit and prestigious Subtilty, and partly by his Authority, have persuaded themselves that such things were most *true* and *clear* to them; which had they

[47]Ibid., p. 684 (V, i). On the following page Cudworth quotes the dismissals of final cause in *Meditations* IV and the *Principles of Philosophy* I, 28 (Cottingham 1:39 and 2:202).
[48]See Cudworth's *True Intellectual System*, p. 761 (V, ii); More's *Immortality of the Soul*, p. 84 (II, v, 10), and More's "The Easy, True and Genuine Notion of a Spirit," in MacKinnon, *Henry More*, p. 211.
[49]Cottingham 2:291–92 ("Sixth Set of Replies to the Objections to the *Meditations*," para. 6).
[50]Cudworth, *True Intellectual System*, p. 646 (V, i).

been not blinded with these Prejudices, they could never have thought to have been so much as possible.[51]

The man who More had hoped would preserve God and incorporeal substance from mechanism now seemed to be delivering them over to the enemy.

In both Cudworth and More, corporeal motion is originated by spirit in the form of a low-level, unconscious incorporeal substance, called "plastic nature" by Cudworth and the "spirit of nature" by More. When Cudworth argues that "he that asserts a *Plastick Nature*, asserts *Mental Causality* in the World," he means that God uses the incorporeal plastic nature to shape the world according to his wisdom and idea; the plastic nature itself has "no *Animal Fancie*, no Express *Con-sense* or *Consciousness* of what it doth." Action in general rather than thought, one of its manifestations, identifies incorporeal substance. The plastic nature is not so much a *res cogitans* as it is "the mere *Umbrage* of *Intellectuality*, a faint and shadowy *Imitation* of *Mind* and *Understanding*."[52] Cudworth insisted that this incorporeal plastic nature is alive: "Though the *Plastick Nature* be indeed the Lowest of all *Lives*, yet notwithstanding since it is a *Life*, or *Internal Energy*, and *Self-activity*, distinct from *Local Motion*, it must needs be *Incorporeal*, all *Life* being Essentially such. But the Hylozoists conceive grossly both of *Life* and *Understanding*, spreading them all over upon Matter, just as Butter is spread upon Bread, or Plaster upon a Wall."[53] Ironically, for his conception of plastic nature Cudworth was to be accused of the hylozoic atheism, the belief that life is a property of matter rather than of spirit.[54]

Where Hobbes leaves us with the problem of how matter can think and Descartes with the problem of how mind and body meet in the pineal gland, the Cambridge Platonists cannot

[51]More, "The Easy, True and Genuine Notion of a Spirit," in MacKinnon, *Henry More*, p. 184.
[52]Cudworth, *True Intellectual System*, pp. 155, 159, 172 (III, xxxvii, 7, 15, 26).
[53]Ibid., p. 173 (III, xxxvii, 26).
[54]See Passmore, *Ralph Cudworth*, p. 23.

make clear the manner in which spirit, whether conscious soul or unconscious plastic nature, interacts with bodies. They subscribed simultaneously to ontological dualism and monism. They spoke of spirit and matter sometimes as separate and incommensurate substances, and other times as mutually interpenetrating and intermixing substances. George Rust writes, as we would expect of a strict ontological dualist, of the moral neutrality of matter: "You are not wont to be so great a friend to Mr. *Hobbes* as to think that *matter* by what name soever it be called, *dead* or *living*, hath any sense or perception at all, much less can it be vertuous or vicious. . . . I believe the matter that makes up the *vehicle* of the Devil is as well content with its lot as that which composes the beautiful robe of an Angel of light."[55] More makes a similar point when he argues that only the soul can make the Platonic ascent. The "great mystery of Christianity" is "The perfecting of the Humane nature by participation of the Divine. *Which cannot be understood so properly of this gross flesh and External senses, as of the Inward humanity*, viz. *our Intellect, Reason, and Fancie.*"[56] These arguments are consistent with the dualism their authors usually endorse. But this position is not consistent with one that posits the moral darkness of matter, and the possibility that it will corrupt spirit. In his explication of Genesis 1:6, More explains why God does not pronounce matter good: "He was not very forward to say it was good, or to please himself much in it; because he foresaw what mischief straying Souls, if they were not very cautious, might bring to themselves by sinking themselves too deep therein."[57] John Smith writes that the divine and incorporeal Reason within us can be

> infected with those evil Opinions that arise from our Corporeal life. The more deeply our souls dive into our Bodies, the more will Reason and Sensuality run one into another, and make up a most dilute, unsavourie, and muddie kinde of Knowledge. We

[55]George Rust, *Letter of Resolution concerning Origen* (1661; facs. rpt. New York: Facsimile Text Society, 1933), p. 129.
[56]More, *Conjectura Cabbalistica*, p. 2 (Preface).
[57]Ibid., pp. 17–18 (Philosophick Cabbala i.7).

must therefore endeavour more and more to withdraw our selves from these Bodily things, to set our Soule as free as may be from its miserable slavery to this base Flesh.[58]

Whichcote condenses this aspect of Cambridge thought into an aphorism: "Good men Study to *Spiritualize* their Bodies; Bad men do *Incarnate* their Souls."[59] The Cambridge Platonists believed that the body can be purified by a moral life. The more the body is denied, the more refined or spiritous it will become. Conversely, the more it is indulged, the more it infects the soul with gross materiality. The thought is inconsistent with the stricter dualism voiced elsewhere, and it certainly is not Cartesian. There is here a vital interaction and something approaching a sharing of essence. The relative fuzziness of the division between substances is a function of their Neoplatonism, in which spirituality and corporeality are measured in relation to emanations above and below, but it jars with the dualistic claims for the absolute immateriality of spirit they make elsewhere in their writings.[60] The interaction of substances owes something to Pauline dualism; More's conflation of ontological and ethical dualism is suggested by his equation of Plato's Cave with a Spenserian "Errour's Den" (*Psychathanasia* I.i.15–16).

For More at least the incarnation of the soul and the spiritualization of the body were not mere metaphors. In a letter to Anne Conway of October 23, 1660, he writes that "excess of passion voluntarily yielded to, addes some soile to the soule, and is probably thought to make her exitus less prosperous

[58]John Smith, "The True Way or Method of Attaining to Divine Knowledge," in *Select Discourses* (1660), pp. 15–16; this essay is reprinted in Patrides, *Cambridge Platonists*, pp. 128–44. See also Rust, *Letter of Resolution*, p. 50; Glanvill, *Lux Orientalis*, p. 150; More, "Cupid's Conflict," in *Poems*, p. 174.

[59]*Moral and Religious Aphorisms*, #367, in Patrides, *Cambridge Platonists*, p. 330.

[60]R. J. Zwi Werblowsky notes: "Almost all historical manifestations of Neoplatonism are caught between the horns of this same dilemma: their ontological monism (the world as a chain of emanations and thence divine) and their axiological dualism which equates the radical contrast between good and evil with that between Spirit and Matter or Soul and Body" ("Milton and the *Conjectura Cabbalistica*," *Journal of the Warburg and Courtauld Institutes* 18 [1955]: 99).

into the other state."[61] I do not think that More is referring to some abstract stain; the "soile" is rather gross corporeal matter, a degenerative incarnation of the immaterial. In this letter More provides a literal example of the second part of Whichcote's aphorism. A letter to Conway of June 7, 1654, contains a literal example of the first part, in the form of a rational explanation of the power of a contemporary faith healer, Matthew Coker: "I have this odd conceit concerning this matter, that the blood and spiritts of this party is become sanative and healing, by long temperance and devotion, as I suppose, nature being so hugely advanced and perfectly concocted, that his blood and spiritts are a true elixir."[62] By virtuous life, More suggests, Coker has rarefied the matter of his blood and spirits; he has moved them toward immateriality.

For all its careful elaboration, More and Cudworth's theory of vehicles served only to deepen the ambiguity of their dualism. According to this theory the soul is always united with a corporeal vehicle.[63] Ficino had described the soul's most refined body, which it receives as it descends from God and relinquishes before merging again into God, as "not body and almost soul, and not soul and almost body."[64] More often leaves the impression that he has such an in-between category in mind, despite his announced dualism. There are three types of vehicles: the terrestrial, the aereal, and the celestial or aethereal. Men and animals inhabit terrestrial vehicles, daemons (the spirits of the middle air) inhabit aereal ones, and angels celestial ones.[65] The

---

[61]*Conway Letters: The Correspondence of Anne, Viscountess Conway, Henry More, and Their Friends, 1642–1684*, ed. Marjorie Nicolson (New Haven: Yale University Press, 1930), p. 169.

[62]Ibid., p. 101.

[63]See, for example, More, *Immortality*, p. 146 (III, i, 2), and Glanvill, *Lux Orientalis* (London, 1662), p. 131. Glanvill does speak of the possibility of "unembodyed Spirits," but argues that their mode of existence is beyond our conception (p. 133). The following discussion draws mainly from Henry More. For Cudworth's discussion of corporeal vehicles for the incorporeal soul, see the *True Intellectual System*, pp. 820–30 (V, iii).

[64]Ficino, *De Vita Coelitus Comparanda* III, 3 (Venice, 1516), fol. 153ʳ, quoted in Walter Pagel, "Paracelsus and the Neoplatonic and Gnostic Tradition," *Ambix* 8 (1960): 128.

[65]More, *Immortality of the Soul*, p. 35 (I, viii, 6).

more tenuous the vehicle, the swifter and keener the perception
they allow the soul; thus angels can know at once and intuitively
what we learn laboriously and discursively. Several of the group,
including More, Rust, and Glanvill, hold that man's soul descended into the terrestrial vehicle at the fall.[66]

Despite what he says about the soul falling "out of her *Airy*
Vehicle into this *terrestrial* Body," More writes that all three
vehicles are to be found in man. More invokes nature's abhor-
rence of a vacuum to demonstrate that the celestial vehicle
resides in the pores or pockets of the grosser aereal vehicle and
that the aereal vehicle resides in the pores of the terrestrial
vehicle.[67] (More does not explain how the "pores" in the terrestrial vehicles of animals do not contain higher vehicles.)
Man's full complement of vehicles in More's system provides
him with the metaphysical mobility familiar in Renaissance
Neoplatonism.

Although there is no one-to-one relationship between the
three vehicles and the Renaissance tripartite soul, there is a
close connection between the animal spirits in man and his
higher vehicles. Rust is consistent with More when he suggests
an equation between the celestial vehicle and the animal spirits:

What she [the soul] *perceives by* is neither flesh nor blood, . . . nor
any other gross part of our bodies, but that purer and subtiler
matter in us which is called *Animal spirits*; . . . if the Soul be an
immaterial substance distinct from the body, 'tis as easily conceived . . . how she should unite with an whole *vehicle* of such
pure matter as with her whole *terrestrial* body; especially she giving us even in this body a *specimen* of that capacity of hers, by
being in her highest degree of vitality united with some portion of
that matter [the animal spirits] already.[68]

---

[66]See ibid., pp. 119–23 (II, xiv–xv), and Rust, *Letter of Resolution*, p. 48. Glanvill
combines the ideas of keener angel perception with man's fall into the body at
the opening of *Vanity of Dogmatizing*: "Adam needed no Spectacles. The acute-
ness of his natural Opticks . . . shew'd him much of the Coelestial magnifi-
cence and bravery without Galilaeo's tube" (p. 5).

[67]More, *Immortality of the Soul*, p. 119 (II, xiv, 3).

[68]Rust, *Letter of Resolution*, p. 66.

The soul after death is united with an aereal or celestial vehicle that does not essentially differ from the tenuous matter of the animal spirits. It is presumably the celestial vehicle in a wicked person that contracts the "soil" of the terrestrial vehicle, and conversely the terrestrial vehicle that is purified and rarefied in the virtuous man. Thus More seems to avoid the charge of intermixing two incompatible substances across a dualism.

But More's theory of vehicles itself harbors some inconsistent implications, for in practice the higher vehicles provide a spirit-matter bridge in a dualist metaphysic that has no room for such a bridge. More verges toward a near equation of higher vehicle or animal spirits and spirit itself, even while repeatedly affirming the materiality of animal spirits and even of angelic vehicles.[69] The souls of the dead retain their perception and are saved from oblivion by their incorporation into a higher vehicle: "For they have no less Body then we our selves have, only this Body is far more active then ours, being more *spiritualized*, that is to say, having greater degrees of Motion communicated unto it; which the whole Matter of the world receives from some *Spiritual* Being or other, and therefore in this regard may be said the more to symbolize with that Immaterial Being, the more Motion is communicated to it."[70] More habitually uses "spirit" and "spiritual" to describe incorporeal substance, referring to the material spirits specifically as the "animal spirits." Has the higher vehicle merged with spirit? As always at a metaphysical crux, More cannot be pinned down. The higher vehicle "symbolizes with that *Immaterial Being*," an obscure construction that suggests a sharing of nature or qualities. Elsewhere More uses the negative of the same verb to suggest the incommensurability of matter and spirit: "It is as much spiritual as before, and does not herein symbolize with Matter, but

---

[69]For an assertion of the materiality of the animal spirits, see *Antidote* I, xi, 2: "these *Animal Spirits* are nothing else but matter very thin and liquid, whose nature consists in this, that all the particles of it be in Motion, and being loose from one another, fridge and play up and down according to the measure and manner of agitation in them" (p. 33).

[70]More, *Immortality of the Soul*, p. 154 (III, ii, 9).

approves itself contrary thereto."[71] If these distinctions seem muddled, then the reader has a taste of More.

Through a theory of vehicles a Neoplatonist emanationist hierarchy entered an avowedly Platonic dualism. Nevertheless, the Cambridge Platonists continued to argue for the distinction between corporeal and incorporeal substance, which is blurred rather than destroyed. In his doctrine of the extension of incorporeal substance, More went farther than the other Platonists in blurring this distinction, and, if one takes extension as the essence of matter, he did destroy it. More saw the extension of spirit as necessary for its role in moving matter—if spirit were not extended, it would not be able to move extended bodies—and also for its very existence. In this unique ontological excursion, More's thought converged, oddly enough, with that of his materialist enemies, who argued that all that exists is extended body.

More had glossed over Descartes's belief in the nonextension of immaterial substance in his early praise of the French philosopher. But later he begins, oddly enough, to sound like Hobbes: "It [is] of the very essence of whatsoever is, to have . . . *Extension* in some measure or other. For, to take away all *Extension*, is to reduce a thing onely to a Mathematical point, which is nothing else but pure Negation or Non-entity; and there being no *medium* betwixt *extended* and *not-extended*, no more then there is betwixt Entity and Non-entity, it is plain that if a thing be at all, it must be *extended*."[72] Recall Hobbes: "The Word *Body*, in the most general acceptation, signifieth that which filleth, or occupyeth some certain room, or imagined place; and dependeth not on the imagination, but is a real part of that we call the *Universe*."[73] More and Hobbes differed on the existence of incorporeal substance, but they agreed that

<hr />

[71]*An Answer to a Learned Psychopyrist*, in Glanvill, *Saducismus Triumphatus*, pp. 222–23. More goes on to argue that an atomist conception of matter can prevent the confusion of spiritual and material substance. If matter is particulate rather than continuous, then the move to immateriality cannot be merely a matter of greater tenuousness.

[72]More, *Immortality of the Soul*, p. 3 (Preface).

[73]*Leviathan*, p. 428 (chap. 34).

whatever is, is extended. Observers who overstress the affinity of More and his Cambridge allies with Descartes and their antagonism to Hobbes should note that Hobbes is reported to have said that after his own philosophy he preferred More's.[74] It is plausible that however much More railed against Hobbes and denounced the new mechanism, he was influenced by the emerging strength of materialism and the new criteria of reality. Looked at from one angle (and from one angle only), More held a monism of extended substance.[75] He maintained a dualism by substituting discerpibility (divisibility) and impenetrability for extension as the essential qualities of matter. Indivisibility and the power of penetration characterize spirit.

More's notion of extension differs from Hobbes's. The "metaphysical extension," although it *does* locate spirit in a place, is not defined by the familiar laws of length, breadth, and depth. Incorporeal substance of x extension can penetrate a body with y extension, and the resulting extension, despite the occupation by each substance of the same site, will be $x + y$. Thus when a metaphysical extension x and a physical extension y are "conjoined into one *Ubi*," they are "not a jot less than when they are separated and occupy an *Ubi* as big again; for the *Extension* in neither of them is diminished, but their *Situation* only changed."[76] This sounds more like density than extension, and in fact More assigns to spiritual extension a fourth dimension exotically named "Essential Spissitude," a term denoting density.[77] Thus spirits can expand or contract the places they fill without affecting their extensions, because of the resulting increase or decrease in essential spissitude. In addition,

[74]See MacKinnon, *Henry More*, p. 290; she cites Richard Ward's *Life of More* (London, 1710), p. 80.

[75]Alexander Koyré does in fact claim this type of monism for More in Koyré, *From the Closed World to the Infinite Universe* (Baltimore: Johns Hopkins University Press, 1957), p. 127; but while More has this monistic tendency, in the final analysis he remains a dualist.

[76]More, "True Notion," sec. xxi, in MacKinnon, *Henry More*, p. 212.

[77]Ibid., sec. xxii, in MacKinnon, *Henry More*, p. 213; for "essential spissitude," see *Immortality of the Soul*, p. 20 (I, ii, 11). This "metaphysical extension," for all of its differences from common extension, seems to share in the spirit of Boyle's investigation into the nature of gases. See the *Antidote against Atheism*, pp. 44–47 (II, ii).

More specifies that what is extended is the "secondary substance" of spirit, emanating from the "center of life," which is itself akin to a mathematical point. The analogy for the rayed extension of secondary spirit is *light*. It is indiscerpible from center to circumference (a ray of light cannot be separated from its fountain), but across these radii it is divisible (otherwise it could not shape and move itself). This discussion further blurs the line between spirit and matter. The tenuous matter of vehicles approaching spirit converges with the secondary substance of spirit approaching matter.

More calls those who deny extension to spirit "Nullibists" and crowns Descartes "Prince of the Nullibists."[78] More charges Descartes with denying spirit existence in denying spirit extension. One wonders whether More ever fully realized that his fellow Cambridge Platonists were by his definition nullibists. One by one his allies rejected More's notion of spirit extension. Cudworth kindly does not mention his friend's name when he denies the extension of spirit. He writes of the body as an "outside thing" and the spirit as an "inside thing": "Now this *Inside* of *Cogitative Beings*, wherein they thus Act or *Think* Internally within themselves, cannot have any *Length*, *Breadth*, or *Thickness* in it, because if it had, it would be again a meer *Outside thing*." Cudworth argues that even if the spirit had extension, it would be a merely "outside" and nonfunctional part of its being. He concludes: "It is Impossible, that One and the self same *Substance*, should be both *Extended* and *Unextended*. Wherefore in this *Hypothesis* of *Extended Understanding Spirits*, . . . there is an Undiscerned *Complication* of *Two Distinct Substances*, *Extended* and *Unextended*, or *Corporeal* and *Incorporeal*, both together; and a *Confusion* of them into One."[79] Cudworth also endorses the scholastic doctrine of the whole soul in the whole body and in every part, a doctrine which More labels "Holenmerism" and yokes with Nullibism, both

---

[78]"True Notion," in MacKinnon, *Henry More*, p. 184 (sec. ii). He coins the term from the Latin for the denial of "ubi" or place.
[79]Cudworth, *True Intellectual System*, p. 831 (V, iii).

forms of the denial of extension to spirit.[80] In this revealing
section of the *True System*, Cudworth makes the connection that
I am asserting here: More's opinion of incorporeal substance is
intertwined with contemporary beliefs in matter. In insisting
that spirit is extended, More accommodated an emerging criterion of reality (i.e., the material, or extended, is the "real")
inimical to the Cambridge program.

Those who struggle, with good reason, with More's conception of the metaphysical extension of spirit will be alarmed or
relieved to hear that More treats an inability to understand this
point as a disease of the mind, "this Corporeal Malady of *Imagination.*"[81] More writes as if one's understanding of the coexistence of metaphysical extension and physical extension in one
site is a matter of one's actively sending one's own mind's extension into matter. The mind of the person who does not grasp
metaphysical extension is unable "to *penetrate* with that *Spiritual*
Extension into the Extension *Material*; but like a stupid beast
stands lowing without, as if the Mind it self were become wholly
corporeal." More writes of "the *Mind* incrassated and swayed
down by the *Imagination,*" becoming "like a gross stupid thing,
and altogether Corporeal."[82] Thus the mind sick with imagination is in a sense another case in More of the immaterial being
soiled. More always qualifies his statements of the material in-
fection of the immaterial with "like's" and "as if's," but the
blurring of categories is always there.

More's particular set of strengths and shortcomings makes
him an invaluable test case in a study such as this. An uncritical
and eclectic thinker, he is a barometer of some interesting intellectual currents in the mid-seventeenth century. Many contemporary trends of thought found their way into his metaphysics,
usually at the expense of clarity and consistency. Probably without being aware of what he was doing, More responded to the

---

[80]See More, "True Notion," secs. xi–xv, in MacKinnon, *Henry More,* pp. 198–
205; the doctrine in question can be found in Aquinas, *Summa theologiae* I,
Q.76, art.8, and *Summa contra gentiles* II, lxxii.
[81]"True Notion," sec. xxi, in MacKinnon, *Henry More,* p. 212.
[82]Ibid.

emerging consensus that materiality is a major criterion of reality. Significantly, he developed his theory of spirit extension late; the traditional and opposed view appears, for example, in his poetry (*Psychathanasia* II.ii). While he continued to defend the existence of incorporeal substance against Hobbes late in his career, he began to describe that substance in terms normally reserved for matter. It is the empiricism that he shared with the new philosophy that moved him to argue that spirit must be extended throughout matter if it is to be able to move it. He was unwilling to accept, as his colleagues did, a spirit that does not need to be coextensive with matter in order to move it.

The Cambridge Platonists represent a vehement, defensive reaction against materialist mechanism and its theological implications in the mid-seventeenth century. Henry More, in his attempt to save spirit, moved beyond his colleagues to accommodate the materialist assertion of extension as criterion of reality. But others at the same time were impatient with any notion of incorporeal substance and were embracing materialism unequivocally. Among them was John Milton.

~ 3

Material Life:
Milton's Animist Materialism

In England the civil and ecclesiastical dislocation of the 1640s opened a space for intellectual innovation, as the successful challenge to the monarch's authority emboldened dissenters from philosophical authority.[1] Milton, among others, was to move toward a radical new conception of the relation between body and soul. By the late 1650s, Milton had become a materialist. Like other radical ideas, Milton's animist materialism responded to contemporary debates while being rooted in older traditions. It is best understood as an original synthesis of ideas, some of them borrowed from Aristotle and the Neoplatonists, which countered the threats to free will and theism posed by the new science and emerging mechanism.

The young Milton's poetry is dualist, that is to say it presupposes a relation of body and soul traceable to Plato and Renaissance Neoplatonists. Embodied souls, having descended from the immaterial and supercelestial realm of the immutable forms, are trapped in alien matter. Properly directed souls aspire to escape the body and to reascend to their natural home; depraved souls descend into grosser bodies, either while alive or

[1] For a discussion of the intellectual consequences of civil dislocation, see P. M. Rattansi, "Paracelsus and the Puritan Revolution," *Ambix* 11 (1963): 24–32.

after death in reincarnation as brutes. The pattern, while familiar in its essentials from the *Phaedrus*, owes much of its elaboration to Plotinus, who introduced the explicit conception of an emanative hierarchy of matter. In "In Obitum Praesulis Eliensis" (1626), the seventeen-year-old Milton has the soul of the dead bishop of Ely escape the "sordid prison" (*"foedum . . . carcerem,"* l. 46) of the body. The poet describes the body as a "darksome House of mortal Clay" in the "Nativity Ode" (1629, l. 14). The speaker of "Il Penseroso" (1631?) hopes to

> unsphere
> The spirit of *Plato* to unfold
> What Worlds, or what vast Regions hold
> The immortal mind that hath forsook
> Her mansion in this fleshly nook.
> (88–92)

In the masque *Arcades* (1632) the poet invokes the cosmology and anthropology of the *Republic*. The body in "On Time" (1633?) is "mortal dross" and "Earthly grosness" from which the soul escapes at death. The mortalism of the mature Milton, an inevitable concomitant of his materialism, is absent from the early poetry. Milton pictures as alive outside of the body the bishop of Winchester (1626) and the marchioness of Winchester (1631). In all these poems, the material body is both the relatively unreal shadow of spirit and the grossly substantial barrier between the incorporeal soul and its heavenly home.

By the time he came to write the Latin prose *Christian Doctrine* and *Paradise Lost* in the late 1650s and after, Milton had unequivocally repudiated the dualism of the early poems and thus separated himself from the Neoplatonism then reigning at Christ's, his undergraduate college at Cambridge. Instead of being trapped in an ontologically alien body, the soul is one with the body. Spirit and matter become for Milton two modes of the same substance: spirit is rarefied matter, and matter is dense spirit. All things, from insensate objects through souls, are manifestations of this one substance. Like Hobbes, Milton circumvented the mind-body problem that vexed Descartes, Gassendi, and the Platonists and that moved them to construct elaborate models of two-substance interaction. But where Hobbes assimilated mind to matter and explained mental events mechanically, Milton assimilated matter to current notions of mind and moved toward the position that all corporeal substance is animate, self-active, and free.

The contrast between the topographies of *Comus* (1634) and *Paradise Lost* (1667) suggests the distance between Milton's early dualism and late monism. In the masque the Attendant Spirit contrasts his home with the Earth:

> Before the starry threshold of *Jove's* Court
> My mansion is, where those immortal shapes
> Of bright aërial Spirits live inspher'd
> In Regions mild of calm and serene Air,
> Above the smoke and stir of this dim spot,
> Which men call Earth.
>
> (1–6)

This picture of Earth and its "rank vapors" (16), like its source in the *Phaedo* (109b–110a), underscores the gap between the terrestrial and the celestial and between the bodily and the spiritual. The variegated topography of Earth collects vaporous pools that prevent men from seeing the real; above the Earth are unblemished spheres. Thirty years later, Milton would cancel this difference between the shapes of Heaven and Earth. There are hills in the epic's Heaven; as Raphael tells Adam, "Earth hath this variety from Heav'n / Of pleasure situate in Hill and Dale" (6.640–41).

How does Milton get from the regular Heaven of *Comus* to the irregular Heaven of *Paradise Lost*? That is to say, how does he work toward a conception of the corporeality of spirit, soul, and Heaven? And just as important, why did he move in this direction? The seeds of the change are already present in *Comus*, which contains Milton's earliest substantial articulation of the nature of body and soul.

The perspective in *Comus*, despite the paraphrase of the *Pha-*

edo in the opening lines, is eclectic rather than uniformly Platonic. The poem reenacts in small compass the interactions among Platonic dualism, Neoplatonist emanation, and Pauline dualism. The enchanter Comus cannot harm the Lady, because he can touch her body only. In keeping her eyes aloft while treading on the ground, the Lady follows the prescription of the *Phaedrus* for release from the body and reascent to Heaven. In his long, Platonizing speech the Elder Brother (418–75) contrasts the purity of soul with the impurity of corporeal nature; angels protect the chaste soul, "Driving far off each *thing* of sin and guilt" (456; my emphasis). But immediately after this, the barriers between soul and body are dismantled:

> Till oft converse with heav'nly habitants
> Begin to cast a beam on th'outward shape,
> The unpolluted temple of the mind,
> And turns it by degrees to the soul's essence,
> Till all be made immortal: but when lust
> By unchaste looks, loose gestures, and foul talk,
> But most by lewd and lavish act of sin,
> Lets in defilement to the inward parts,
> The soul grows clotted by contagion,
> Imbodies and imbrutes, till she quite lose
> The divine property of her first being.
>
> (459–69)

In this Neoplatonic version of body and soul, creatures are arranged along an emanative hierarchy; the purer the soul, the more refined the body. The step from Plato's strict dualism to Neoplatonism and its monist tendencies is mediated by Pauline dualism, constructed as it is on a Hebraic monistic conception of soul and body. Despite his talk of the dangers of the flesh and the cultivation of the spirit, Saint Paul did not attack the body in order to celebrate the soul. According to the Hebraic conception that he shared, man is not a composite creature of soul and body, but rather "flesh-animated-by-soul, the whole conceived as a psycho-physical unity."[2] As William Kerrigan

---

[2]John A. T. Robinson, *The Body: A Study in Pauline Theology*, Studies in Biblical Theology, no. 5 (London: SCM Press, 1952), p. 14. Robinson demonstrates how Paul's use of Greek inevitably introduces distortions of Hebraic conceptions.

notes, Paul's "flesh" is not the body as opposed to the soul, but "a diagnostic category in the pathology of the will, . . . a symbol in moral psychology."[3] One becomes more fleshly or more spiritual to the extent that one is directed away from or toward God. A literalized version of Pauline symbolism superimposed on Platonic dualism results in ontological mobility very much like that familiar from Neoplatonism. To the extent that Neoplatonists such as the Cambridge Platonists leaned toward Plato's dualism of mind and body, the chain of emanation remained incoherent. The mature Milton would dissociate himself from the Platonism of *Comus*, but not from its intuition of the spiritualization of body or the materialization of soul. He would find a place for this intuition in a non-Platonic and materialist metaphysic.

Intimations of Materialism in Milton's Prose

Most of Milton's prose works date from two decades, beginning in 1641, during which he set aside his poetry to serve his nation as a prose controversialist. The polemical works provide glimpses of Milton's changing metaphysical assumptions. Like *Comus*, the early prose works reveal the influence of both Plato and Saint Paul, often in the same passages. Milton's attack on Anglican ritual in *Of Reformation* (1641) is cast in Paul's language. Anglicans think "they could make *God* earthly, and fleshly, because they could not make themselves *heavenly*, and *Spirituall*" (*CP* 1:520). To the carnal, everything is carnal, even the supposed worship of God. To this Pauline picture of spiritual bondage Milton adds, straight from the *Phaedrus*, an allegory of the priest at mass:

> then was the *Priest* set to *con his motions*, and his *Postures* and *Liturgies*, and his *Lurries*, till the Soule by this meanes of overbodying her selfe, given up justly to fleshly delights, bated her

---

[3]William Kerrigan, *The Sacred Complex: On the Psychogenesis of "Paradise Lost"* (Cambridge: Harvard University Press, 1983), p. 31. Kerrigan also points to the persistence of Greek dualism in *Comus*, particularly in its emphasis on the "tainted physicality of the world" (p. 32).

wing apace downeward: and finding the ease she had from her visible, and sensuous collegue the body in performance of *Religious* duties, her pineons now broken, and flagging, shifted off from her selfe, the labour of high soaring any more, forgot her heavenly flight, and left the dull, and droyling carcas to plod on in the old rode. (*CP* 1:521–22)[4]

Milton charges the Anglican clergy with a fault for which he himself would be taxed nearly a century later: "corrupting our Notions of spiritual Things, and sensualizing our Ideas of Heaven."[5] For obviously polemical reasons, Milton zealously guards the Platonist division between matter and spirit that he will abandon later and that he had shown signs of abandoning in *Comus*.

In the early 1640s Milton oscillates between Platonist and Pauline conceptions of the relation of soul and body. He copies into his Commonplace Book John Chrysostom's Christian Platonist conception of soul and body: "A good man by some reckoning seems to surpass even the angels, to the extent that, enclosed in a weak and earthly body and always struggling with his passions, he nevertheless aspires to lead a life like that of the inhabitants of heaven" (*CP* 1:364). In *The Reason of Church-Government* (1642) Milton contrasts God's "work[ing] from within himself" with the bishops' working "by the heavy luggage of corporeal instrument" (*CP* 1:855). Milton here, like Chrysostom before him, views the body as a drag on the soul, or as a barrier separating the soul from an incorporeal Heaven. Elsewhere Milton echoes Paul, regarding the body not as the material shell of the incorporeal soul, but as a symbol for the soul's direction toward the world. "Man," Milton writes in *The Reason of Church-Government*, "consisting of two parts the inward and the outward, was by the eternall providence left un-

---

[4]See *Phaedrus* 246b–248e. In *Milton and the Pauline Tradition* (Lanham, Md.: University Press of America, 1982), Timothy O'Keefe argues for a Pauline reading for this passage; although he cites Plato (the *Phaedo* rather than the *Phaedrus*), he sees only a slight influence of Platonism.

[5]Anonymous letter to the *Gentleman's Magazine*, March 1738, in *Milton 1732–1801: The Critical Heritage*, ed. John T. Shawcross (London: Routledge & Kegan Paul, 1972), p. 101.

der two sorts of cure, the Church and the Magistrat. The Magistrat hath only to deale with the outward part, *I mean not of the body alone, but of the mind in all her outward acts*, which in Scripture is call'd the outward man" (*CP* 1:835; my emphasis). The Pauline and Platonist perspectives merge in a passage from the 1642 *Apology against a Pamphlet* in which man is said to see "as through the dim glasse of his affections which in this frail mansion of flesh are ever unequally temper'd" (*CP* 1:909). The famous passage from 1 Corinthians 13 jostles here with the Platonist picture of the soul in the shell of the body. While this juxtaposition seems natural to the heirs of centuries of Platonized Christianity, it conceals an incoherence between dualist and monist conceptions of soul and body.

Eventually, Milton was to work his way out of this incoherence with a materialism that allowed him to literalize Paul's figurative economy of the will and to eliminate the Platonists' ontological gap between soul and body. Considered as a tenuous substance not different in kind from the body, the soul can become carnal and fleshly in more than symbolic terms. There are intuitions of this monistic conception of soul and body in the early prose tracts. Elaborating on his discussion of the minister and the magistrate quoted above, Milton writes that the minister's "end is to recover all that is of man both soul and body to an everlasting health: and yet as for worldly happinesse, which is the proper sphere wherein the magistrate cannot but confine his motion without a hideous exorbitancy from law, so little aims the Minister, as his intended scope, to procure the much prosperity of this life, that oft-times he may have cause to wish much of it away, as a diet puffing up the soul with a slimy fleshinesse, and weakning her principall organick parts" (*CP* 1:845–46). The reference to the "everlasting health" of the body is arresting, the tradition of Christ as physician notwithstanding. The body converges with the "inner man" to which the church ministers.[6] The larger surprise

---

[6]Returning to this conception much later in *The Likeliest Means to Remove Hirelings out of the Church* (1659), Milton, by now a radical in politics and a heretic in theology, praised the heretical Waldensian preachers for combining knowledge and practice of "physic and surgery" with "the studie of scripture" (*CP* 7:306).

comes at the end of the passage. Material wealth puffing up the soul with fleshiness is conventional (though the term "slimy" is unconventionally concrete), but what might Milton mean by the reference to the "principall organick parts" of the soul? The phrase probably marks an inchoate intuition rather than a precise conception of the metaphysics of the soul, but it does suggest Milton's dissatisfaction with the common view of the soul as indivisible and incorporeal. The *Areopagitica* (1644) offers a further hint of the direction in which Milton is moving: "For as in a body, when the blood is fresh, the spirits pure and vigorous, not only to vital, but to rationall faculties, . . . it argues in what good plight and constitution the body is" (*CP* 2:557). These are the corporeal Galenic spirits, refined from the blood. Milton's contemporaries normally excluded the corporeal spirits from the operations of reason and will—Descartes and Gassendi are cases in point.

Whereas Paul had described the upright and depraved wills with the symbolic categories of flesh and spirit, Milton prefers imagery of the healthy and diseased body. This imagery mediates between Plato and Paul. For the Plato of the *Phaedrus*, the body is a disease of the soul; for Milton, vice is described in terms of diseased bodies. For Paul, the attack on the flesh as a category of the will does not entail a repudiation of the body, as it could not for one sharing a Hebrew conception of the person; for Milton, the healthy body becomes an image for spiritual health.[7]

In *Of Reformation* (1641), Milton rewrites Livy's story of Menenius Agrippa, who calmed a mutinous army with the fable of the revolt of man's members against the belly. Milton likens the episcopate to a diseased growth on the body politic, "a huge

---

[7]Milton was to gain too close a knowledge of disease and medicine in the years to come. When he began to lose his sight around 1644, he commenced a course of "tampering with Physick to preserve it" (Edward Phillips's *Life of Milton*, in *The Early Lives of Milton*, ed. Helen Darbishire [London: Constable, 1932], p. 72). Among the cures Milton underwent was the excruciating and gruesome process of setoning (drawing a thread through a fold in the skin in order to maintain an opening for discharges); see William Riley Parker, *Milton: A Biography*, 2 vols. with continuous pagination (Oxford: Clarendon Press, 1968), p. 992. Milton was troubled also with headaches and flatulence.

and monstrous Wen [or tumor] little lesse then the Head it selfe" (*CP* 1:583). A philosopher called to judge the Wen's defense of its utility reverses Menenius's defense of the belly that nourishes the entire body: "Wilt thou (quoth he) that art but a bottle of vitious and harden'd excrements, contend with the lawfull and free-borne members?" (*CP* 1:584) The Wen receives a sharp rebuke for its contention that it is a retreat for the soul when the soul leaves the body for contemplation: "Lourdan, quoth the Philosopher, thy folly is as great as thy filth; know that all the faculties of the Soule are confin'd of old to their severall vessels, and *ventricles*, from which they cannot part without dissolution of the whole Body; and that thou containst no good thing in thee, but a heape of hard, and loathsome uncleannes, and art to the head a foul disfigurment and burden" (*CP* 1:584). Milton likens the bishops' spiritual pride to a "noysom, and diseased tumor," which must be "cut away from the publick body" (*CP* 1:598). Significantly, this is an excrement of flesh and not the flesh itself; the zeal of the bishops is "a meere ague-cake coagulated of a certaine Fever they have" (*CP* 1:582). Because of the bishops' insistence on external forms of worship "all the inward acts of *worship* issuing from the native strength of the SOULE, run out lavishly to the upper skin, and there harden into a crust of Formallitie" (*CP* 1:522). This scabby crust, not the body itself, imprisons the soul. The crust is formed, as is the Wen, by the leaking of fluid, a violation of the integrity of the body. This leaking leaves an empty crust or shell.

To images of leaking bodies Milton opposes images of healthy, compact ones. In a passage foreshadowing the opening of *Leviathan*, he describes episcopacy as a disease of the commonwealth: "How to soder, how to stop a leak, how to keep up the floting carcas of a crazie, and diseased Monarchy, or State betwixt wind, and water, swimming still upon her own dead lees, that now is the deepe designe of a politician. Alas Sir! a Commonwelth ought to be but as one huge Christian personage, one mighty growth, and stature of an honest man, as big, and compact in vertue as in body" (*CP* 1:572). In these antiepiscopal images from *Of Reformation*, Milton substitutes disease for Paul's "flesh" and suggests metaphorically that vice is tied to a violation of the integrity of soul and body. Compactness opposes leaking. In the tracts to follow, there are indications that Milton viewed this matter more than metaphorically. In the *Apology against a Pamphlet* (1642), he describes his daily exercises, "usefull and generous labours preserving the bodies health, and hardinesse; to render lightsome, clear, and not lumpish obedience to the minde, to the cause of religion, and our Countries liberty" (*CP* 1:885–86). *Mens sana in corpore sano* takes on a new meaning for one who writes of "the organick parts" of the soul. In *Of Education* (1644) Milton prescribes music after exercise and meals for its salutary effects upon the "spirits":

> The interim of unsweating themselves regularly, and convenient rest before meat may both with profit and delight be taken up in recreating and *composing their travail'd spirits* with the solemn and divine harmonies of musick heard, or learnt. . . . [Musical performances], if wise men & prophets be not extreamly out, have a great power over dispositions and manners, to smooth and make them gentle from rustick harshnesse and distemper'd passions. The like also would not be unexpedient after meat to assist and cherish nature in her first concoction, and send their *mindes* backe to study *in good tune* and satisfaction. (*CP* 2:409–11; my emphasis)

While editors normally point to Plato and Aristotle for this tradition, a more pertinent parallel is Francis Bacon, who borrowed from Plato's and Aristotle's taxonomies of music's psychological effects, but who attributed those effects to music's power to move (literally) the corporeal spirits. "Harmony," Bacon writes,

> coming with a *manifest motion*, doth by custom of often affecting the spirits and *putting them into one kind of posture*, alter not a little the nature of the spirits. . . . And therefore we see that tunes and airs, even in their own nature, have in themselves some affinity with the affections: as there be merry tunes, doleful tunes, solemn

tunes; tunes inclining men's minds to pity; warlike tunes, &c. So as it is no marvel if they alter the spirits, considering that *tunes have a predisposition to the motion of the spirits in themselves*.[8]

Like Bacon, Milton follows Plato and Aristotle on the effects of music but suggests that the medium of the effect is corporeal motion.

In the divorce tracts of 1643–45 Milton feels his way toward his mature, materialist metaphysics. If Milton's denunciation of worldly bishops in the antiprelatical tracts invited metaphors of body and spirit, his argument in the divorce tracts required a close anatomy of the interrelationship of spirit and body. Despite their undermining of spirit-body dualism, at first glance they appear aggressively dualistic, intent on reordering mistaken priorities and placing the claims of the separable spirit over the claims of the body.[9] Insisting that marriage properly is a union of fit minds rather than a conjunction of bodies, Milton attacks the inversion of the priority between mind and body institutionalized in English church law, which allowed for divorce only in cases of adultery, impotence, frigidity, and consanguinity. Marriage, Milton writes, "must proceed from the mind rather then the body, els it would be but a kind of animal or beastish meeting"; he faults current notions of marriage for placing the fitness of minds "beneath the formalities and respects of the body, to make it a servant of its owne vassall" (*CP* 2:275, 598). Physical desire hands us over to inner servitude or necessity; in the absence of love sexual need is a "bestiall necessitie" (*CP* 2:259–60).

---

[8]*Sylva Sylvarum* 114, in *The Works of Francis Bacon*, ed. James Spedding, Robert Leslie Ellis, and Douglas Denon Heath, 14 vols. (London: Longman, 1858–74), 2:389; my emphasis.

[9]For a fuller discussion of the emergence of materialist monism in the divorce tracts and of the resistance of entrenched dualist modes of thought, see my "Metaphysics of Milton's Divorce Tracts," in *Politics, Poetics, and Hermeneutics in Milton's Prose*, ed. David A. Loewenstein and James Grantham Turner (Cambridge: Cambridge University Press, 1990), pp. 69–83.

Despite their strident and dualist attack on sexuality,[10] the divorce tracts offer brief and incomplete indications of a more balanced view. Milton not only acknowledges the need for sexual release even among the godly but also goes so far as to suggest that a proper union of minds can lead to a better sex life: "the deed of procreation . . . it self soon cloies, and is despis'd, unless it bee cherisht and re-incited with a pleasing conversation" (*CP* 2:740).

The conflict of perspectives on sexuality in the tracts does not betray incoherence; rather it results inevitably from Milton's decision to address two audiences: conventional, unreflective persons are dualists, who find food for the soul outside of marriage and food for the body within marriage; unconventional men, almost invariably labeled "gentle," are monists, for whom there can be no merely physical sexual life. Milton will reorder dualism for the benefit of "grunting Barrows," but to "persons of gentle breeding" he will demonstrate that the claims of the body and soul are inseparable (*CP* 2:747).[11]

"Gentle" spirits sense that sexual relations touch the soul as well as the body and that loveless sexual relations brutalize and corporealize the soul. When there is no union of minds in marriage, all that is left is "a displeasing and forc't remedy against the sting of a brute desire; which fleshly accustoming without the souls union and commixture of intellectual delight, as it is rather a soiling then a fulfilling of mariage-rites, so is it anough to imbase the mettle of a generous spirit, and sinks him to a low and vulgar pitch of endeavour in all his actions, or, which is wors, leavs him in a dispairing plight of abject and hard'n'd thoughts" (*CP* 2:339). As Milton discusses the plight of the gentle soul, the terms relating to body and soul interpenetrate. The "imbased mettle" of the soul and the "hardened thoughts" are more than metaphorical in this new monistic

---

[10]The best analysis of this aspect of the divorce tracts can be found in James Grantham Turner, *One Flesh: Paradisal Marriage and Sexual Relations in the Age of Milton* (Oxford: Clarendon Press, 1987), chap. 6 and passim.

[11]Earlier, Milton had divided the audience of *The Reason of Church-Government* into the corrupt and the "gentler sort" and directed his comments to the latter alone (*CP* 1:802, 808).

world; the "soil" here and in a later reference to the "soiling" of
souls (*CP* 2:619) savor of corporeal materialization. The interpenetration of terms culminates in the suggestion that the soul
is expended with the semen; it "is the most injurious and un-
naturall tribute that can be extorted from a person endew'd
with reason, to be made to pay out the best substance of his
body, and of his soul too, as some think, when either for just
and powerfull causes he cannot like" (*CP* 2:271).[12] With the
paying out of the soul, the individual is threatened with bestial-
ization and loss of identity.

Given the ascetic polemic against the body and the insistence
on the importance of spiritual union, Irene Samuel's judgment
that the tracts are informed by a "Platonic dichotomy of the
world into two realms," the material and the spiritual, is explicable; in light of the monist suggestions of the inseparability of
body and spirit, however, it is inadequate.[13] Milton writes dualism into his text, but he imputes it as a scandal to his opponents.
The strategy of dividing the audience into the fit and the unfit
(and accommodating the teaching accordingly) that I ascribe to
Milton here is one that Milton ascribes to Christ in *The Doctrine
and Discipline of Divorce*. Christ's apparently unambiguous pro-
hibition of divorce except in the case of adultery (Matthew
5:31–32) should be regarded, Milton writes, as directed only to
the Pharisees, who misinterpreted the Mosaic law in order to
justify divorce for trivial reasons: "In such cases that we are not
to repose all upon the literall terms of so many words, many
instances will teach us: Wherin we may plainly discover how
Christ meant not to be tak'n word for word, but like a wise
Physician, administring one excesse against another to reduce
us to a perfect mean" (*CP* 2:282–83).[14] Whatever the exegeti-

---

[12]Renaissance sexual physiology assumed the presence of refined corporeal
spirits in the semen. The term "spirit," as we saw in the preceding chapter,
invited equivocation (see Shakespeare's Sonnet 129). In this passage, Milton
gestures toward his later identification of soul or spirit and the refined corporeal spirits.

[13]Irene Samuel, *Milton and Plato* (Ithaca: Cornell University Press, 1947), p. 157.

[14]Milton echoes this argument in *Tetrachordon*: "as the offense was in one extreme, so the rebuke, to bring more efficaciously to a rectitude and mediocrity,
stands not in the middle way of duty, but in the other extreme" (*CP* 2:668).

cal value of this argument, Milton follows this teaching method himself: the extreme deference to the body over the mind in English church teaching on divorce is countered with the extreme denigration of body and emphasis on aphysical spiritual union. But for those who have eyes to see and ears to hear (and skin to touch?), Milton offers quietly and briefly an indication of the godly joy of sex (see, e.g., *CP* 2:597). In metaphysical terms, the "perfect mean" between the two "excesses" of disordered and reordered dualisms is monism, which repairs the disintegration of body and spirit that characterizes either extreme.

The attempt to separate body from spirit is absurd from a monist point of view; it results paradoxically in the despiritualization of the one substance. If there is only one substance, and if body is conceived as separate from spirit, then the body must be dead and spiritless. "Who," Milton asks in *Tetrachordon*, "that is not himselfe a meer body, can restrain all the unfitnes of mariage only to a corporal defect?" (*CP* 2:711). The answer will be those like the "Pork" of *Colasterion*. And while Milton exploits the emotive force of this bestial characterization, he hints in a deceptively simple passage of *Tetrachordon* that these "meer bodies" are below animals: "the Soul as much excells the body, as the outward man excells the Ass and more; for that *animal* is yet a living creature, perfet in it self; but the body without the Soul is a meer senseles trunck" (*CP* 2:624). The "outward man" or body excels the ass as we begin, but it is inferior to the ass as we conclude. To be a mere body is to be dead and senseless, to be an inanimate lump. This passage, with its opposition of soul and body, is rooted in the dualism that Milton questions in the divorce tracts. If it seems an uncomplicated affirmation of dualism, we should note a passage from the *Christian Doctrine*, written after his unambiguous commitment to monism: "Where 'body' is spoken of as a merely physical trunk [*truncus*], 'soul' [*anima*] may mean either the spirit [*spiritus*] or its secondary faculties, such as the vital or sensitive faculty" (*CP* 6:318; *Works* 15:40; I have modified Carey's translation). If all substance is both vital and tangible inseparably, it can nevertheless be spoken of as one or the other in turn.

Milton picks up on the conception of the dead and senseless mere body when he describes the Answerer as a "fleamy clodd" (*CP* 2:740). The vital spirits are refined from the blood, one of the two elements missing from this combination of phlegm and earth. Interestingly, the terms of this denunciation echo precisely a description of the errant wife: the virtuous man can find himself "bound fast to an uncomplying discord of nature, or, *as it oft happens, to an image of earth and fleam*" (*CP* 2:254; my emphasis). The wife, like the Answerer, is dismissed by implication as a mere body; in *The Doctrine and Discipline* she is a "mute and spiritles mate" (*CP* 2:251).

It is also significant that the unfit wife is an "*image* of earth and fleam." Behind the image of the errant wife lies emptiness.[15] The tracts' many metaphors of outsides-without-insides embody the monist's view of dualist matter: dead, inert, cut off from its vivifying force. Behind the "veile" of the "appearance of modesty" in a virgin, a husband may find, "if not . . . a body impenetrable," a mind "uselesse and almost liveles" (*CP* 2:250). The "liveles" mind is almost no mind at all; one can penetrate the body, but one will find it empty. More to the point, a marriage without union of minds is "but the empty husk of an outside matrimony" and "the meer carcas of a Mariage" (*CP* 2:256, 603).[16]

The most striking image of an outside without an inside comes in the allegory of Error and Custom in the letter prefacing the second edition of *The Doctrine and Discipline*. Custom, a "meer face," "count'nances" Error, a "blind and Serpentine body without a head" (*CP* 2:223). Like a bad marriage, which Milton elsewhere calls "a most unreal nullity, . . . a daring phantasm, a meer toy of terror" (*CP* 2:666–67), the monster is all show and no substance. Another notable "image" in the divorce tracts is the cloud given to Ixion by Zeus in place of

[15]In another series of metaphors growing out of the antiprelatical tracts, the image of the wife conceals a repulsive and diseased interior. This series of images has been anatomized in Turner's *One Flesh*, pp. 194–203.

[16]For Milton's use of the image of interiority for spirit despite his monism, see *Paradise Lost* 3.194; 4.20; 6.158; 7.204; 8.221; 9.96, 121; 10.221; 12.101, 488, 523, 587.

Hera, which gave him "a monstrous issue . . . , the fruits of a delusive mariage" (*CP* 2:597). The renounced interiors of the metaphors of outsides-without-insides resurface as metaphors of insubstantiality. The cloud given to Ixion and the "unreal nullity" and "daring phantasm" of a bad marriage shimmer in the tracts like the separated spirits of the dualist, spirits that have left behind in their flight hard crusts and "empty husks."[17] The dualist barters his living body and substantial soul for a hardened, lifeless body and an insubstantial soul. In place of and opposed to these images of outsides-without-insides and of phantoms, Milton constructs images of Truth in which inside and outside are inextricably involved. As Custom provides a face for Error, so Milton, with his unconventional argument, will be the face of "discount'nanc't truth" (*CP* 2:224). On the same page truth is both a mother and a child, both a womb and that which is born from the womb. The womb itself is at once the inside of the woman and the outside that contains the child. If we can place the two metaphors together, truth is the solid interior of the living exterior. Yet, in apparent opposition to these gestative metaphors, truth is something intangible: "Truth is as impossible to be soil'd by any outward touch, as the Sun beam" (*CP* 2:225). It is simultaneously body, interior of the body, and incorporeal substance; the divisions cherished by the dualist are obliterated in the figurative economy of the letter. In metaphors such as these, we can witness Milton working intuitively toward the monism that he will lay out discursively in the *Christian Doctrine*.

Sexual relations in a fit marriage, like these metaphors, involve a seamless interpenetration of inner and outer. In *Colasterion* Milton writes that the "*Metaphorical* union of two bodies into one flesh, cannot bee likn'd in all things to . . . that natural union of soul and body into one person" (*CP* 2:734). The loveless but sexually active couple "grind in the mill of an undelighted and servil copulation" (*CP* 2:258); such relations amount not to a union of bodies but to a friction of surfaces. To overcome this impediment to bodily union Milton pieces to-

---

[17]Milton had used the myth of Ixion at the end of his (significantly) abortive "Passion" of 1630. He returned to it in *Paradise Regained* 4.318–21.

gether a metaphysics of sexuality in the tracts. The union of minds is more than metaphorical. He writes in *Tetrachordon* that "the unity of minde is neerer and greater then the union of bodies" (*CP* 2:606); this union of minds generates a true union of bodies: "Wee know that flesh can neither joyn, nor keep together two bodies of it self; what is it then must make them one flesh, but likenes, but fitnes of mind and disposition, which *may breed the Spirit of concord*, and union between them?" (*CP* 2:605; my emphasis). One of the inescapable and disturbing facts about the divorce tracts is that Milton does not seem concerned about and indeed rarely mentions children; here the issue of procreation surfaces in a displaced form. The vision of the birth of the spirit of concord can be read as a metaphysical obstetrics. The child of a fit couple is a "Spirit of concord," a spirit that fills the husk and enlivens the carcass of an otherwise empty matrimony. This "Spirit" can help us to gloss the enigmatic claim in *The Doctrine and Discipline* that "the fit union of their souls be such as may even incorporate them to love and amity" (*CP* 2:326). The spirit of concord is incorporated, made flesh, in the sexual union of the fit couple.

In the divorce tracts, Milton confronts the inadequacy of dualist conceptions of man from both sides. Ascetic counsels, including the Roman command of celibacy (*CP* 2:595), affront human nature, which is inseparably corporeal and spiritual. Contemporary teachings on divorce, "reformed" in name only, privilege the body at the expense of the soul. A proper perspective mediates these extremes; one can describe a person interchangeably as an animated body or an incorporated soul. In a poem written less than two years after *Tetrachordon*, Milton made a significant emendation pointing in the new direction. In a draft, he addressed his deceased friend Catharine Thomason: "Meekly thou didst resign this earthly *clod* / Of *flesh and sin*, which *man* from *heav'n* doth sever." In the final version, the italicized words are changed: "Meekly thou didst resign this earthly *load* / Of *Death, call'd Life*, which *us* from *Life* doth sever."[18] After the divorce tracts, the "clod of flesh" no longer

---

[18]Sonnet XIV. The original readings can be found in *John Milton: Complete Shorter Poems*, ed. John Carey (London: Longman, 1971), p. 296.

adequately describes those who fail to see the unity of spirit and body. And by the time of *Paradise Lost*, Milton will have come to believe firmly that it is not corporeality that separates us from heaven.

The intimations of materialist monism in the divorce tracts and the other works of the early 1640s are just that. The articulation of a mature and thoroughgoing monism will wait until the late 1650s and 1660s. Little conclusive evidence of Milton's metaphysical thought can be gathered from the work of the intervening years. In the *Second Defence of the English People* (1654), Milton taunts his controversial opponent: "you . . . have afflicted your mind and senses with such a callus (unless your mind is one great callus)" (*CP* 4:637). While this can be made to fit with Milton's monism, according to which the vicious mind becomes more corporeal, it is probably no more than a conventional and crude jeer. In the same work Milton compliments Queen Christina in Platonist (or dualistic Neoplatonist terms): "we marvel at that vigorous mind of yours, plainly of heavenly origin [*aethereum*], that purest particle of the divine air [*purissimam divinae aurae partem*] which has fallen, so it seems, into those remote regions" (*CP* 4:605). We seem to be back in the Platonizing mood of the opening of *Comus*. But if the harsh words for More are conventional abuse, the kind words for Christina are conventional praise.

Nevertheless, by the end of the 1650s Milton had worked his way to the unequivocal materialist monism of the *Christian Doctrine* (c. 1656–60) and *Paradise Lost*. In the decade and a half after 1644, the conception of the corporeal spirits as giving rise to the rational as well as the vital faculties has graduated from speculation to firm assertion. Our knowledge of the metaphysical debate going on around Milton, and especially of the implications of that debate for freedom of the will, gives us a sense of the external pressures that moved Milton from fitfully expressed intuitions to an articulated materialist system.

I observed in Chapter 1 that Hobbes's strict determinism is inseparable from his version of mechanist materialism, although it is difficult to say which gives rise to the other. With

Milton, freedom of the will might be the key to the development of animist materialism. From the very beginning, Milton
affirms his unshakable conviction of the freedom of the will.
The early *Comus*, like the late *Paradise Lost* and *Paradise Regained*, is a drama of free choice. The *Areopagitica* (1644) assumes freedom of the will even as it argues for freedom of the
press; its famous claim (*CP* 2:527) that "when God gave
[Adam] reason, he gave him freedom to choose, for reason is
but choosing; he had bin else a meer artificiall *Adam*, such an
Adam as he is in the motions" contrasts sharply with the neces-
sitarian arguments of Hobbes. Hobbes observes that while pre-
Christian philosophers recognized that actions spring from
chance or necessity, *"freewill,* is a thing that never was mentioned among them, nor by the Christians in the beginning of
Christianity."[19] At roughly the same moment in the late 1650s
when Hobbes was belaboring Bramhall for his affirmation of
freedom of the will, Milton was arguing that "From the concept
of freedom . . . all idea of necessity must be removed" (*CP*
6:161).

William Riley Parker has suggested that as Milton developed
his defense of Christian liberty in the early 1640s his works
became more philosophical, but that even the divorce tracts of
the end of this period contain "more *feeling* than philosophy."[20]
Milton, Parker suggests, undertook from the late 1640s on the
construction of a coherent theological system to serve as a
foundation for his convictions. I contend that Milton undertook the construction of his metaphysical model out of the
same motivation. Around him during these years, and especially from the publication of *Leviathan* in 1651, raged a debate in
which the question of freedom of the will was inseparable from
the debate over the nature of substance and the relation of
mind and body. Milton's Christian materialism shows signs of

[19]*The Questions concerning Liberty, Necessity, and Chance*, in *The English Works of
Thomas Hobbes*, ed. Sir William Molesworth, 11 vols. (London: John Bohn,
1839–45), 5:1. This work dates from 1656, but the quoted passage represents
thinking consistent with Hobbes's work from 1640 on.
[20]Parker, *Milton: A Biography*, p. 293.

the influence of the contemporary debate; it is a shelter for freedom of the will in an increasingly hostile climate.[21] Like the Cambridge Platonists, Milton felt the threat of Hobbes; unlike them, he was prevented by his intuitions from taking the dualist route to answer Hobbes.

Milton's Animist Materialism

By the late 1650s, having concluded that everything that exists is a parcel of what he calls in *Paradise Lost* "one first matter," Milton broke with centuries of Christian orthodoxy. The anxiety accompanying Milton's arguments for the corporeality and mortality of the soul surfaces in the defensive asides and prefaces of the *Christian Doctrine*. "I hope," he writes, "that all my readers will be sympathetic, and will avoid prejudice and malice, even though they see at once that many of the views I have published are at odds with certain conventional opinions" (*CP* 6:121).[22] Milton's heresies are philosophical as well as theological. Viewed from the perspective of the middle of the seventeenth century, Milton's views on the soul's relation to the body broke ranks with the defense against the materialist Hobbes, who denied free will and the natural immortality of the soul. Descartes, Cudworth, and More viewed the existence of a separable, incorporeal soul as an essential pillar of the free-will defense and as the metaphysical warrant of immortality.[23] Milton, on the other hand, was willing to drop natural

[21]The connection between Milton's monism and his conception of liberty is adumbrated in the prominence of a monistic conception of the text in his great early work on liberty of the press. In the *Areopagitica*, books contain "a potencie of life" and "that ethereall and fift essence, the breath of reason it selfe"; they "preserve as in a violl the purest efficacie and extraction of that living intellect that bred them" (*CP* 2:492–93). Books are not collections of signs pointing toward disembodied thought; they are vital repositories of the body of reason.
[22]Ironically, the *Christian Doctrine* was not published until the nineteenth century. Its publication prevented by Milton's enemies or friends, it was discovered among some papers in Whitehall in 1823 and published in 1825.
[23]Despite his attempt to reconcile Aristotle and the new mechanical philosophy in his *Two Treatises* (1644), Sir Kenelm Digby also follows the orthodox line in tying freedom of the will and immortality to the soul's incorporeality (see *A Treatise on Mans Soule*, especially chap. 8, secs. 1–2, and chap. 9, secs. 1–5).

immortality and was confident that freedom could be defended by other metaphysical means.

Milton's monistic conception of the relationship between body and soul is an affront to any of the available dualist conceptions, including the Platonic, the Christianized Aristotelian, and the Cartesian. "Unless we prefer to be instructed about the nature of the soul by heathen authors," Milton argues, we must conclude that "Man is a living being [*animal*], intrinsically and properly one and individual. He is not double or separable: not, as is commonly thought, produced from and composed of two different and distinct elements, soul and body. On the contrary, the whole man is the soul, and the soul the man [*totum hominem esse animam, et animam hominem*]: a body, in other words, an individual substance, animated, sensitive, and rational" (*CP* 6:317–18; *Works* 15:40). While Milton points to the Bible for authority and claims explicitly to shun "heathen authors," his conception here stems from Aristotle's hylomorphism: for Aristotle the form is the organization of body, not a superadded entity, and the soul is the form of a living body. Significantly though, Milton insists, unlike the great Christian Aristotelian Thomas Aquinas, that the rational soul is not different in kind from the sensitive and vegetative souls. Where Thomas thought that the vital and sensitive souls are transmitted in the semen while the rational or intellectual soul is incorporeal and infused by God, Milton agrees with Aristotle that the semen contains the entire soul (*CP* 6:319–22).[24] Milton claims disingenuously that "Nearly everyone agrees that all form—and the human soul is a kind of form—is produced by the power of matter [*ex potentia materiae produci*]" (*CP* 6:322; *Works* 15:48).[25] In fact, Christian Aristotelians followed Aqui-

---

While Digby illustrates one more attempt at mid-century to articulate a new metaphysical system, I do not treat him at length here because his work neither closely parallels Milton's nor presents, like Hobbes's, a particular threat to Milton's beliefs.

[24]See *Summa theologiae* I, Q. 118.

[25]Following William Hunter, I have modified the Yale translation. See "Milton's Power of Matter," *Journal of the History of Ideas* 13 (1952): 551–62. My discussion of Milton and Aristotelian hylomorphism is indebted to this brief article, which contains a lucid discussion of Milton's conception of *potentia materiae*.

nas in excluding the production of the soul from the power of matter.

Milton, as we have seen, does distinguish between spirit and body (*CP* 6:318). But neither the incorporeality of the soul nor the actual separability of body and soul follows from the lawfulness of distinguishing between them: "The idea that the spirit of man is separate from his body, so that it may exist somewhere in isolation, complete and intelligent, is nowhere to be found in scripture, and is plainly at odds with nature and reason" (*CP* 6:319).

Despite his hylomorphism, Aristotle equivocates on the inseparability and immortality of the soul. If soul is the act or form of a body, then it makes no sense to speak of it as either separable or immortal. Aristotle seems to make this clear in *De anima*: the soul is "a ratio or formulable essence, not a matter or subject. . . . The soul cannot be without a body, while it cannot *be* a body; it is not a body but something relative to a body. That is why it is *in* a body, and a body of a definite kind." But this follows on the heels of a speculation that some "parts" (i.e., the rational part) might be separable from the body, and hence immortal.[26]

Milton breaks with Aristotle's ambiguity or indecisiveness on these points by moving from hylomorphism to materialism. The soul for Milton is a substantial, corporeal entity, not an abstract combination of the shape, internal organization, or faculties of the body. While it is separable after death (though not before death), it separates only to dissolve, like the relatively more corporeal body, into its constituent elements. What are these elements? According to Genesis, the soul is breathed into man by God. Citing Ecclesiastes 12:7 and Isaiah 57:20, Milton acknowledges that "the soul, on account of its origin, returns again at death to elements different from those of the body" (*CP* 6:323). In some sense, the soul returns to God, but

---

[26]*De anima* 414a.13–22 and 413a.3–8, in *The Basic Works of Aristotle*, ed. Richard McKeon (New York: Random House, 1941), pp. 559 and 556. With a metaphor borrowed by Descartes, Aristotle adds that "we have no light on the problem whether the soul may not be the actuality of its body in the sense in which the sailor is the actuality of the ship."

in what sense? Fully aware of the heterodoxy of his argument, Milton embraces the mortalism that follows from his materialism. If his opponents cite Ecclesiastes 12:7, "Then the dust shall return to the earth as it was: and the spirit unto God who gave it," Milton is ready: "*returning to God* must be understood in a very broad sense: after all the wicked do not go to God at death, but far away from him" (*CP* 6:407). For scriptural passages in which God is said to take spirits and souls to himself while the flesh dies (Job 34:14–14 and Psalms 104:29–30), Milton audaciously calls upon Euripides for aid in interpretation:

> Euripides, in the *Suppliants*, has given a far better interpretation [of Job 34] than my opponents, without knowing it:
>
> > *Each various part*
> > *That constitutes the frame of man returns*
> > *Whence it was taken; to th'ethereal sky*
> > *The soul, the body to its earth*
>
> that is, when soul and body part each component returns to the place it came from, to its own element. (*CP* 6:407–8)

Yet even here, where Milton diverges from Aristotle on the disposition of the soul after death, there is an echo of Aristotle. In his discussion of reproduction, Aristotle speaks of a tenuously corporeal element in which the soul participates and which resembles the elements of the superlunar sphere:

> Now so far as we can see, the faculty of Soul of every kind has to do with some physical substance which is different from the so-called "elements" and more divine than they are; and as the varieties of Soul differ from one another in the scale of value, so do the various substances concerned with them differ in their nature. In all cases the semen contains within itself that which causes it to be fertile, . . . the *pneuma* which is enclosed within the semen or foam-like stuff, and the natural substance which is in the *pneuma*; and this substance is analogous to the element which belongs to the stars.[27]

[27]Aristotle, *Generation of Animals* 736b.30–737a.1, in the Loeb edition, trans. A. L. Peck (Cambridge: Harvard University Press, 1943), p. 171.

Aristotle apparently thought of the pneuma as a tenuous physical substance higher than the four elements to which the faculties of the soul (or *psyche*) are connected; this substance mediates between the body and the incorporeal *psyche*. The pneuma neither consumes fuel nor destroys like fire, but supplies the vital heat of living things. In the *Parts of Animals* (II, vii) Aristotle separates himself from those who identify soul with fire and stipulates that the soul "is carried in" or "exists in" a body similar to fire.[28] Milton in his new materialist metaphysic has moved toward a pneumatic conception of the soul itself.

Milton's materialist monism treats spirit and matter as manifestations, differing in degree and not qualitatively, of the one corporeal substance. Milton's spirit does not coexist with an alien matter; it contains matter: "Spirit, being the more excellent substance, virtually, as they say, and eminently contains within itself what is clearly the inferior substance [matter]; in the same way as the spiritual and rational faculty contains the corporeal, that is, the sentient and vegetative faculty" (*CP* 6:309).[29] Milton struggles here to articulate monism with a vocabulary tempered by centuries of dualism. The inferiority of matter is neither moral nor dependent on an ontological gulf separating it from spirit; matter is merely more gross and less vital spirit.

When redefining Aristotle's conception of the pneuma in the *Christian Doctrine*, Milton moves away from hylomorphism toward materialism. In *Paradise Lost* that materialistic turn finds expression in an idiosyncratic version of Galen. Milton addresses the relationship between body and soul or matter and spirit in Raphael's lecture to Adam on the continuity between man and angel:

> O *Adam*, one Almighty is, from whom
> All things proceed, and up to him return,

---

[28]Aristotle, *Parts of Animals* 652b.9, in the Loeb edition, trans. A. L. Peck (Cambridge: Harvard University Press, 1937), p. 151.
[29]John Rumrich illuminates this difficult passage with the analogy of the manner in which gases contain liquids and solids (*Matter of Glory: A New Preface to "Paradise Lost"* [Pittsburgh: University of Pittsburgh Press, 1987], p. 67).

If not deprav'd from good, created all
Such to perfection, one first matter all,
Indu'd with various forms, various degrees
Of substance, and in things that live, of life;
But more refin'd, more spirituous, and pure,
As nearer to him plac't or nearer tending
Each in thir several active Spheres assign'd,
Till body up to spirit work, in bounds
Proportion'd to each kind. So from the root
Springs lighter the green stalk, from thence the leaves
More aery, last the bright consummate flow'r
Spirits odorous breathes: flow'rs and thir fruit
Man's nourishment, by gradual scale sublim'd
To vital spirits aspire, to animal,
To intellectual, give both life and sense,
Fancy and understanding, whence the Soul
Reason receives, and reason is her being,
Discursive, or Intuitive; discourse
Is oftest yours, the latter most is ours,
Differing but in degree, of kind the same.

(5.469–90)

The affinities with the tradition of the chain of being should
not obscure the distinctive features of this passage. The "one
first matter" extends from what we think of as matter to reason, the "being" of the soul. In this emanative chain, moral
purity is measurable in the degree of rarefaction of body, but
even the most pure and spiritous substance remains corporeal.
The chain is dynamic; direction is more important than position. Milton's devils, as we shall see, are less corporeal than his
men, but they are moving toward greater relative corporeality.
Movement is presented in *Paradise Lost* in metabolic language.
The ascent of good creatures is modeled on metabolic sublimation, and the descent of the evil on excretion and expulsion.
The relation of plant to the one first matter is synecdochic. The
plant not only represents in its root and flowers the poles between grossly corporeal and relatively incorporeal matter, it
also enacts the process of digestion by which individuals ascend
the chain. The metabolism of the plant transforms matter from

the gross to the tenuous. Milton's picture of the mind and soul as the flower of matter recalls Gassendi.

At the upper end of the spectrum, or at the end of the process of digestion, come the spirits. The sublimed matter of plants, the fruit, becomes food, which in man is further sublimed to vital spirits and then animal spirits. Milton here follows Galen, whose articulated theory of the spirits or pneumas corresponded imperfectly with the Aristotelian tripartite soul. But Milton skips the first spirit, the natural spirits, to begin with the vital spirits, and adds his own invention, the "intellectual" spirits, which "give both life and sense, / Fancy and understanding, whence the Soul / Reason receives, and reason is her being." While the construction is remarkably fluid—the soul receives something from the intellectual spirits, and thus seems separate from them, but what the soul receives, reason, is "her being"—to save the coherence of this passage one must take the "intellectual spirits" as interchangeable with the soul.[30] In identifying the soul with the tenuously corporeal intellectual spirits, Milton modifies Galen in the same direction that he modified Aristotle in the *Christian Doctrine*, toward unambiguous materialism. Galen considered identifying the soul with the corporeal pneuma but declined to discard categorically the possibility of an incorporeal soul: "The brain necessarily contains within itself the substance of the soul, and this must be either the natural heat, or the pneuma, or the form of the composition taken as a whole [i.e., the form of the brain], or some incorporeal power beyond it."[31] Thus Milton articulates his conception of the relationship between soul and body with the help of Aristotle in the *Christian Doctrine* and of Galen in *Paradise Lost*. The alliance was not new: Galen borrowed several

[30]This is how the passage is read by Lawrence Babb, who notes correctly that the term "intellectual spirits" would have initially suggested angels to Milton's contemporaries, and angels were understood by both scholastic and Neoplatonic readers as analogous to soul (*The Moral Cosmos of "Paradise Lost"* [East Lansing: Michigan State University Press, 1970], p. 41).

[31]*On the Use of Breathing*, chap. 5, in *Galen on Respiration and the Arteries*, ed. and trans. David J. Furley and J. S. Wilkie (Princeton: Princeton University Press, 1984), p. 131. For a Renaissance adaptation of Galen, see *The Epitome of Andreas Vesalius*, trans. L. R. Lind (Cambridge: M.I.T. Press, 1949).

central ideas from Aristotle, including the crucial conception of vital heat, and Renaissance Galenic medical texts were often founded on Aristotelian philosophy. R. Bostocke, a Paracelsan antagonistic toward both Aristotle and Galen, wrote in 1585 that "The heathnish Phisicke of Galen doth depende uppon that heathnish Philosophie of Aristotle, (for where the Philosopher endeth, there beginneth the Phisition)."[32] In like fashion, where the theological treatise ends the epic begins.

In Raphael's speech the plant begins as a metaphor for the steps of the hierarchy of matter only to become a synecdoche for the process by which creatures ascend the hierarchy. The focus shifts from synchronic image to diachronic process. The spiritous nature of the matter closer to God is analogized progressively in flower, fruit, and perfume (the "spirits odorous," a later version of the intellect preserved in a vial in *Areopagitica?*), but these phenomena, present all at once to our senses, are themselves serial products of metabolism. The flowers and fruit, then, become man's food and are progressively metabolized into the faculties and, apparently, the soul itself. At the end of the process of digestion, the tenuously corporeal takes over the role normally reserved for the incorporeal by Platonists and scholastic Aristotelians. The tenuous intellectual spirits give rise to life, sense, fancy (or imagination), and understanding, and through them to reason, the being of the soul. Human discursive reason and angel intuitive reason differ "but in degree, of kind the same." This relation continues the principle of organization of the one first matter. When Milton has Raphael say, immediately after the long passage quoted above,

> Wonder not then, what God for you saw good
> If I refuse not, but convert, as you,
> To proper substance; time may come when men
> With Angels may participate, and find
> No inconvenient Diet, nor too light Fare:
> And from these corporal nutriments perhaps

[32]R. Bostocke, *The Difference betwene the auncient Phisicke . . . and the latter Phisicke*, sig. A5ᵛ, quoted in Allen G. Debus, *The English Paracelsians* (London: Oldbourne, 1965), p. 58.

> Your bodies may at last turn all to spirit,
> Improv'd by tract of time, and wing'd ascend
> Ethereal, as wee, or may at choice
> Here or in Heav'nly Paradises dwell,
>
> (5.491–500)

the roles of digester and digested are interchanged. The refined spirits in the plant are a product of the digestion of crude
materials. The logic of the plant simile asks us to see man as
digested by the world. From crude material to odorous spirits
in the metabolism of the plant, from human being to angel in
the metabolism of the animate world.

The animation of the world was established in the prologue
to Raphael's lecture, when he assures Adam that he can eat
earthly food:

> food alike those pure
> Intelligential substances require
> As doth your Rational; and both contain
> Within them every lower faculty
> Of sense, whereby they hear, see, smell, touch, taste,
> Tasting concoct, digest, assimilate,
> And corporeal to incorporeal turn.
> For know, whatever was created, needs
> To be sustain'd and fed; of Elements
> The grosser feeds the purer, Earth the Sea,
> Earth and the Sea feed Air, the Air those Fires
> Ethereal, and as lowest first the Moon;
> Whence in her visage round those spots, unpurg'd
> Vapors not yet into her substance turn'd.
> Nor doth the Moon no nourishment exhale
> From her moist Continent to higher Orbs.
> The Sun that light imparts to all, receives
> From all his alimental recompense
> In humid exhalations, and at Even
> Sups with the Ocean.
>
> (5.407–26)[33]

---

[33]The beginning of this passage exemplifies the manner in which, according to
Christian Doctrine, the spirit as the more excellent substance contains matter.

The turning of the corporeal to the incorporeal in this passage must be taken as relative. In conventional seventeenth-century discourse the incorporeal soul is immortal because it is immutable, a condition violated by the physiological origin described here. For Milton, soul, and the life which springs from it, are not anomalies in a dead material world; instead, life is the usual condition of matter. Milton gladly strips soul of its special status—and, as we shall see, of its natural immortality—in order to celebrate the vitality of all matter. It is as if he is saying that the deadness of the material world is too great a price to pay for the immortality of a separable soul.

The Reaction to Mechanism

Milton's animist materialism allows him to forgo making a case for incorporealism without admitting a mechanism threatening to his conception of freedom of the will. This materialism should be viewed as a subtle and ingenious contribution to the metaphysical debate of the mid-seventeenth century. The standard view of his diametric opposition to Hobbes is inadequate and misleading. If the criterion for grouping thinkers is acceptance of the immortality and incorporeality of the soul, a criterion central to the seventeenth-century debate, then Milton and Hobbes belong in the same camp. Whatever their great differences in politics and ethics, Milton and Hobbes shared a significant assumption: all that exists is body, even if the type of body that goes under the name of incorporeal is inaccessible to the senses. Of course Milton is not a Hobbesian. If both agree that there is no such thing as incorporeal substance, they disagree on the nature of corporeal substance. Hobbes views life, for example, as the mechanical motion of a complex of essentially inert parcels of matter; Milton views matter as essentially alive. Nevertheless, Milton participates in the same materialist project as other thinkers of his time, including Hobbes. In the next chapter I will examine more closely the relation of Milton to Hobbes.

What moved Milton to break with tradition and to articulate

an animist materialism? The philosophies of Descartes and Hobbes, with their enormous influence, made business-as-usual impossible. The loose Neoplatonism of the early poetry was inadequate armor against the mechanism of both and the determinism of Hobbes. Hobbes's mechanism spelled the end of liberty and probably of God. Descartes's conception of the *res cogitans* paradoxically marginalized incorporeal substance, making it seem irrelevant to the operation of the natural universe. While Descartes argued for the freedom of the will, he lodged it in the small corner of this substance, thus giving it a tenuous hold in philosophy. If thinkers accepted Descartes's *res extensa* without his *res cogitans*, as many feared Hobbes and Spinoza did (with some sort of justification for Hobbes but little for Spinoza), then liberty would be lost. Moreover, Descartes need not be truncated or misread to yield a world equaling Hobbes's in its mechanism. Milton could hardly fail to be aware of the momentous developments in philosophy unfolding around him.

The Cambridge Platonists felt the same challenge. Milton shared More's and Cudworth's sense of the danger posed to theism, the soul, and free will by mechanism, as he could hardly have failed to do, but he did not take the same route to counter it. During a time when, as More wrote to Robert Boyle, "the notion of a spirit is so hooted at by so many for nonsense,"[34] Milton moved toward a materialist conception of the soul and mind. In this, he reflected his time. Hobbes had argued for a reduction of thought to corporeal motions, Spinoza and Leibniz were developing different arguments that thought and extension were two aspects of the same substance. Locke in 1690 was to point out that it is "not much more remote from

[34] *The Works of the Honourable Robert Boyle*, ed. Thomas Birch, 2d ed., 6 vols. (London, 1772), 6:514 (letter from More to Boyle, December 4, 1671). Birch places the letter in 1665; for the correct date, see Alan Gabbey, "Philosophia Cartesiana Triumphata: Henry More (1646–1671)," in *Problems of Cartesianism*, ed. Thomas M. Lennon, John M. Nicholas, and John W. Davis (Montreal: McGill-Queens University Press, 1982), p. 248. For More's concern that the assertion of the incorporeality of the soul could lead to doubt in its existence, see his *Psychathanasia* II, ii, 1.

our Comprehension to conceive that GOD can, if He pleases, superadd to Matter a Faculty of Thinking, than that he should superadd to it another Substance with a Faculty of Thinking."[35] Milton hoped to preserve freedom not by insisting on the immateriality of the soul, but by redefining matter away from mechanism. Given the precarious state of incorporeal substance, itself reflected in the vehemence of the Cambridge Platonist defense, this was an understandable move.

Moreover, as in the case of Hobbes, political as well as ethical imperatives may have played a role in the development of Milton's new metaphysical model. *Leviathan* links mechanistic determinism with a severely restrictive view of the liberty of subjects. One can see how Milton, a revolutionary who distrusted the masses, could find attractive a picture of a scale of homogenous matter crowned by rare spirits. The fictions of *Eikon Basilike* might impress "an inconstant, irrational, and Image-doting rabble . . . a credulous and hapless herd," Milton argues in *Eikonoklastes*, but would not "stirr the constancie and solid firmness of any wise Man" (*CP* 3:601). In the *Defence of the People of England* (1651), Milton distinguishes between "the dregs of the populace" and "the middle class, which produces the greatest number of men of good sense and knowledge of affairs" (*CP* 4:171). With the other revolutionaries, Milton struggled through the 1650s with the paradox of bringing liberty to people who did not seem to want it, and concluded in *The Readie and Easy Way* (1660) that it is just and right "that a less number compell a greater to retain . . . thir libertie" (*CP* 7:455). Presumably, middle-class Independents such as Milton himself could speak for the people, as a monarch could not, because they were the flower of the nation, "more refin'd, more spiritous, and pure." As Milton casts about in *The Readie and Easy Way* for a workable model of representative government, he imag-

---

[35]John Locke, *Essay concerning Human Understanding*, ed. Peter H. Nidditch (Oxford: Clarendon Press, 1975), p. 541 (IV, iii, 6). John W. Yolton traces the reaction to this observation in *Thinking Matter: Materialism in Eighteenth-Century Britain* (Minneapolis: University of Minnesota Press, 1983).

ines a progressive sifting reminiscent of the distillation of the spirits in Raphael's lecture on the one first matter:

> Another way will be, to wel-qualifie and refine elections: not committing all to the noise and shouting of a rude multitude, but permitting only those of them who are rightly qualifi'd, to nominat as many as they will; and out of that number others of a better breeding, to chuse a less number more judiciously, till after a third and fourth sifting and refining of exactest choice, they only be left chosen who are the due number, and seem by most voices the worthiest. (*CP* 7:442–43)

The scale that both unites and holds apart the refined spirits and the clotted and imbruted dregs is the metaphysical counterpart of a political vision of republican rule of and for all the people by the chosen few. The animism of Milton's version of materialism accounts for the freedom that sets it apart from Hobbes's, as Milton's politics finds a central place for a kind of freedom denied by Hobbes. But in the descent along the graded scale of animate matter we witness the metaphysical version of Milton's distaste for the unruly material of the mass of his countrymen.

~ 4

Milton and Anne Conway

Several influential voices in seventeenth-century England proposed a principle of life neither incorporeal nor mechanical, and it is among these thinkers that Milton takes his place. Advocates of vitalism—the belief that life is a property traceable to matter itself rather than to either the motion of complex organizations of matter or an immaterial soul—included Francis Bacon, whom the young Milton read and admired at Cambridge, William Harvey, the Aristotelian physiologist and pioneer of the circulatory system, and Lady Anne Conway, a brilliant and neglected metaphysician whose thought offers illuminating similarities to Milton's.[1]

Francis Bacon and William Harvey

After flirting with atomism, Bacon developed a philosophy of substance based on the interaction of tangible and gross matter on the one hand and tenuous pneumatic matter on the other. This pneumatic matter is practically but not theoretically intangible; to our senses it is invisible and weightless. In the context of a rationalized version of Paracelsus's confused and

---

[1] Animist materialism—the belief, shared by Milton, that matter can possess the traits of mind—is an extension of vitalism.

inconsistent doctrine of the three principles (salt, mercury, and sulphur) and four elements (the Aristotelian elements)—Paracelsus never decided whether the principles were the foundation of the elements or vice versa—Bacon suggested that inert grosser matter is moved by tenuous pneumatic matter. Pneumatic matter, existing independently above the moon and trapped below the moon in tangible bodies, is the cause of change in those tangible bodies. The spirits fall into three categories: inanimate spirits, or spirits that are dispersed and "cut off" in tangible bodies (*spiritus abscissi*); vital spirits, or spirits that are organized in branches (*spiritus ramosi simpliciter*); and finally vital spirits that are attached to a cell or brain (*spiritus ramosi simul et cellulati*).[2] This trichotomy roughly echoes both the Aristotelian theory of the souls and the Galenic division of the spirits. Inanimate spirits are present in all tangible bodies, as is evidenced by the dissolution of bodies brought about by the "desire" of these spirits to escape; vital spirits are present in plants; and vital spirits organized with a cell (or brain) are peculiar to animals, including man.[3] While it has been suggested that Bacon rejected atomism for his pneumatic conception of matter for methodological reasons (i.e., the impossibility of verifying atomism empirically),[4] the move

---

[2]*De Viis Mortis*, fol. 16ʳ. This Bacon manuscript was published for the first time recently in Graham Rees, *Francis Bacon's Natural Philosophy: A New Source* (Chalfont-St. Giles: The British Society for the History of Science, 1984). I have taken the Latin descriptions from *Novum Organum* II, xl, in *The Works of Francis Bacon*, ed. James Spedding, Robert Leslie Ellis, and Douglas Denon Heath, 14 vols. (London: Longman, 1858–74), 1:311. References to Bacon, with noted exceptions, are from this edition, indicated in the notes as Spedding. For Paracelsan elements in Milton, see William Empson, *Milton's God* (1961; Cambridge: Cambridge University Press, 1981), pp. 169–72; William Kerrigan, *The Sacred Complex: On the Psychogenesis of "Paradise Lost"* (Cambridge: Harvard University Press, 1983), pp. 199–200, 219–21; John Rumrich, *Matter of Glory: A New Preface to "Paradise Lost"* (Pittsburgh: University of Pittsburgh Press, 1987), pp. 76, 85.

[3]Bacon hoped for the prolongation of life through intervention in the balance between the inanimate spirits, which desire to escape the tangible body, and the vital spirits, which desire to hold the body together.

[4]Robert Kargon, *Atomism in England from Hariot to Newton* (Oxford: Clarendon Press, 1966), pp. 46–48.

toward pneumatism is consonant with Bacon's interest in alchemy.[5]

Bacon argued for the seamless continuity of inanimate and animate spirits. He writes of the "kindling" of inanimate spirits, by which he means the transformation of inanimate spirits into animate spirits: "But when the [inanimate] spirit is neither wholly detained [i.e., cut off in dispersed pockets] nor wholly discharged [i.e., escaped from the tangible body altogether], but only makes trials and experiments within its prison-house, and meets with tangible parts that are obedient and ready to follow, so that whithersoever the spirit leads they go along with it, then ensues the forming of an organic body, and the development of organic parts, and all other vital actions as well in vegetable as in animal substances."[6] Here life appears to be a function of a rudimentary organization of tenuous matter rather than of either an incorporeal principle or a mechanical motion of parts. Even the inanimate spirits are potentially alive; it is only the restriction of being "cut off" that keeps them in their inanimate state. Moreover, Bacon writes in *De Augmentis Scientarum* that "it is now known that [the sensible soul] is itself a corporeal and material substance (*substantiam corpoream et materiatam*)."[7] While arguing that sense, imagination, and

---

[5]For Bacon's interest in theoretical alchemy, as opposed to the sooty business of attempting to transmute base metals into gold, see Paolo Rossi, *Francis Bacon: From Magic to Science*, trans. Sacha Rabinovitch (Chicago: University of Chicago Press, 1968), pp. 13–22.

[6]*Novum Organum* II, xl, in Spedding 4:196. For the language of "kindling," see *De Viis Mortis*, fol. 26ᵛ (Rees, *Bacon's Natural Philosophy*, pp. 158–59). In this passage, Bacon also uses language that suggests a debt to the Aristotelian conception of the power of matter: "*if it* [the inanimate spirit] *has the resources* for joining itself up and through that for exercising and enjoying its own nature, then indeed it kindles and conducts itself *according to its capability*" (my emphasis).

[7]IV, iii, in Spedding 4:401 and 1:610. Francis Glisson also argued that life is a function of the arrangement of apparently inanimate matter; Glisson's hylozoic treatment of fibrous solids can be found in his *Treatise on the Energetic Nature of Substance* (1672) and his *Treatise on the Stomach and Intestines* (1677). For Glisson see Thomas S. Hall, *Ideas of Life and Matter: Studies in the History of General Physiology*, 2 vols. (Chicago: University of Chicago Press, 1969), 1:396–97.

memory in animals derive from concentrations of spirit in the brain, Bacon stops short of completely corporealizing the human soul for reasons that are not quite clear. According to Graham Rees, "Bacon probably thought that human voluntary motion, sensation, sense, imagination, memory, and even reason were all products of vital spirit operating in the nerves and ventricles of the brain. But if he thought that why did he claim repeatedly that human reason, imagination, and memory belonged to the incorporeal rational soul?"[8] Rees concludes that Bacon envisioned some unspecified intercourse between the incorporeal soul and the vital spirits in the brain corresponding to the various faculties. Considering the ill success of Descartes's pineal-gland model, Bacon may have been wise to leave this question unaddressed. In any event, in Bacon the young Milton would have found a natural philosophy in which the inanimate and animate are located along a continuum of matter, and in which life and thought are functions of rarefied and active matter rather than of the motion of corpuscles of inherently inert matter. Facing the mechanist challenge some years later in the middle of the century, Milton would also write of life as an essential property of tenuous matter.

A contemporary of Bacon at times mentioned in conjunction with Milton is Robert Fludd, a thinker of central importance in English and Continental philosophy in the early seventeenth century.[9] Fludd attempted to base a cosmogonical natural philosophy on the Bible and hermetic texts. While there are intriguing similarities between, for example, Fludd's discussion of light and Milton's invocation to light (*Paradise Lost*, Book 3), Fludd's occult, enthusiastic, and allegorical temperament is al-

---

[8]Rees, *Bacon's Natural Philosophy*, p. 41.

[9]Allen G. Debus labels Fludd "the best-known English scientist of his generation on the Continent," in *The English Paracelsians* (London: Oldbourne, 1965), p. 123. Denis Saurat claims that Robert Fludd's cabbalism is an important source for Milton's materialism in *Milton: Man and Thinker* (New York: Dial Press, 1925), pp. 301–9, and *Milton et le matérialisme chrétien en Angleterre* (Paris: Rieder, 1928), pp. 13–97. But R. J. Zwi Werblowsky points out the incoherence and inauthenticity of Fluddean cabbalism and undermines Saurat's claims for its influence on Milton; see "Milton and the *Conjectura Cabbalistica*," *Journal of the Warburg and Courtald Institutes* 18 (1955): 90–113.

ien to Milton. Milton was skeptical of occult phenomena and alchemical experiments (although he viewed digestion as a kind of natural alchemy).[10] Most important, Milton repudiates the dualist distinction between the imprisoned soul and the imprisoning body maintained by Fludd, who for example speaks of

> mÿ self and other spirits of this present and succeeding race as Wel alreadÿ captiued in prisons of claÿ, [and] thos, that ar ÿet at libertÿ, and haue not tasted the calamitÿ of bondage, but swim and bathe themselues in the vast and liquid Ocean of the Worlds uni-uersal spirit, til bÿ inevitable fate and destinye theÿ be included to finishe a Times portion also in dark dungeons of Woe.[11]

There is an initial resemblance between the tenuous athereal vehicles or astral bodies of the Christian cabbalist and the corporeal soul of Milton.[12] Emanation is central to Christian cabbalism, which is infused with a strong dose of Neoplatonism, and the proliferation of intermediate and tenuous vehicles of the soul tends in the same direction as Milton's denial of the incorporeality of the soul, but it stops short of Milton's forthright materialism.

Fludd owed more to Plato than to Aristotle, whom he attacked violently. Milton shared the animus of his time toward the scholastics, but he never joined in the chorus against Aristotle. A glance at the Aristotelian William Harvey, the discoverer of the circulation of the blood, helps us to see how far Milton's conception of the relation of mind and body differs from Fludd's and More's theories of vehicles. In a work of 1649 answering objections to his famous work of 1628 on the circula-

---

[10]For Milton's skepticism, see *Paradise Lost* 1.784 and 5.441.

[11]*Robert Fludd and His Philosophicall Key*, intro. Allen G. Debus (New York: Science History Publications, 1979), p. 83. In this book, Debus presents, with an excellent introduction, a transcription of a Fludd manuscript composed between late 1618 and early 1620.

[12]Werblowsky describes the irony of the term "Christian cabbalist," but insists that the adjective be used when discussing writers such as Fludd and Henry More who appropriated poorly understood Hebrew cabbala for their own purposes.

tion of the blood (but significantly not in the work of 1628 itself), Harvey makes clear his opposition to incorporeal spirits:

> Some speak of corporeal, others of incorporeal spirits; and they who advocate the corporeal spirits will have the blood, or the thinner portion of the blood, to be the bond of union with the soul, the spirit being contained in the blood as the flame is in the smoke of a lamp or candle . . . ; others, again, distinguish between the spirits and the blood. They who advocate incorporeal spirits have no ground of experience to stand upon; their spirits indeed are synonymous with powers or faculties, such as a concoctive spirit, a chylopoietic spirit, a procreative spirit, &c.—they admit as many spirits, in short, as there are faculties or organs.[13]

Working with a pneumatic conception of the spirits derived explicitly from Aristotle's *Generation of Animals*, Harvey argues that the soul is indistinguishable from the spirits, which are analogous to the matter of the stars but which are engendered by natural means in the blood. "The blood," he writes,

> does not seem to differ *in any respect* from the soul or the life itself (anima); at all events, it is to be regarded as the substance whose act is the soul or the life. Such, I say, is the soul, which is neither wholly corporeal nor yet wholly incorporeal; which is derived in part from abroad, and is partly produced at home; which in one way is part of the body, but in another way is the beginning and cause of all that is contained in the animal body, viz. nutrition, sense, and motion, and consequently of life and death alike.[14]

[13]William Harvey, *Two Anatomical Disquisitions on the Circulation of the Blood, Addressed to John Riolan*, in *The Works of William Harvey, M.D.*, trans. Robert Willis (1847; rpt. Annapolis, Md.: St. John's College Press, 1949), p. 116.
[14]William Harvey, *Anatomical Exercises on the Generation of Animals* 71 ("Of the Innate Heat"), in *Works*, pp. 501–12; my emphasis. The quoted passage is from p. 511. Citing this same section of Harvey, William Hunter argues incorrectly that Harvey "splits the organism apart, with the soul originating from one principle, the body from another" ("Milton and the Thrice Great Hermes," *Journal of English and Germanic Philology* 45 [1946]: 328). Hunter does not recognize that Harvey follows Aristotle in the claim that the spirits are identical in essence to ethereal matter but are engendered in the blood. This supposed difference is crucial to Hunter's attempt to relocate Milton from Aristotelian to Hermetic contexts.

The alternatives offered here resolve Aristotle's ambivalence and, despite the language of corporeal and incorporeal, move Aristotle's equivocation toward a clearly materialist solution. The soul for Harvey and for Milton is not "wholly corporeal" in the qualified sense of accessibility to the senses. By its very tenuousness, pneumatic matter is "incorporeal," but only relatively. Harvey straddles Aristotle's pneumatic and hylomorphic conceptions of the soul with his conclusion that the soul is "in one way part of the body" (i.e., the blood) and "in another way" the principle of bodily structures, or "the beginning and cause" of corporeal actions.

Milton resembles Bacon and Harvey in his belief that life is neither the sum of mechanical motions, as Descartes and Hobbes would have it, or an attribute of an incorporeal substance superadded to body, as the Cambridge Platonists insisted. He resembles them also in invoking corporeal spirits to explain physical and mental operation. Nevertheless, in his thinking on substance and life Milton most closely resembles Anne Conway, who developed an animist materialism in response to mechanist philosophies that threatened the existence of freedom. Unlike Milton, she left a record of her opinions of her philosophical adversaries.

Lady Anne Conway

Conway, unfortunately, seems to be better known for the lifelong and severe headache that exhausted the resources of seventeenth-century medicine than for her contribution to philosophy. The center of a circle of intellectuals including Cudworth, Whichcote, Rust, Glanvill, John Worthington, and Francis Mercury van Helmont, Conway was also a special friend and pupil of More, who dedicated his *Antidote against Atheism* to her.[15] No docile disciple, Conway sensed the confusion be-

[15]For Conway's life and circle, see Marjorie Nicolson's introduction to her edition of the *Conway Letters: The Correspondence of Anne, Viscountess Conway, Henry More, and Their Friends, 1642–1684* (New Haven: Yale University Press, 1930).

tween dualism and monism in her mentor. She avoids the inconsistencies into which More falls by explicitly rejecting dualism in her own philosophy and articulating a thoroughgoing monism. Her one book, *The Principles of the Most Ancient and Modern Philosophy*, was published in 1690, eleven years after her death.[16] While her work can obviously have had no influence on Milton, it deserves to be more widely known among Miltonists, for Conway's monism is in many respects remarkably similar to Milton's own.[17]

Her philosophy deserves to be known on its own merits also. Her monism anticipates that of Leibniz, who in fact read her book and praised her: "*Les miens en philosophie approchent un peu d'avantage de ceux de feu Madame la Comtesse de Conway*, et tiennent le milieu entre Platon et Democrite, puisque je crois que tout se fait mechaniquement, comme veulent Democrite et Descartes, contre l'opinion de Mr. Morus et ses semblables; et que néanmoins tout se fait encore vitalement et suivant les causes finales, tout étant plein de vie et perception, contre l'opinion des Democritiens."[18] Leibniz admires Conway for re-

---

[16]Conway wrote the work in English, probably shortly before her death in 1679. More and/or Francis Mercury van Helmont edited and translated her manuscript for the first Latin edition; the 1692 edition is a retranslation into English. I will cite the edition by Peter Lopston (The Hague: Martinus Nijhoff, 1982) by page number in the text. Lopston prints the Latin translation of 1690 and the English retranslation of 1692; the second number in parenthetical references refers to the Latin text.

[17]The *Principles* is influenced by van Helmont's cabbalism. But because there is no question of Conway's influence on Milton, there is no need here to separate the strands of Conway's originality and the presence of van Helmont in her work. Moreover, the *Principles*, precisely in its downplaying of cabbalist elements, is closer to the thought of Milton than is the published work of van Helmont.

[18]Leibniz, letter to Thomas Burnet (1697), quoted in *Conway Letters*, p. 456. Carolyn Merchant translates this passage in *The Death of Nature: Women, Ecology, and the Scientific Revolution* (San Francisco: Harper & Row, 1983), p. 257: "My philosophical views approach somewhat closely those of the late Countess of Conway, and hold a middle position between Plato and Democritus, because I hold that all things take place mechanically as Democritus and Descartes contend against the views of Henry More and his followers, and hold too, nevertheless, that everything takes place according to a living principle and according to final causes—all things are full of life and consciousness, contrary to the views of the Atomists."

pairing the defects of both More and Descartes (and by extension Plato and Democritus): all takes place both mechanically
on the one hand and vitally and according to final causes on the
other.

While her teacher More modified Descartes's dualism by arguing that all substance, corporeal and incorporeal, is extended, Conway moved closer to Milton and to Hobbes by arguing that there is only one type of substance in creation.
Conway writes that all creatures, by whom she means everything from rocks to angels, "in regard of their First Substance
and Essence [*primae substantiae & essentiae*], . . . were all one and
the same Thing, and as it were Parts and Members of one
Body" (pp. 199, 111). She adds that "the whole Creation is still
but one Substance or Entity" (p. 206). This conception closely
echoes Milton's conception of the "one first matter" from
which all things, both corporeal and "incorporeal," spring. For
both Conway and Milton, the corollary of this unity of substance is ontological mobility. Conway insists, for example, that
a rock could become a plant, an animal, or a man. She writes,
"An Horse in divers Qualities and Perfections draws near unto
the Nature and *Species* of a Man, and that more than many
other Creatures; Is therefor the nature of a Man distant from
the Nature of an Horse, by Infinite Degrees, or by Finite only?
If by Finite, then certainly a Horse may in length of Time be in
some measure changed into a Man, (I mean his Spirit; as for
his Body that is a thing evident)" (p. 182). The position of a
creature along the hierarchy of being is in part determined by
moral worth. Virtue in life will lead to spiritualization of the
body, much in the manner of the atherealization promised to
obedient human beings by Raphael in *Paradise Lost*; Conway's
fallen angels undergo, like Milton's, a corporealizing metamorphosis. She writes that "if it be here demanded, Whether
those Spirits became more Corporeal by their Transgression,
than they were in their Primitive State before they fell? I answer, Yes" (pp. 193–94).

All is body in Conway's monist metaphysic, but body is best
understood as an expression or mode of spirit: "Indeed every
Body is a Spirit, and nothing else, neither differs any thing

from a Spirit, but in that it is more dark; therefore by how much the thicker and grosser it is become, so much the more remote is it from the degree of a Spirit, so that this distinction is only modal and gradual, not essential or substantial" (p. 190). This conception of the relation of spirit and body is shared by Milton, who agrees that "Spirit and Body are originally of one Nature and Substance, and that a Body is nothing but a fixed and condensed Spirit, and a Spirit nothing but a subtile and volatile Body" (p. 217).

Like Milton again, Conway elaborates on the relationship between spirit and matter alternately in hylomorphic and pneumatic terms. Spirit and body, while parcels of the first substance differing in degree rather than kind, act as the active and passive principles of creatures. Conway expresses her hylomorphism with a metaphor of the mirror:

> The Spirit is an Eye or Light beholding its own proper Image [*propriam suam imaginem*], and the Body is a Tenebrosity or Darkness receiving that Image, when the Spirit looks thereinto, as when one sees himself in a Looking-Glass; for certainly he cannot so behold himself in the Transparent Air, nor in any Diaphanous Body, because the reflexion of an Image requires a certain opacity or Darkness, which we call a Body: Yet to be a body is not an Essential property of any Thing; as neither is it a property of any Thing to be dark; for nothing is so dark that it cannot be made Light. (pp. 189, 100)

On this model one cannot divide spirit and body except conceptually. Conway refers later to Aristotle's hylomorphic conception of *entelechy* to explicate the relation of soul and body. But more often Conway speaks of the spirit as a kind of subtle body located within the grosser matter of the visible body. If the description of the body as the mirror of the mind sounds like an attempt to express hylomorphism in language borrowed from theosophy, Conway's descriptions of the spirit as subtle body bring us back to ground familiar from Bacon and Harvey and Milton: "a Body is the grosser part of a thing, and Spirit the subtiler, whence also Spirit hath it's name from the Air, which is the most subtile nature in this visible World" (p. 205).

As with Milton, the fact that Conway conceives of spirit and body as ontologically continuous and not as separate substances does not prevent her from talking alternately about them. While spirit is a tenuous, rarefied body, one can use the term "body" in many contexts. With a credulity reminiscent of More, Conway notes that "the Spirit or Soul so loveth the Body wherewith it is united, and so unwillingly departs out of it, that it has been manifestly notorious, the Souls of some have attended on, and been subject to their Bodies, after the Body was dead, until it was corrupted, and dissolved into dust" (p. 200). This dead body parallels Milton's special use of "body" as "merely physical trunk" (*CP* 6:318). If Milton nevertheless implies in *Paradise Lost* a living universe, in which even supposedly "inanimate" objects are "instinct with spirit," Conway insists explicitly that everything that God created is capable of life and sense, that is to say, every stone is a condensed spirit waiting to come to life.

Conway echoes Milton in employing digestion as an analogy for and example of the ascent along the hierarchy of being:

> For Nature still works to a farther perfection of subtilty and spirituality; even as this is the most natural Property of all Motion and Operation: For all Motion wears and divides, and so renders a Thing subtile and spiritual. Even thus in Man's Body, the Meat and Drink is first changed into Chyle, then into Blood, afterwards into Spirits [*in spiritus*], which are nothing else but Blood brought to perfection [*sanguis in perfectionem deductus*]; and these Spirits, whether good or bad, still advance to a greater subtilty or spirituality, and by these Spirits which come from the Blood, we see, hear, smell, taste, feel, and think, yea meditate, love, hate, and do all things whatsoever we do. (pp. 218, 132)

In her monist system, these "Spirits," at once body and spirit, do not involve her in contradiction and inconsistency, as those of the Cambridge Platonists do. Conway goes as far as Milton in extending the chain of one matter from food to angel when she concludes that "these [Spirits] are the proper Angels, or ministering Spirits of a Man."

In pushing her monism to its limits, Conway provides for a mental obstetrics that recalls the metaphysical obstetrics of Milton's divorce tracts (or the birth of the "new soul" in Donne's "Extasie"). Having described reproduction in terms of the mixing of the spirits of the male and female, Conway argues that the process is continuous with the birth of thoughts, which themselves have bodies: "And after the same manner also, the Internal Productions of the Mind, *viz.* Thoughts are generated, which according to their Kind are true Creatures, and have a true Substance [*veram substantiam*], proper to themselves, being all our Internal Children, and all of them Male and Female, that is, they have Body and Spirit [*corpus habent & spiritum*]" (pp. 189, 101). Like other animists and anti-mechanists in the seventeenth century, including More, Conway resorts to a mechanical model to explain her psychology: "for if they [thoughts] had not a Body, they could not be retained, nor could we reflect on our own proper Thoughts; for every reflection is made by a certain Tenebrosity or Darkness, and this is a Body; so the memory requires a Body, to retain the Spirit of the Thing thought on" (pp. 189–90). This insistence on the material existence of thoughts (as opposed to the tracks in the brain favored by Hobbes, Glanvill, and others) recalls Milton's monistic conception of the book as the "pretious life-blood of a master spirit" of *Areopagitica* (CP 2:493).

Conway's belief in three classes of substance—God, Christ as medium, and creature—mirrors Milton's. God is eternal and immaterial, creatures are temporal and simultaneously spiritual and material, and Christ is the created medium who translates God's goodness into creation. Milton's God is eternal and ineffable (if not clearly immaterial). And for both Milton and Conway, the Son substantially expresses God and his goodness. In this they both resemble ibn Gabirol [Avicebron], the Iberian Jewish philosopher and poet of the eleventh century.[19] This sense of the ontological distance between Father and Son leads Conway, like Milton, to unorthodoxy on the Trinity.[20]

---

[19]Peter Lopston cites Martin Tweedale for the resemblance of Conway and ibn Gabirol in "Anne Conway's Philosophy of Substance and Essence," a paper delivered at the 1984 meeting of the Canadian Society for Eighteenth Century Studies. I thank Professor Lopston for sharing this paper with me. For Milton and ibn Gabirol, see Rumrich, *Matter of Glory*, p. 188.
[20]See chapter 1 of the *Principles*.

Several issues separate Conway from Milton, most importantly those stemming from the cabbalist influence of van Helmont: Conway argues that each creature is made of a multitude of spirits (organized under one spirit) and each body, of a multitude of bodies. This aspect of her thought foreshadows Leibniz and may have contributed to his theory of monads.[21] Conway asserts the immortality and transmigration of souls and denies eternal damnation. Taking an extreme Neoplatonist stance on the eternal necessity of God's creation of the universe, she argues against biblical creation and for the eternity of the world.[22] Nevertheless, in her insistence that all creation is derived from one substance, that spirit and body are rare and dense manifestations of the one matter, and in her attempt to save spirit during a time when materiality was emerging as the test of reality, Conway resembles Milton very closely.

The relation of Conway and Milton suggests the degree of engagement of Milton with the central philosophical debates of his time. Conway is particularly valuable in this attempt to relate Milton to his contemporaries, because while Milton is silent about the relationship between his monism and the systems of contemporary philosophers, Conway is outspoken, explicitly contrasting her philosophy with those of Descartes, Hobbes, and the Platonists. In the following section I will use her book as a touchstone. Because her own vitalist monism is so close to Milton's and diverges from Cartesian dualism, Hobbesian mechanism, and Cambridge incorporealism in the same ways, her reaction to these philosophers is a valuable clue to Milton's.

Milton, Conway, and Their Adversaries

In the prospectus to the final chapter of *The Principles of the Most Ancient and Modern Philosophy*, Conway draws hostile boundaries:

[21]See Carolyn Merchant, "The Vitalism of Anne Conway: Its Impact on Leibniz's Concept of the Monad," *Journal of the History of Philosophy* 17 (1979): 255–69.
[22]On seventeenth-century expressions of the Neoplatonist imperative of eternal creation, see my "'To Act or Not': Milton's Conception of Divine Freedom," *Journal of the History of Ideas* 49 (1988): 431–32.

The Philosophers (so called) of all Sects, have generally laid an ill Foundation to their Philosophy; and therefore the whole Structure must needs fall. 2. The Philosophy here treated on is not Cartesian. 3. Nor the Philosophy of *Hobbs* and *Spinosa*, (falsely so feigned,) but diametrically opposite to them. 4. That they who have attempted to refute *Hobbs* and *Spinosa*, have given them too much advantage. 5. This Philosophy is the strongest to refute *Hobbs* and *Spinosa*, but after another method. 6. We understand here quite another thing by Body and Matter, than *Hobbs* understood; and which *Hobbs*, and *Spinosa*, never saw, otherwise than in a Dream. (p. 221)

This passage bristles with antagonism toward Descartes, Hobbes, and Spinoza, prime examples of "Philosophers (so called)." The main focus here is on Hobbes and Spinoza for two reasons: they are the closest to Conway and the farthest. That is to say, Conway articulates a version of materialist monism as they do, but at the same time she abhors the determinism of both and the panmechanism of Hobbes. As in the case of Milton, the philosophical battle is to be fought on the fields of materialism, an area in which the dualisms of Descartes and the Cambridge Platonists are decreasingly relevant.

In her treatment of Descartes, Conway focuses on his deanimation of *res extensa*, thus providing a clue to Milton's probable reaction to Cartesian thought:

As touching the *Cartesian* Philosophy, this saith that every Body is a mere dead Mass, not only void of all kind of Life and Sense, but utterly uncapable thereof to all Eternity. . . . Although it cannot be denied that *Cartes* taught many excellent and ingenious Things concerning the Mechanical part of Natural Operations, and how all Natural Motions proceed according to Rules and Laws Mechanical, even as indeed Nature her self, *i.e.* the Creature, hath an excellent Mechanical Skill and Wisdom in it self, (given it from God, who is the Fountain of all Wisdom,) by which it operates: But yet in nature, and her Operations, they are far more than merely Mechanical; and the same is not a mere Organical Body, like a Clock, wherein there is not a vital Principle of Motion, but a living Body . . . far more sublime than a mere Mechanism, or Mechanical Motion. (pp. 221–22)

Conway charges that while Descartes argues for a free incorporeal substance, he delivers *res extensa* over to a mere mechanism. This perception was shared by many of Milton's contemporaries, some of whom feared that mechanism was but a short step from atheism. Pascal is reported to have said he "cannot forgive Descartes: in his whole philosophy he would like to do without God; but he could not help allowing him a flick of the fingers to set the world in motion; after that he had no more use for God."[23] Like Cudworth, Conway recognizes the operation of mechanical laws while insisting on their inadequacy to explain phenomena; spirit and life must also be invoked.

We can be certain that Milton would have opposed Cartesian mechanism as firmly as Conway did. His disagreement is demonstrable from the monist metaphysic defined in the *Christian Doctrine* and the natural philosophy incorporated into *Paradise Lost*. The vigor of the creation scene in Book 7 attests to his conviction of the life of the material universe:

> The Earth obey'd, and straight
> Op'ning her fertile Womb teem'd at a Birth
> Innumerous living Creatures.
>
> (7.453–55)

"Waters generate / Reptile" and "grassy Clods . . . Calv'd" (7.387–88, 463). These images themselves are born from Milton's unshakable animist conviction. His conception of the celestial as in some way animate would have struck Descartes with his blind vortices as old-fashioned and unscientific:

> other Suns perhaps
> With thir attendant Moons thou wilt descry
> Communicating Male and Female Light
> Which two great Sexes animate the World.
>
> (8.148–51)

The procreative metaphor here confirms that in Creation Milton's intuition met its proper theme. His universe, like the Son's

---

[23]"Sayings Attributed to Pascal," in Blaise Pascal, *Pensées*, ed. A. J. Krailsheimer (Harmondsworth: Penguin, 1966), p. 355.

chariot, is "instinct with Spirit" (6.752). Descartes's abstraction
of spirit from matter, leaving a mere mechanism, is foreign to
Milton's intuition of universal life.

Conway's criticism points to another issue separating Descartes and Milton. Descartes removed from natural philosophy
the *final cause*, the cause *for the sake of which* a thing is what it is.
Descartes believed that the preoccupation with final causes
leads natural philosophy into dead ends. *Res extensa* can be
discussed only in terms of efficient and material causation.
Conway counters this position with her argument that "Nature
her self, *i.e.* the Creature, hath an excellent Mechanical Skill
and Wisdom in it self" (p. 222). Despite the label of "mechanical," "skill" and "wisdom" here suggest both activity and inten-
tionality, as opposed to the blind reaction of mechanism. Milton
also affirmed the principle of final cause and intention in nature. In both the *Christian Doctrine* (I, vii) and the *Art of Logic* (I,
ix), he endorses the Aristotelian division of causation into four
categories: efficient, material, formal, and final. Milton finds
final cause explicit in the Bible and incorporates it into *Paradise
Lost*:

> And God made two great Lights, great for thir use
> To Man, the greater to have rule by Day,
> The less by Night altern: and made the Stars,
> And set them in the Firmament of Heav'n
> To illuminate the Earth, and rule the Day
> In thir vicissitude, and rule the Night,
> And Light from Darkness to divide.
>
> (7.346–52)

The heavenly bodies are not the chance products of vortices or
gravity, but lights set about Earth by a solicitous God, animate
bodies to illuminate an animate home. In his attack on final
cause, Descartes carried the present and future with him; the
seventeenth century saw the death of final cause in scientific
discussion, despite its defense by Conway and by the more
influential voices of Gassendi, Boyle, and Leibniz.

It is conventional to speak of the absolute opposition of Milton and Hobbes. One is an active social and political reformer,

the other an authoritarian defender of the status quo; this political hostility, in all likelihood, lies at the heart of Elizabeth Milton's statement that the views of her husband and Hobbes "did run counter to each other."[24] The political disagreement reflects fundamental philosophical oppositions: Milton's unshakable conviction that man is free versus Hobbes's methodical destruction of that freedom, and Milton's realist belief in the availability of absolute truth to right reason versus Hobbes's nominalist assertion that abstractions are relative and manmade. The Hobbesian citizen whose actions are to be determined by a government takes his place in a universe governed by physical causation. Because good and evil are relative terms defined by those in power, there is no basis for principled action against the government. The Miltonic citizen who must sometimes oppose the government is the man who is accountable for his own free actions. Because absolute standards of goodness and truth may conflict with the wishes of those in power, there are occasions when Milton's citizen must resist legally sanctioned authority.

But the extremity of these political and psychological differences has obscured the complex relationship between the metaphysics of the two men. Blanket statements of the affinity of Milton to the anti-Hobbesian Cambridge school distort this relationship, for in a few important ways Milton is closer to Hobbes than he is to More.[25] There is a remarkably broad range of agreement between the two authors, deriving from their shared monism. One technical instance of agreement is their mutual rejection of atomism in favor of the plenum, the distribution of homogeneous matter throughout the universe.[26] More generally and significantly, both challenge the incorporeality of spirit and thus the usual readings of the meaning of "spirit" in the Bible. Hobbes suggests that the term means "any eminent abili-

---

[24]See Introduction, note 13.

[25]One of these ways is temperament. Milton's skepticism, revealed in his treatment of elves even in a poem (*PL* 1.781–84), is reminiscent of Hobbes and a far cry from More's credulous recital of the tale of the Pied Piper of Hamlin (*Antidote against Atheism* III, vi, 2).

[26]See A.S.P. Woodhouse, *The Heavenly Muse*, p. 156.

ty, or extraordinary passion, or disease of the mind."[27] Both offer lists of meanings for "spirit" in Scripture, and of the seven possible meanings mentioned by Hobbes, three are echoed by Milton.[28] In most cases, they agree, "spirit" is used to denote a power or attribute of God or a creature; angels themselves are corporeal creatures. Taking their mutual position to its logical conclusion, Milton and Hobbes both reject the orthodox conception of the Holy Spirit as a person in the sense that the Father or Son is.

According to Hobbes, where "spirit" in the Bible cannot be understood to mean either an attribute or a subtle body, "the place falleth not under humane Understanding; and our Faith therein consisteth not in our Opinion, but in our Submission; as in all places where God is said to be a *Spirit*; or where by the *Spirit of God*, is meant God himselfe."[29] Hobbes continues, "For the nature of God is incomprehensible; that is to say, we understand nothing of *what he is*, but only *that he is*; and therefore the Attributes we give him, are not to tell one another, *what he is*, nor to signifie our opinion of his Nature, but our desire to honor him with such names as we conceive most honorable amongst our selves."[30] In an oblique but interesting way, Hobbes's stance on the attributes of God is related to Milton's. Milton is more confident in the truth of the divine attributes as found in Scripture than Hobbes seems to be, but he admits that the Bible offers only a partial truth: "It is safest for us to form an image of God in our minds which corresponds to his representation and description of himself in the sacred writings. Admittedly, God is always described or outlined not as he really is but in such a way as will make him conceivable to us. Nev-

[27]*Leviathan*, ed. C. B. Macpherson (Harmondsworth: Penguin, 1968), p. 430 (chap. 34).
[28]*Leviathan*, pp. 430–34 (chap. 34); *CP* 6:282–86.
[29]*Leviathan*, p. 430 (chap. 34).
[30]The bow toward incorporeality is related to the admission of incomprehensibility; the former implies the latter, because knowledge for Hobbes derives from the senses. The difficulty, of course, lies in gauging Hobbes's sincerity when he implies that God is incorporeal (see Chapter 1, note 56, for Hobbes's assertion of God's corporeality).

ertheless, we ought to form just such a mental image of him as he, in bringing himself within the limits of our understandings, wishes us to form" (*CP* 6:133). For Milton as for Hobbes, God is the one ineffable entity in the universe.

Shared materialism leads to shared mortalism; there is no incorporeal soul to survive the death of the body.[31] Milton denies that the spirit is either separable from the body or immortal: "once it is agreed that spirit is not divine but merely human, . . . It must also be conceded that no cause can be found why, when God sentenced the whole sinful man to death, the spirit alone should have been exempted from the punishment of death" (*CP* 6:404). "Eternal life" is to be enjoyed after the general resurrection and Last Judgment. Hobbes's position is the same: "That the Soul of man is in its own nature Eternall, and a living Creature independent on the body; or that any meer man is Immortall, otherwise than by Resurrection in the last day, (except *Enos* and *Elias*,) is a doctrine not apparent in Scripture. The whole 14. Chapter of *Job* . . . is a complaint of this Mortality of Nature; and yet no contradiction of the Immortality at the Resurrection."[32] Milton cites the same chapter in his own mortalist argument (*CP* 6:401). Norman Burns has argued that Milton and Hobbes derived their mortalism from Scripture and not from philosophical commitments.[33] But the fact remains that these philosophically adept thinkers found mortalism in the Bible when other sophisticated readers, including Calvin, did not.[34] We have witnessed

---

[31]Maurice Kelley has remarked on the weakness of Milton's arguments for mortalism relative to his arguments for other unorthodox positions in the *Christian Doctrine* (*CP* 6:94–95), a weakness that might betray a distorting effect of Milton's philosophy on his reading of Scripture.

[32]*Leviathan*, p. 483 (chap. 38).

[33]Norman Burns, *Christian Mortalism from Tyndale to Milton* (Cambridge: Harvard University Press, 1972), p. 9.

[34]Burns himself discusses Calvin and quotes Bullinger (p. 25), whose interpretation of Scripture on this point is the inverse image of Milton's: "We say . . . that man doth consist of two, and those diverse substances in one person; of a soul immortal . . . and a body mortal" (*The Second Helvetic Confession* [1566]).

Gassendi moving toward an affirmation of the incorporeal and immortal soul in response to the insistent demands of Christian orthodoxy. Walter Charleton wrote in 1656 that in his time "the Metaphysicks have, doubtless, received a very great encrease of clearness, and mens Speculations seem to be highly refined, in regard of sundry lively and fruitful hints, that are inspersed upon the leaves of sacred Writ, concerning as well the Original and Nature of the Soul, as the state of it after death."[35] What one finds in the Bible depends in part on what one takes to it. If Milton and Hobbes are able to find mortalism in the Bible, it is because they have broken free of the Platonist and scholastic dualisms that colored the reading of others.

Simple diametrical opposition thus does not suffice as a description of the relationship between Milton and Hobbes. At a time when others responded to Hobbes by defending incorporeal substance, Milton's opposition to him took another form, one that adopted an assumption shared by Hobbes and the new science: the materiality of all entities. It is against this common background that Milton's opposition to Hobbes must be viewed, for the similarities make Milton's ultimate repudiation of him more significant.

To understand how Hobbes's monism would have appeared from the specific perspective of Milton's, we can again turn to Conway. While the label of Hobbesian was, along with atheism, a red flag in the mid and late seventeenth century, Conway acknowledges her convergence with Hobbes. Anticipating the objection that her argument for the materiality of all creatures and actions makes her a Hobbesian, she writes: "although *Hobbs* saith the same, yet that is no prejudice to the Truth of it, as neither are other parts of that Philosophy where *Hobbs* affirms something that is true, therefore an *Hobbism*, or an Opinion of *Hobbs* alone" (p. 223). Having made this defiant admission, Conway differentiates her own conception of body from Hobbes's conception of matter and Descartes's *res extensa*. While

---

[35]Walter Charleton, *Epicurus's Morals*, intro. Frederic Manning (London: Peter Davies, 1926), sig. d1r.

Hobbes and Descartes listed extension, figure, site, motion, and impenetrability as the qualities of matter,

> they were plainly ignorant of the noblest and most excellent Attributes of that Substance which they call Body and Matter, and understood nothing of them. But if it be demanded, what are those more excellent Attributes; I Answer, these following, Spirit, or Life, and Light, under which I comprehend a capacity of all kind of Feeling, Sense, and Knowledge, Love, Joy, and Fruition, and all kind of Power and Virtue . . . ; so that even the vilest and most contemptible Creature; yea, Dust and Sand, may be capable of all these Perfections, *sc.* through various . . . Transmutations from the one into the other. (p. 225)

Descartes posits a gulf between matter and spirit that does not exist. Hobbes is a monist, but one who has it all backward, treating mental activity as a by-product of matter rather than treating body as congealed spirit. Conway finds fault with both Cartesian and Hobbesian mechanism, but the latter is worse because it is more universal. The freedom, life, and self-activity that Milton and Conway ascribe to the one first substance find no place in Hobbesian matter, as they do in the incorporeal substance of classical and Cartesian dualisms. It is revealing that Conway substitutes for Hobbes's litany of extension, figure, site, and motion the simpler formula of "life and figure." Under "figure" fall the undeniably mechanical relations of bodies, but under "life" fall "Knowledge, Love, Joy, and Fruition, and all kind of Power and Virtue." Conway acknowledges both spiritual and bodily functions in her monist substance: "a Vital Action is plainly distinct from Local, or Mechanical Motion, although it is not nor cannot be separated from it" (p. 225). Among these vital actions are thought and will, both of which are for Hobbes mechanical phenomena.

Perhaps Conway is so determined to set herself apart from Hobbes precisely because of their shared monism. And perhaps Milton's attack on Hobbesian determinism, to be examined in the final chapter, owes some of its vigor to his need to distance his own materialist monism from the "monster of

Malmesbury's." In any event, Hobbes's mechanization of mind and will is an affront to Milton's and Conway's shared belief in the life of the one substance, a life that guarantees the freedom denied by Hobbes.

Conway's book also provides clues of Milton's probable attitude toward the Cambridge Platonists. Conway attacks at length Cambridge assertions of the essential difference between spirit and matter. More, Cudworth, and the others hammered at the theme that matter alone is mere dead mass, and that all life and motion reside in spirit. Cudworth speaks for all the Platonists when he writes, as we saw in the second chapter, that *"Life, Cogitation* and *Understanding* can be no Corporeal things, but must needs be the Attributes of another kind of Substance distinct from Body."[36] Conway has in mind Platonists as well as Cartesians when she writes, "nothing in the whole World can be conceived so contrary to any Thing, as Body and Spirit, in the opinion of these Men" (p. 201). She, on the other hand, sets out to prove "that Spirit and Body differ not essentially, but gradually (*non . . . essentialiter, sed gradibus*)" (pp. 211, 125).[37] Conway articulates a theory of corporeal vehicles for the soul (pp. 194, 198, 200, 215), but in a metaphysical framework that saves the theory from the confusion and inconsistency from which it suffers in More's dualistic setting. She questions the logic of More's principle of "vital congruity" between a soul and its body, arguing that if body and spirit are separate substances with attributes defined in opposition to each other, then there is no basis for such congruity. Bodies can spiritualize and spirits can corporealize because, as in Milton, there is no ontological divide to cross. Graded steps of ascent in a pneumatic hierarchy account for the union of corporeal soul

---

[36]Ralph Cudworth, *The True Intellectual System of the Universe* (London, 1678; facs. rpt. Stuttgart-Bad Cannstatt: Friedrich Frommann Verlag, 1964), p. 50 (II, xl).

[37]Conway dwells on More's claim that penetrability and discerpibility (divisibility) separate spirit from matter, though she tactfully does not mention her friend and former teacher's name. She argues in response that both bodies and spirits can be more or less penetrable, and that, properly understood, body is as indivisible as spirit (pp. 202–10). She caustically dismisses More's idea of "essential spissitude" (pp. 202–6).

and corporeal body: "the most subtile and Spiritual Body may be united with a Body that is very gross and thick, *sc.* by means of certain Bodies, partaking of subtility and grossness, according to divers degrees, consisting between two Extreams, and these middle Bodies are indeed the Links and Chains, by which the Soul, which is so subtile and Spiritual, is conjoined with a Body so gross" (p. 214).

Conway challenges the Cambridge thinkers and other dualists when she asks, "If Spirit and Body are so contrary one to another, so that a Spirit is only Life, or a living and sensible Substance, but a Body a certain Mass merely dead . . . : What (I pray you) is that which doth so join or unite them together?" (p. 211). The question stumped Glanvill, who shared dualism with Descartes and the Platonists: "That we are a Compound of beings distant in extreams, is as clear as Noon. But how the purer Spirit is united to this clod, is a knot too hard for fallen Humanity to unty. What cement should untie [sic] heaven and earth, light and darkness, natures of so diverse a make, of such disagreeing attributes, which have almost nothing, but *Being*, in common; This is a riddle, which must be left to the coming of Elias."[38] Others were not as patient. Some followers of Descartes, notably Nicholas Malebranche, turned to the occasionalist argument that *God* moves bodies at the instigation of souls. Descartes and More themselves, as we have seen, envisioned a kind of hydraulic system in which the soul uses animal spirits to move the gross body, a solution that displaces the dilemma without resolving it.[39]

Like Conway, Milton avoids this dilemma of his anti-Hobbesian allies by his explicit rejection of dualism. His monism allows him to posit the interpenetration of mental and physical activity in terms similar to More's, but without the inconsistency. Milton can attribute spiritual and physical properties to the "intellectual spirits" in men without contradiction, for he does not separate incorporeal and corporeal substance.

Milton's ontology had a further advantage over that of the

[38]Glanvill, *The Vanity of Dogmatizing* (London, 1661), pp. 19–20.
[39]See More, *Immortality of the Soul* II.xiv.8, II.xv.3, II.xvii.3 (pp. 120, 123, and 134).

Cambridge Platonists in the seventeenth-century battle of ontologies. The Platonists' own perception that Hobbesian materialism was an extension of Cartesian dualism testifies to the rise in the ontological status of matter in the seventeenth century. With the rapid advance of the new science, materiality (which allowed for observation, quantification, and measurement) increasingly became a leading test of reality or existence. Proponents of active incorporeal substance, by definition imperceptible, scrambled to provide empirical evidence of the activity of that substance; More's *Antidote against Atheism* and Glanvill's *Saducismus Triumphatus* are in this genre. The tenuousness of the belief in spirit or incorporeal substance, not long before considered "more real" than material, is evidenced by its voluminous and vociferous defense by the Cambridge Platonists, a defense that would have been superfluous in earlier centuries. Milton can afford to be more skeptical of spirit phenomena than are the Cambridge thinkers; his monist ontology does not require him to provide evidence of the mysterious workings of incorporeal substance. In this he is more in tune with his time than the group of religious philosophers with whom his name is often linked. Faced with a growing consensus on the priority of material existence, Milton responds not with a defense of incorporeal substance, but with an insistence that body and spirit are not different in kind. If materiality was to become the sine qua non for the reality of all creation, Milton's conception of soul, mind, and angel would remain intact. Milton's ontology is a hybrid amalgam of Hobbesian materialism, Galenic-Aristotelian pneumatism, and Aristotelian hylomorphism, containing elements of all while denying aspects of each.[40] He agrees with Hobbes that all creation is material, but he adds that it is simultaneously spiritual. And he agrees with the Aristotelians (and Cambridge Platonists, for that matter) that spirit is active and body passive, but again he insists that spirit is corporeal and differs from body in degree only.

---

[40]In a shrewd aside, George Williamson remarked in 1935 that in his philosophy of form "Milton interprets Aristotle by approaching Hobbes." See "Milton and the Mortalist Heresy," reprinted in *Seventeenth Century Contexts* (London: Faber and Faber, 1960), p. 159.

Philosophies are inevitably shaped to their authors' deepest assumptions. In his animist materialism, Milton finds a philosophy congenial to his temperament: he does not share in his mature works the distrust of the body and of physical pleasures rightly used that is pervasive even in More (to whose sensuous heaven Nicolson rightly compares Milton's) and that is so prominent in the Christian tradition. In enjoying the world, Milton enjoys not a dangerous and tainted substance, but a substance for which God is the material as well as the efficient cause.

Milton's monism helps to explain the vexed issue of Milton's ambivalence about the new science. Critics point to Milton's Baconian enthusiasm in the "Third Prolusion" and to the eager commendation of scientific endeavor in the "Seventh Prolusion" and contrast these with the tentativeness of the astronomy in *Paradise Lost* and the outburst against vain knowledge in *Paradise Regained*. Babb demonstrates that the scientific program outlined in *Of Education* is out of date.[41] He suggests that Milton's temperament is "bookish and authoritarian" and that he holds himself back from the new science out of a deep-seated conservatism. D. C. Allen goes even farther, implying that Milton is guilty of obscurantism for endorsing a literal belief in the narrative of the Bible at the expense of more scientifically correct alternatives.[42] Both of these views present Milton as opposing the new science only because it is not congruent with the wisdom of the past. I suggest, on the other hand, that Milton's lack of enthusiasm for the new science from the 1640s on has rational and not merely nostalgic grounds. It should not be surprising that Milton did not wholeheartedly support a project that eagerly co-opted the metaphysics of Descartes. Right or wrong, Milton fundamentally opposed the separate existence of an aspiritual material universe, which was the laboratory of the new philosophy.

Such are the main differences between Milton and all of the

[41]Lawrence Babb, *The Moral Cosmos of "Paradise Lost"* (East Lansing: Michigan State University Press, 1970), pp. 20–25.
[42]Don Cameron Allen, *The Legend of Noah: Renaissance Rationalism in Art, Science, and Letters*, Illinois Studies in Language and Literature, vol. 33, nos. 3–4 (Urbana: University of Illinois Press, 1949), p. 39.

combatants in the battle of ontologies that unfolded during his maturity. That his monism is the product of the years when Descartes, Hobbes, and the Platonists held center stage in English intellectual life suggests that it is in part a response to that battle. The consistency of the metaphysics of *Paradise Lost*, unique in seventeenth-century poetry (as the next chapter will show), will itself be evidence of the importance that Milton must have placed on the metaphysical issues under debate. And in that metaphysics Milton will have a poet's revenge, dressing the philosophies of Descartes and Hobbes in diabolic clothing.

~ 5

Milton's True Poem and the
Substance of Epic Angels

Legions of angels inhabit the pages of English epic and philosophical poetry in the seventeenth century, their way prepared
by the religious subject matter of many of the poems and by the
epic convention of supernatural machinery. Beliefs about angels involve answers to metaphysical questions: Can a separable, incorporeal substance exist? Are all substances material?
Thus the poetic use of angels inevitably reveals something
about an author's conception of the relation between spirit and
matter, even if it is only his or her inconsistency or carelessness
with the metaphysical frame of the narrative. Samuel Johnson
accused the author of *Paradise Lost* of just such limitations:

> Another inconvenience of Milton's design is that it requires the
> description of what cannot be described, the agency of spirits. He
> saw that immateriality supplied no images, and that he could not
> show angels acting but by instruments of action; he therefore
> invested them with form and matter. This, being necessary, was
> therefore defensible, and he should have secured the consistency
> of his system by keeping immateriality out of sight, and enticing
> his reader to drop it from his thoughts. But he has unhappily
> perplexed his poetry with his philosophy. His infernal and celes-

tial powers are sometimes pure spirit and sometimes animated body.[1]

The result, he continues, is a "confusion of spirit and matter" that mars the epic. But Milton's angels are never pure spirits in either the scholastic or the Cartesian sense. Ironically, a reading of contemporary long poems reveals that Milton is unusual in the rigor with which he reconciles philosophy and the poetry of angels. More important than Johnson's misreading of Milton's angels is its source, an assumption that Johnson shared with his age: if angels exist at all they are purely immaterial. The assumption and its consequence are embedded in Johnson's confident assertion that Milton "saw that immateriality supplied no images." One assumption leads to another, that Milton "invested" immaterial angels "with form and matter." But Johnson's certainties were anything but certainties in the turbulent philosophical climate of the 1640s through the 1660s.[2] Milton was far from alone, however, in challenging the scholastic dualism of his predecessors and the related Cartesian dualism. The outcome of the debate in which Milton played his part determined the next world-view, the next set of assumptions about the nature of reality. For a brief and exciting period, reality was up for grabs, and the monism of Milton and others was not a quaint and curious fringe opinion, but a contender for the minds of future Englishmen.

The Philosophers and the Angels

Henry More summarizes contemporary thought on the nature of angels: "Concerning angels, some affirm them to be *fiery* or *airy* Bodies; some pure spirits; some Spirits in airy or

[1]Samuel Johnson, "Life of Milton," in *Johnson's Lives of the English Poets: A Selection*, ed. J. P. Hardy (Oxford: Clarendon Press, 1971), p. 107.
[2]Johnson wrote a half-century before the rescue of Milton's *Christian Doctrine* from oblivion. The indisputably monist statements of this treatise might well have perplexed Johnson, but they might also have alllowed him to see that Milton's poetry and philosophy are consistent and are mixed without confusion in *Paradise Lost*.

fiery bodies."[3] The choices Milton's contemporaries made among these alternatives owed as much to assumptions about the nature of substances as to the reading of Scripture. The ontologies of Descartes, Hobbes, and the Cambridge Platonists held contrasting implications for angelology.

Unlike the other thinkers, Descartes was reticent on the subject of angels. He declined requests from Sir Kenelm Digby and Thomas White to address the topic.[4] Shortly before his death Descartes did respond to a query from More concerning whether or not angels are corporeal and have sensations: "I reply that the human mind separated from the body does not have sensation strictly so called; but it is not clear by natural reason whether Angels are created like minds distinct from bodies, or like minds united to bodies. I never decide about questions on which I have no certain reasons and I never allow conjectures into my system."[5] As far as Descartes was concerned, his conception of *res cogitans* was compatible with belief in either corporeal or incorporeal angels.

Hobbes thought that if angels exist at all they must be subtle bodies. As usual in his writings, there is a bow to orthodoxy: while casting doubt on conventional beliefs about spirits, Hobbes carefully sets himself apart from the Sadducees, a Jewish sect which denied the existence of spirit and angels altogether.[6] Of course Hobbes cannot share the scholastic belief in purely incorporeal angels. Incorporeal substance, Hobbes is adamant, is "*Nothing*; and consequently *no where*." As philosophy is vexed by meaningless Aristotelian terms, so angel lore is vexed by the errors of Gentile epic tradition: "The Gentiles did vulgarly conceive the Imagery of the brain, for things really

---

[3]Henry More, *An Explanation of the Grand Mystery of Godliness* (London, 1660), I, iii, 6.

[4]Sterling P. Lamprecht, "The Role of Descartes in Seventeenth-Century England," in *Studies in the History of Ideas*, vol. 3, ed. Columbia University Department of Philosophy (New York: Columbia University Press, 1935), pp. 189, 195.

[5]Letter of August 1649, in *Descartes: Philosophical Letters*, ed. and trans. Anthony Kenny (Oxford: Clarendon Press, 1970), p. 256.

[6]*Leviathan*, ed. C. B. Macpherson (Harmondsworth: Penguin, 1968), p. 145 (chap. 8). For the Sadducees, see Acts 23:8.

subsistent without them, and not dependent on the fancy; and out of them framed their opinions of *Daemons*, Good and Evill; which because they seemed to subsist really, they called *Substances*; and because they could not feel them with their hands, *Incorporeall*."[7] Most often, according to Hobbes, an Old Testament angel is "some image raised (supernaturally) in the fancy, to signifie the presence of God in the execution of some supernaturall work."[8] These angels are not self-existent or permanent, but temporary manipulations of men's imaginations by God.

In the New Testament the evidence for self-existent spirits is unequivocal, and here Hobbes changes tack. He argues that these angels are not incorporeal, but only seem so because their matter is so diffuse: it is incorporeal as far as our senses go, but not metaphysically. Clearly, Hobbes would prefer these angels to be temporary, disposable tools of God, but he grudgingly admits evidence from the New Testament for permanent, subsistent angels. His final position reveals his dutiful belief in official orthodoxy (prescribed in *Leviathan*) combined with his innate skepticism:

> Considering therefore the signification of the word Angel in the Old Testament, and the nature of Dreams and Visions that happen to men by the ordinary way of Nature; I was enclined to this opinion, that Angels were nothing but supernaturall apparitions of the Fancy, raised by the speciall and extraordinary operation of God. . . . But the many places of the New Testament, and our Saviours own words, and in such texts, wherein is no suspicion of corruption of the Scripture, *have extorted from my feeble Reason, an acknowledgment, and beleef,* that there be also Angels substantiall, and permanent. But to beleeve they be in no place, that is to say, no where, that is to say, nothing, as they (though indirectly) say, that will have them Incorporeall, cannot by Scripture bee evinced.[9]

---

[7]*Leviathan*, p. 435 (chap. 34).
[8]*Leviathan*, p. 436 (chap. 34).
[9]*Leviathan*, pp. 439–40 (chap. 34); my emphasis.

Angels embarrass Hobbes—he will make a place for them as corporeal beings, but he is disturbed by their scholastic and occult associations.

As might be expected from their theory of soul vehicles, the Cambridge Platonists held that angels were dualist creatures, souls in corporeal vehicles, and explicitly rejected the purely immaterial angels of Aquinas. More anticipates the charge that he had "offended against the authority of the *Schools*": his opponents should "remember that the *Schools* trespass against a more ancient authority then themselves, that is to say, the *Pythagoreans*, *Platonists*, *Jewish Doctours*, and the *Fathers* of the Church, who all hold *That even the purest Angels have corporeal Vehicles*."[10] Angels have bodies, however tenuous. The dualist, corporeal angels of the Cambridge Platonists were to enjoy a vogue and were to influence the literary presentation of angels in the mid-seventeenth century, but in the final analysis they are quite different from Milton's, which resemble those to which Hobbes granted lukewarm belief.

Milton's Material Angels

As with Hobbes and Henry More, Milton's conception of angels derives from his ontological assumptions. The central proof text for the materiality of angels in *Paradise Lost*, and one that makes explicit the monist basis of that materiality, is Raphael's speech on the "one first matter." Raphael ends his analogy between plant metabolism and the sublimation of body into spirit by holding out the possibility, made plausible by the ontological continuity that he has just illustrated, that man can turn into angel:

> time may come when men
> With Angels may participate, and find

[10]Henry More, *The Immortality of the Soul* (1659), rpt. in *A Collection of Several Philosophical Writings*, 2 vols. (1662; facs. rpt. New York: Garland, 1978), 1:6 (Preface).

> No inconvenient Diet, nor too light Fare:
> And from these corporal nutriments perhaps
> Your bodies may at last turn all to spirit,
> Improv'd by tract of time, and wing'd ascend
> Ethereal, as wee, or may at choice
> Here or in Heav'nly Paradises dwell.
>
> (5.493–500)

While this passage indicates the potential spiritualization of man, it also implies the corporeality of angels. Like his contemporaries, Milton viewed angels and human souls as similar in substance; the tenuously corporeal angels of *Paradise Lost* resemble the tenuously corporeal souls of *Christian Doctrine*. Milton's angels are not Aquinas's disembodied spirits; their substance, like their mode of reason, differs from man's "but in degree, of kind the same."

Milton does use the terms "incorporeal" and "pure spirit" to refer to angels. Raphael will speak of the warring angels by "lik'ning spiritual to corporal forms" (5.573); he describes angels as both "purest Spirits" and "those pure / Intelligential substances" (5.406,407–8); the narrator calls the devils "incorporeal Spirits" (1.789). But especially in the seventeenth century the meaning of the terms "incorporeal" and "spiritual" must be gathered from context. Milton's "incorporeal" is not Aquinas's or Descartes's. The devils must contract to enter Pandemonium: "Thus incorporeal Spirits to smallest forms / Reduc'd thir shapes immense" (1.789–90). The necessity for the actual physical contraction of these "incorporeal Spirits" is a far cry from the proverbial scholastic wrangle about the dancing room for angels on the head of a pin. Nor is the corporeality of angels overthrown by Gabriel's comment to Uriel, "hard thou knows't it to exclude / Spiritual substance with corporeal bar" (4.584–85). The point here is that Gabriel says "hard" and not "impossible." Satan must wait for the opening of the gates to leave Hell, and he must find material access to Paradise, either by leaping over a wall or by wriggling up through the plumbing. Significantly, almost all of Johnson's evidence for Milton's confusing corporeal and incorporeal in his angels points to their corporeality: Satan supports his weight with a lance, he is blown up by vapors in chaos, he is afraid of material weapons, the devils and angels are hampered by crushed armor, etc.[11] That the few counterexamples suggest incorporeality is debatable; Johnson mentions Satan's animation of the toad and the ability of the devils to be "at large, though without number" in the enclosed Hall of Pandemonium. As for the first example, no one in Milton's time who held the materiality of soul would deny it the ability to penetrate visible and gross bodies. As for the second, it is clear that the phrase "without number" is figurative; neither Milton nor anyone else claims that the number of angels is infinite. And the passage Johnson quotes follows the one in which the narrator specifies that the "incorporeal" devils must reduce in size to enter the hall.

If "incorporeal" and "spiritual" can be read as relative terms in Milton, what about the description of angels as "intelligences," another scholastic term? Belial fears the loss of "this intellectual being" (2.147) and Adam addresses Raphael as a "pure / Intelligence of Heav'n" (8.180–81). But Raphael shows that to be an "Intelligence" is not to be purely incorporeal; in contrasting angels and men he sets "intelligential" not against corporeal, but against "rational": "food alike those pure / Intelligential substances require / As doth your Rational" (5.407–9).

Milton consistently minimizes the ontological distance between angels and men. Thus follows his unorthodox assertion that angels really eat and digest. Milton directly confronts the conventional interpretations of angelic eating:

> So down they sat,
> And to thir viands fell, nor seemingly
> The Angel, nor in mist, the common gloss
> Of Theologians, but with keen dispatch
> Of real hunger, and concoctive heat
> To transubstantiate; what redounds, transpires
> Through Spirits with ease.
>
> (5.433–39)

---

[11]Johnson, "Life of Milton," pp. 107–8.

Milton asserts here the basic unity of substance, whether "spiritual" or bodily, against the discontinuity of spirit and matter in the schools and even in the Neoplatonizing dualism of More.[12] For Milton, "transubstantiate" can mean only such a refinement of substance as is outlined in Raphael's plant metaphor. In the *Christian Doctrine*, Milton heaps scorn on the Catholic notion of Eucharistic transubstantiation, with its claim that a substance can be transformed ritually into a substance of another kind: "Consubstantiation and particularly transubstantiation and papal *anthropophagy* or cannibalism are utterly alien to reason, common sense and human behavior. What is more, they are irreconcilable . . . with the normal use of words" (*CP* 6:554).

Milton's assertion through Raphael of angel sexuality also highlights his belief in their materiality:

> Whatever pure thou in the body enjoy'st
> (And pure thou wert created) we enjoy
> In eminence, and obstacle find none
> Of membrane, joint, or limb, exclusive bars:
> Easier than Air with Air, if Spirits embrace,
> Total they mix, Union of Pure with Pure
> Desiring; nor restrain'd conveyance need
> As Flesh to mix with Flesh, or Soul with Soul.
>   (8.622–29)

As the final line indicates, the intercourse of Milton's angels is neither the conjunction of gross animal bodies nor a disembodied meeting of minds or souls.[13]

As Milton presents them, angels modify their appearance by

---

[12]It is true that angels "transpire" while men excrete waste (despite his validation of material life, Milton apparently was never reconciled to excretion, as the poem's diabolical imagery suggests). Nevertheless, the distinction is between varieties of physiology, not between corporeality and incorporeality.

[13]Milton's direct affirmation of angel digestion and sexuality differs from More's dualist and inconsistent speculations on these same matters, as Robert H. West has shown; see *Milton and the Angels* (Athens: University of Georgia Press, 1955), pp. 162–74. Later in life, moreover, More backed away from his early speculations on angel sex, which even at their most extreme stopped well short of Milton's.

shaping their subtle material bodies, rather than by manipulating assumed bodies as do scholastic angels. His narrator explains how the fallen angels appear to be both male and female:

> For Spirits when they please
> Can either Sex assume, or both; so soft
> And uncompounded is thir Essence pure,
> Nor ti'd nor manacl'd with joint or limb,
> Nor founded on the brittle strength of bones,
> Like cumbrous flesh; but in what shape they choose
> Dilated or condens't, bright or obscure,
> Can execute thir aery purposes.
>
> (1.423–30)[14]

The substance of Milton's angels is not compounded or complex as are the bodies of men and animals, but it is by the same token not immaterial. Milton differs from Platonists such as More who write of the materiality of angels; Milton insists that the angel's body is not a separable vehicle for an intelligence, but an aspect of the intellectual being. While Milton at one point suggests the infinite fluidity of angel bodies,

> All Heart they live, all Head, all Eye, all Ear,
> All Intellect, all Sense, and as they please,
> They limb themselves, and color, shape or size
> Assume, as likes them best, condense or rare,
>
> (6.350–53)

at other times he imagines a physical embodiment for angels remarkably like our own. He describes the flight of Raphael from heaven down through the spheres,

> till within soar
> Of Tow'ring Eagles, to all the Fowls he seems

[14]Milton borrows from Michael Psellus in his portrayal of material angels in this passage. Psellus, a Byzantine theologian, argued that angels have tenuous material bodies. See Robert West, "Milton and Michael Psellus," *Philological Quarterly* 28 (1949): 477–89.

> A *Phœnix*, gaz'd by all, . . .
>
> .   .   .
>
> At once on th'Eastern cliff of Paradise
> He lights, and to his proper shape returns
> A Seraph wing'd.
>
> (5.270–77)

The narrator describes Raphael's "six wings," "shoulder broad," "waist," "loin . . . thigh . . . heel" (the picture derives from Isaiah 6:2). Milton here suggests that angels do indeed have proper shapes to which they return after any metamorphosis into "what shape they choose," and that that shape resembles our material bodies, with wings added.[15] The Platonists, on the other hand, tend to make the bodies of angels increasingly abstract even while asserting their materiality. More's angels, for example, have spherical bodies.[16]

If the materiality of Milton's angels is not unique in seventeenth-century poetry, the rigor with which Milton fits his narrative to his metaphysical stance might be, as a brief survey of contemporary long poems will show. When reading the minor religious epics of the century one becomes accustomed to a wide array of beliefs about angels and to the poets' carelessness in fitting narrative to those beliefs, a carelessness that makes the integrity of *Paradise Lost* stand out by contrast. The works I have examined vary greatly in quality, but we should resist the temptation to assume that Milton must have held these largely forgotten poems in contempt. The young Milton prized Joshua Sylvester's du Bartas (1605), in which lines as grotesque and unintentionally comic as these occur:

---

[15]One definition of the word "shape" is "body" (*OED* 6b), a meaning often employed unambiguously in the poem to describe a variety of creatures, including Satan at 3.634, Adam and Eve at 4.288, the snake at 10.495, and Michael at 11.239.

[16]See More, *Immortality of the Soul*, p. 166 (III, v, 6). It should be noted that More confesses on the next page that he does not know how there can be conversation between "two such heaps of living Aire." He suggests that for communication angels might appear to each other in "a more operose and articulate form."

Almighty Father, as of watery matter
It pleas'd thee make the people of the Water;
So, of an earthly substance mad'st thou all
The slimie Burgers of this Earthly Ball.[17]

Literary Angels

Despite the Renaissance and Reformation revolt against scholasticism, the purely immaterial angels of scholastic orthodoxy survive in English literature through at least the early seventeenth century. Scholastic immaterial angels were retained even by Protestant theologians who otherwise rejected Aquinas and all his ways.[18] The popularity of John Salkeld's scholastic *A Treatise of Angels* (1613) illustrates the momentum of this aspect of the stalled scholastic movement. But in England, as the seventeenth century progressed, the literary presentation of angels began to reflect emerging, antischolastic ontologies. The angels encountered in poems by the youthful Milton were likely to be purely immaterial; those created by his contemporaries were likely to be tenuously incarnate, designed to fit a new view of the nature of reality. The fashion was to be short-lived. Aquinas's immaterial angels, displaced for a historical moment, won a pyrrhic victory after the seventeenth century, as an age that placed little credence in angels imagined these objects of disbelief to be immaterial.

Milton's education in literary angelology derived in part from Catholic poets such as Tasso and Marco Giralamo Vida, who could employ immaterial angels unself-consciously. The angels of Vida's Latin *Christiad* (1535), a remarkable synthesis of aggressive classicism and Gospel narrative, are pure spirits

---

[17]Joshua Sylvester, *Divine Weekes* I.vi.512–15, in *The Complete Works of Joshua Sylvester*, ed. Alexander Grosart, 2 vols. (New York: AMS, 1967), I:76; further references to this poem will be indicated in the text by book, section, and line number. There are several echoes of this poem, a translation of du Bartas's *Semaines*, in *Paradise Lost*; see George Coffin Taylor, *Milton's Use of Du Bartas* (Cambridge: Harvard University Press, 1934).

[18]West, *Milton and the Angels*, pp. 43–60 and passim.

who must put on bodies of foreign matter in order to be seen, rather than "dilating" or "condensing" their own matter: "Each spirit fits wings to the body he has made for himself, assuming airy limbs and a fitting image, so that he can make possible his appearance to humans."[19]

Adherence to scholastic orthodoxy is natural in Catholic poets; what is a bit surprising is the tenacity with which this type of angel hangs on in Protestant England. Representative of the survival of scholastic angels in long poetry of the early seventeenth century is Thomas Heywood's profoundly conservative *Hierarchie of the Blessed Angells* (1635). This massive verse and prose treatise focuses relentlessly on the nature and operation of angels, conceived of as scholastic and incorporeal. Though an ardent Protestant, Heywood retains more scholastic trappings than even the Jesuit-trained Salkeld. The nine books of his treatise, for example, are named for the nine orders of pseudo-Dionysius. Heywood, following Aquinas's bias, denies that the devils became corporeally gross at their fall, an important article in the beliefs of both Platonist dualists such as More and the monists Milton and Conway.[20] Like Aquinas again, Heywood denies that angels can truly eat (p. 230).[21]

Whatever its shortcomings as a work of art, Heywood's book is a storehouse of patristic, medieval, and Renaissance angel lore. Heywood, like Robert Burton, repeats a range of opinions on the nature of angels and devils, but unlike Democritus Junior he firmly takes a stand on the question. Identifying himself with the Thomist position, Heywood offers various refutations of the arguments of the corporealists.

It was not only Anglican poets like Heywood who retained scholastic angels; the Huguenot du Bartas, for one, includes

---

[19]Vida, *Christiad* 5.540, 542–46, in *The Christiad: A Latin-English Edition*, ed. and trans. Gertrude C. Drake and Clarence A. Forbes (Carbondale: Southern Illinois University Press, 1978), pp. 216–19 (I have modified the translation). The young Milton in his unfinished "Passion" praised the *Christiad*: "Loud O'er the rest Cremona's trump doth sound." See also Tasso's *Jerusalem Delivered* I.xiii.
[20]Thomas Heywood, *The Hierarchie of the Blessed Angells* (1635; facs. rpt. New York: The English Experience, 1973), p. 214; further citations of this work will be indicated in the text by page number.
[21]See the *Summa theologiae* I, Q.51, art. 3.

them in his *Semaines*. Du Bartas's formula of wholly incorporeal angels who assume temporary bodies to appear to us agrees in every detail with Aquinas's, as can be seen from this comparison:

> It is, further, impossible for an intellectual substance to have any kind of matter. For the operation belonging to anything is according to the mode of its substance. Now to understand is an altogether immaterial operation. . . . Hence it must be that every intellectual substance is altogether immaterial. (*Summa theologiae* I, Q.50, art. 2)[22]

> Angels need an assumed body, not for themselves, but on our account. . . . The assumed body is united to the angel not as its form, nor merely as its mover, but as the mover represented by the assumed movable body. (*ST* I, Q.51, art.2)

Du Bartas follows Aquinas point by point, as we see in Sylvester's translation:

> For, Angels, being meer Intelligences
> Have (properly) no Bodies, nor no Senses:
> But (sacred Legats of the *Holy-One*)
> To treat with us, they put our Nature-on;
> And take a body fit to exercise
> The Charge they have, . . .
> 　　　　　　　　. . . and, that past,
> Turns t'Elements, whence first it was ammast.
> A simple Spirit (the glittering Childe of Light)
> Unto a bodie doth not so unite,
> As to the Matter Form incorporates:
> But, for a season it accomodates,
> As to his Tool the quaint Artificer,
> (That at his pleasure makes the same to stir)
> Yet in such sort that th'instrument (we see)
> Holds much of him that moves it actively.
> 　　　　　　　　　(II.iii.1.1090–1105)

[22]This and other passages from the *Summa* are quoted from the *Basic Writings of Saint Thomas Aquinas*, ed. Anton C. Pegis, 2 vols. (New York: Random House, 1945).

The relationship between these passages does not depend on du Bartas having read Aquinas, whose writings had become the stuff of commonplaces. Nevertheless, whether by coincidence or not, the last few lines of du Bartas explicate by analogy the thorny passage about the "mover represented by the assumed movable body."

On the composition of man, though, du Bartas does deviate from Aquinas. Du Bartas subscribes to a pneumatic conception of the bond between soul and body:

> For spirits, by faith religiously refin'd,
> 'Twixt God and man retain a middle kinde:
> And (Umpires) mortall to th'immortall joine;
> And th'infinite in narrow clay confine.
>
> (II.i.1.390–93)

To Aquinas this is a denigration of the power of the incorporeal soul:

> It is clear how false are the opinions of those who maintained the existence of some mediate bodies between the soul and body of man. Of these, certain Platonists said that the intellectual soul has an incorruptible body naturally united to it, from which it is never separated, and by means of which it is united to the corruptible body of man. Others said that the soul is united to the body by means of a corporeal spirit. . . . Now all this is fictitious and ridiculous, . . . because the soul is immediately united to the body as the form to matter. (*ST* I, Q.76, art.7)

Although Aquinas and du Bartas comment on souls rather than angels here, the Neoplatonist "middle term" between incorporeal and corporeal was to play an increasingly large role in theological and poetic angelology as the seventeenth century progressed.

The combination of scholastic and Neoplatonist thought in du Bartas recurs in the narrative poems of the brothers Giles and Phineas Fletcher, who were active shortly after the publication of the complete version of Sylvester's du Bartas in 1608. The angels in Giles's *Christs Victorie and Triumph* (1610), and in

Phineas's *Locusts* (1627) and *Purple Island* (1633), are scholastic immaterial spirits who assume bodies. But in the *Purple Island*, as in du Bartas, the spirits play an intermediate role between soul and matter. Phineas Fletcher describes caverns in the brain: "Here first are born the spirits animall, / Whose matter, almost immateriall, / Resembles heavens matter quintessentiall."[23]

In the dozen long poems in my survey, the poems written up to 1635 almost all feature scholastic, incorporeal angels. In this group fall those by du Bartas, the Fletchers, and Heywood, and the "vast and unreadable" *Doomes-Day* (1614) of Sir William Alexander, the earl of Stirling.[24] Heywood's scholastic verse treatise of 1635 marks the end of an era. Afterward the dualist, partly corporeal angels of Platonist and Neoplatonist speculation ushered immaterial angels off the literary stage for a time.[25] It is perhaps natural that in an age intensely speculative about the nature of spirit and matter poets would be more careful to reject an angelology that violated emerging scientific orthodoxy as well as established Protestant orthodoxy.

Two long poems with unequivocally material angels, and a third treating the soul in a way that implies the materiality of angels, appeared between 1640 and the composition of *Para-*

[23]Phineas Fletcher, *Purple Island* V.xiv, in *Giles and Phineas Fletcher: Poetical Works*, ed. Frederick M. Boas, 2 vols. (Cambridge: Cambridge University Press, 1909), 2:56; references to poems by the Fletchers will be taken from this edition and indicated by book and canto number in the text.
[24]The judgment is offered by Douglas Bush (*English Literature of the Earlier Seventeenth Century* [Oxford: Clarendon, 1945], p. 278). Bush adds that if *Doomes-Day* "did not . . . add a new sting to death, at least [it] shortens the life of the literary historian" (p. 356).
[25]A notable exception to this chronology is Thomas Peyton's *Glasse of Time* (1620). Peyton, a fierce Anglican and anti-Puritan whose poem is punctuated by furiously paranoid outbursts, presents tenuously material angels "compacted of pestiferous fire" (I.lxvii) (*The Glasse of Time, in the First and Second Ages* [New York: John B. Alden, 1886]). Peyton's poem foreshadows the conception of the world as clockwork that was to dominate poetic cosmology in the eighteenth century—God constructs the universe "Like to the wheels within a clock or chime" (I.xix). Other poems are impossible to classify in terms of angel ontology. Joseph Beaumont's *Psyche* seems to lean toward both absolute incorporeality and subtle materiality. See *Psyche: Loves Mysterie in XX Canto's* (London, 1648).

dise Lost. The angels in the poems are dichotomous constructions of immaterial spirit and subtly material body. The three authors represent a full spectrum of interests and denominational background. Henry More was an Anglican divine with a Calvinist upbringing, Edward Benlowes was raised a Catholic and became a zealous Anglican, and Samuel Pordage was a Behmenist.

More packs the Spenserian stanzas of the *Platonick Song of the Soul* (1647) with intricate Neoplatonic speculation. Although the poems comprising the *Platonick Song* were written well before the prose exposition of More's spirit ontology, in most respects they anticipate that ontology. Souls in More's poem— and More saw no essential difference between the glorified souls and angels—are immaterial creatures always tied to material vehicles. This matter may be highly sublimated and "ethereal"; More refers to "ethereall corporeity / Devoid of all heterogeneall organity" (*Psychathanasia* I.ii.24).[26]

Despite his belief in the materiality of souls and angels, More explicitly rejects the Miltonic conception of the ontological unity of the stuff of minds and bodies. In doing so he indulges in a rare flight of satiric whimsy. If spiritual substance is not different in kind from material substance,

> then bodies may
> So changed be by nature and stiff fight
> Of hungry stomacks, that what erst was clay
> Then herbs, in time itself in sence may well display.
> For then our souls can nothing be but bloud
> Or nerves or brains, or body modifide.
> Whence it will follow that cold stopping crud,
> Hard moldy cheese, dry nuts, when they have rid
> Due circuits through the heart, at last shall speed
> Of life and sense, look thorough our thin eyes

[26]*The Complete Poems of Dr. Henry More*, ed. Alexander B. Grosart (1878; facs. rpt. New York: AMS Press, 1967), p. 48; all references to this edition, which follows the revised edition of 1647, appear in the text under the names of the individual poems: *Psychozoia, Psychathanasia, Democritus Platonissans, Antipsychopannychia, The Præexistency of the Soul, Antimonopsychia,* and *The Oracle.*

And view the Close wherein the Cow did feed
Whence they were milk'd; grosse Pie-crust will grow wise,
And pickled Cucumbers sans doubt Philosophize.

(Præxistency of the Soul 89–90)

Milton, on the other hand, agrees with the health-food industry: you are what you eat. The difference between More's argument on digestion and Raphael's (5.404–33, 469–505) measures the distance between *Paradise Lost's* monist angels and More's dualist, material ones.

In Edward Benlowes's *Theophila, or Loves Sacrifice* (1652), a heroic poem of the soul's ascent to God, the angels appear initially to be scholastic immaterial ones: "Invisible, impassive, happy fair, / High, incorporeal, active, rare, / Pure, scientifick and illustrious SPIRITS You are."[27] But in a preface that is a model of subtle equivocation, Benlowes aligns himself with those who use incorporeal and immaterial in a relative sense:

> *Super-coelestials* are Intelligencies [*sic*], altogether Spiritual and Immortal, excellent in their Beings, intuitive in their Conceptions; such are the . . . *Apostles*, the . . . *Prophets*, the . . . *Martyrs*, . . . *Virgins*, . . . *Confessors*, &c. or the blessed Hierarchie of *Angels*, participating somewhat of GOD and Man; . . . void of all Mixture, as is GOD, and yet consisting of Matter and Form, as doth Man; Subsisting in some Subject and Substance as doth Man, yet being incorporeal, as is GOD. (Preface)

But Benlowes ultimately rejects the scholastic definition of angel essence, reserving absolute, as opposed to relative, immateriality for God alone.

If Benlowes's spirit ontology is marked by equivocal subtlety, it is simplicity itself next to Samuel Pordage's. A disciple of Jacob Boehme, Pordage published his 13,000-line *Mundorum Explicatio* in 1661. He asserts that angels or spirits are not vis-

---

[27]Edward Benlowes, *Theophila, or Loves Sacrifice* (London, 1652), 6.73; further references to this poem will be indicated by canto and stanza in the text.

ible to our "outer eyes" because, like God, they have no "Matter, Form, or corporeity." But they are not scholastic angels:

> *Mistake* me not, that *Spirits* bodies have
> I'le not deny: but these I do believe
> *Spiritual*, and incorporeal are,
> And of their Natures very much do share:
> These also to our outward sences be
> Not subject.[28]

Pordage "explains" in a note that these spiritual bodies make spirits visible to our "internal eyes." The bodies allow angels and glorified souls to feel the blessings of heaven and devils and the damned to feel "the wrath and fiery property of the dark hell: For, without bodies there could be not sensibility." The plot thickens when Pordage informs us that these inner bodies of immaterial spirits are composed of the three Paracelsan elements: "Their bodies likewise are of a spiritual substance made out of Sulphur, Mercury, and Sal [salt]; in the inward ground of Eternal Nature the bodies both of Angels and Devils being of the same Matter, but that those are Harmoniz'd by the property of the Light or second Principle; these Harmoniz'd by that of the dark or first Principle" (p. 40). Through this body, Pordage suggests (p. 314), one can see heaven, which is invisible to mortal eyes. Pordage's angels, despite having pure bodies of sulphur, mercury, and salt, gather other bodies from the material world in order to be seen, rather than manipulating the bodies they naturally have (p. 42). Furthermore, the devils, unlike Milton's, do not suffer material pains, as even Aquinas thought they could. Instead, the Paracelsan bodies of the devils allow them to feel "harsh desire . . . rage . . . enmity." While both Milton and Pordage employ nonscholastic angels in their epics, their practices are in fact opposed. Milton removes the gulf between spirit and matter, while Pordage's insertion of spiritual bodies, if anything, widens the gulf by adding a third category of substance.

[28]Samuel Pordage, *Mundorum Explicatio* (London, 1663), p. 40; further references to this poem will be indicated in the text by page number.

Ontological Confusion among
Milton's Contemporaries

More often than not, the poets under discussion violate their own philosophical principles in the course of their narratives, precisely the error with which Johnson charges Milton. Against this background, the integrity of Milton's art and philosophy stands out. There are three main types of ontological inconsistency in these poems: the deformation of ontology under the pressure of allegory; vagueness in the ontological framework itself; and clear violation of a stated ontology for narrative expedience.

Phineas Fletcher's *Purple Island*, in which purely incorporeal angels fight physical battles, exemplifies the first and least important sort of inconsistency. As in other unremittingly allegorical narratives, the characters in *Purple Island* are not meant to be taken as substantial creatures. Nevertheless, as the next chapter will demonstrate, Milton devises even for allegory a role that underscores the ontological integrity of his epic.

Indecision, the second source of inconsistency, is exemplified by du Bartas, who waffles on the substance of the devil and his assumed body. Having declared for purely immaterial spirits, du Bartas seems to have second thoughts when discussing the devil's temptation of Eve. To speak with her, the devil must assume a body,

> For had he been of an ethereall matter,
> Of fiery substance, or aëreall nature;
> The needful help of language had he wanted,
>
> . . .
>
> Sith such pure bodies have nor teeth, nor tongues,
> Lips, art'ries, nose, palate, nor panting lungs.
>
> (II.i.2.86–91)

Du Bartas has changed angelological camps. He describes here the familiar fiery bodies of "ethereal matter" of the Platonist dualists in the tradition of Michael Psellus. Was he even aware that they do not fit with the scholastic model he asserts else-

where? What makes this departure so surprising is its gra-
tuitousness: du Bartas could have made the same point about
the purely immaterial Thomist angels he otherwise employs.[29]

The third type of ontological confusion is the most important, for here the poets contradict themselves and are caught in
a "confusion of spirit and matter" in which philosophy and
poetry do indeed perplex each other. The confusion in every
case takes the form censured by Johnson, the narrative treatment of relatively or purely incorporeal beings as corporeal
ones. Heywood, for example, despite his assertion of the pure
incorporeality of souls and angels and his explicit denial that
the devils fell into corporeality (p. 214), posits a corporeal hell
with corporeal pains:

> Torments in ev'ry Artyre, Nerve, and Vaine,
> In ev'ry Ioint insufferable paine.
> In Head, Brest, Stomake, and in all the Sences,
> Each torture suting to the foule offences,
> But with more terror than the heart can thinke:
> The Sight with Darknesse, and the Smel with Stinke;
> The Taste with Gall, in bitternesse extreme;
> The Hearing, with their Curses that blaspheme:
> The Touch, with Snakes & Todes crauling about them,
> Afflicted both within them and without them.
>
> (p. 347)

In his corresponding "Observations," Heywood acknowledges
that corporeal torments may seem to contradict the incorporeality of the sufferers: "After what manner this corporeall
fire shall torment the Diuels and the damned Ghosts, it is not
for vs to define." But, quoting Ruffinus and Hugo respectively,
he sticks to his guns: "Hee who denieth the Diuell to be
doomed to everlasting fire, shall have part with him in those
eternall flames, and so be sensible of that which hee would not
beleeue. . . . Better it is to doubt of things hid, than to contend

---

[29]Giles Fletcher, another of the scholastic-minded poets of the earlier part of
the century, seems undecided whether the devil hovers around or dwells within
a body he has fashioned (*Christs Victorie* [1610] II.21). In contrast to Milton,
Fletcher seems indifferent to the mechanics of angel apparition.

of what is vncertaine. And let no man rashly meddle about things that are not reuealed" (p. 397). Like many other theological controversialists, Heywood gleefully assigns his doctrinal adversaries to this strange fire.

Joseph Beaumont runs into the same difficulty in accommodating purely incorporeal angels in a narrative that mixes allegorical and nonallegorical characters. The prince of hell sends the devil Aphrodisus, the spirit of Lust, to Earth in order to tempt Psyche, or the soul. Aphrodisus gathers a body (I.37–43) from Earth's courts and spice hoards in Beaumont's poetic and polemic translation of the Thomist metaphysic of borrowed bodies. Aphrodisus, a spirit, is thwarted in his attempt on Psyche by Phylax, her guardian angel, who ties him to a tree and strips him of his borrowed rags, in a scene reminiscent of the stripping of Duessa at the end of Spenser's first book. Later on, in the fourteenth canto, Beaumont speaks of the physical chaining of the devil.

Thomas Peyton's angels modulate into allegorical figures. Beings introduced as Cherubim are transmuted into Justice and Mercy to enact the traditional debate before God (I.161 ff.). The uncertainty as to whether Mercy and Justice are aspects of God, independent entities in a realist universe, personal created angelic beings, or mere poetic abstractions betrays Peyton's confusion or carelessness about ontology, a carelessness one can safely call conventional in long poems of Milton's time. Milton, Johnson notwithstanding, stands out for guarding the coherence of narrative with its philosophical frame.

Milton's Material Angels and True Poetry

Why are Milton's angels material? C. S. Lewis and Robert West share the historical argument that material angels have ample precedent among Milton's contemporaries. Lewis relates Milton's angels to the dualist angels of Platonic theology, who have souls lodged in attenuated bodies.[30] Alastair Fowler picks

[30]C. S. Lewis, *A Preface to "Paradise Lost"* (1942; rpt. London: Oxford University Press, 1961), pp. 108–15.

up Lewis's argument that "Milton . . . rejects the Scholastic view that angels are immaterial. In emphasizing 'the reality of angel nourishment' [he quotes Lewis] he adopts instead the view of Platonic theology, according to which all created spirits are corporeal."[31] Henry More is, of course, a systematizer of Platonic angelology, and Lewis and Fowler follow the lead of Nicolson in suggesting a close similarity between Milton's angels and More's. But the opposition of both of these angelologies to the more familiar scholastic one blinds these scholars to the fundamental difference between Milton's monist angels and More's dualist ones.

West does recognize this difference. He demonstrates that Milton's monist angels have seventeenth-century precedents and argues that Milton uses material angels to celebrate man's material life. He places Milton in the tradition of the Puritan angelologists Henry Lawrence and Isaac Ambrose, exemplars of the "Puritan Reserve," or a reluctance to elaborate on matters not revealed in Scripture.[32] Following patristic texts, Lawrence and Ambrose were advocates for tenuously corporeal, nondichotomous angels. But the differences between these Puritan angels and Milton's, both in form and rationale, are great. Lawrence and Ambrose, as West himself demonstrates, believed that angels, even though corporeal in a sense, must assume temporary bodies to appear on earth, a scholastic view that Milton explicitly rejects. Milton's lengthy digression on angel sexuality and digestion makes no sense from the perspective of the "Puritan Reserve"; it would seem to Lawrence and Ambrose to involve a confusion of an angel's proper body with his assumed one. In Milton, there is no "assumed body," and Raphael eats in his "proper shape." Inasmuch as the writers of the "Puritan Reserve" are marked by a reticence to say more on the particulars of angel essence and operation than is clear from Scripture, they differ from Milton. The angelology embodied in *Paradise Lost* is audacious, original, and still unique. It

---

[31]*Paradise Lost*, ed. Alastair Fowler (London: Longman, 1971), p. 282 (note for 5.407–13).
[32]West, *Milton and the Angels*, pp. 52–57; Lawrence's book is *Of our Communion and Warre with Angels* (1646) and Ambrose's is *War with Devils and Ministration and Communion with Angels* (1662).

rushes boldly where Aquinas and More either feared or did not want to tread.

One of West's main textual examples of Milton's reticence to speculate on angels evaporates when the passage is compared with du Bartas. West cites Milton's indecision on the precise manner of Satan's speaking to Eve (9.529–30): "It is, he says indifferently, either 'with Serpent Tongue Organic, or impulse of vocal Air. . . .' In these passages, which express no choice between alternatives, Milton seems to indicate both his acquaintance with angelological detail and his Puritan indifference to it."[33] But Milton has specified clearly, as Giles Fletcher for example did not, that the devil enters the body. A much better example of "Puritan indifference" can be found in the Huguenot du Bartas, who devotes over seventy lines to recounting five opinions on this same question (II.i.2.142–213). Du Bartas leaves open the possibilities that Satan (1) speaks to Eve as he did in her dream, through her fancy; (2) makes appear before her a phantom snake; (3) appears before her *in* a phantom snake; (4) directs a real snake from without; and (5) appears *in* a real snake. Du Bartas does give priority to the final two options; nevertheless, his survey of possibilities is much closer to Puritan indifference than Milton's indecision between two options that would themselves come under only one (the fifth) of du Bartas's categories.

Elsewhere du Bartas shows reluctance to descend into angelological detail. In his detailed retelling of the Abraham story (II.i.2), he pointedly omits the patriarch's dinner with the angel (Genesis 18:8), a biblical episode that became the subject of the theologians' glosses that were rejected by Milton in his own account of the angels eating. Du Bartas believes in immaterial angels, but in temperament he is much closer to the angelological indifference West finds in his Puritan divines.[34] Milton, in

[33]West, *Milton and the Angels*, p. 126.
[34]Peyton, an anti-Puritan, seems also to exemplify the "Puritan Reserve." His angel ontology is hard to pin down, but seems to involve tenuous corporeality. And when discussing the coupling of Sons of God and daughters of men in Genesis 6:2, Peyton offers three interpretations indifferently: the Sons of God may have been angels, devils, or the sons of Seth (II.142–44). Milton's narrator alludes to the belief that these Sons of God may have been angels at 3.460–65, but he concludes unequivocally at 11.621 ff. that they were men.

pointed contrast, seems to look for opportunities to explore details of angel ontology and operation, and in this he sets himself outside of the "Puritan Reserve."

The second part of West's thesis, that Milton uses his unorthodox angelology to make an argument for the goodness of matter and man's material nature, is more persuasive.[35] Milton, for example, celebrates unfallen sexuality in *Paradise Lost*, a departure from both his early poetry and Christian ascetic tradition. But this is only a partial answer. The angel lore of *Paradise Lost* has as much to do with Milton's ontological convictions and his defense of angels against the assaults of skepticism as it does with his celebration of earthly life. Milton's unusual conception of the truth of poetry requires that he place material angels in *Paradise Lost*.

Milton was not satisfied with a poetic "lie" that points to an abstract truth.[36] Such a substitution was carried on explicitly and self-consciously by Abraham Cowley in the notes to his *Davideis*. Cowley in his verse has his angels move orbs, orchestrate the music of the spheres, and appear on earth, only to debunk these "fictions" in his notes. Here he annotates a passage on the music of the spheres:

> In this, and some like places, I would not have the Reader judge of my opinion by what I say; no more than before in divers expressions about *Hell*. . . . It is enough that the Doctrine of the *Orbs*, and the *Musick* made by their motion had been received very anciently. . . . And to speak according to common opinion, *though it be false, is so far from being a fault in Poetry* [my emphasis], that it is the custom even of the Scripture to do so; and that not only in the Poetical pieces of it; as where it attributes the *members* and *passions* of mankind to *Devils*, *Angels*, and *God* himself; where it calls the *Sun* and *Moon* the two *Great Lights*, whereas the latter is in truth one of the smallest; but is spoken of, as it *seems*, not as it *Is*.[37]

[35]This argument is convincingly expanded by Dennis Burden in *The Logical Epic* (London: Routledge & Kegan Paul, 1967).

[36]For the idea of an artistic lie pointing to the truth, see Don Cameron Allen, *The Legend of Noah: Renaissance Rationalism in Art, Science, and Letters*, Illinois Studies in Language and Literature, vol. 33, nos. 3–4 (Urbana: University of Illinois Press, 1949), pp. 178–81.

[37]Cowley, *Davideis*, I, n. 24, in *The English Writings of Abraham Cowley: Poems*, ed. A. R. Waller (Cambridge: Cambridge University Press, 1905), p. 272; further references to this poem will be cited in the text by book and page number.

Cowley cites the practice of Virgil, Homer, and Statius. He elsewhere warns that some of his statements "must be taken in a Poetical sense" (I, n. 11; p. 268). The most revealing of these notes explains this instance of angel apparition: "*Gabriel* (no blest *Spirit* more kind or fair) / Bodies and cloathes himself with thickned ayr" (II; p. 304). Cowley, the future encomiast of the Royal Society, *seems* to endorse the scholastic opinion here, but his note effectively prevents our assigning any opinion to the author. He cites the opinion of Aquinas on angel apparition and goes on to say that "It is necessary that the Air should be *thickned*, till it come near to the propriety of earth; that is, to be capable of *Figuration*, which cannot be but in a solid body, &c. And this way of *Spirits* appearing in bodies of condensed air (for want of a better way, they taking it for granted that they do frequently appear) is approved by all the *Schoolmen*, and the *Inquisitors* about Witches. But they are beholding for this Invention to the ancient *Poets*" (II, n. 95; p. 321). And Cowley again cites Homer and Virgil. The dialogue between Cowley's verse and his notes sets up a double truth—not Pompanazzi's opposition of the truths of faith and of reason, but that between the truths of fiction and of science.[38]

One might expect this attitude in Cowley, the poet of the Royal Society, but it is interesting to see a hint of it in the ardent angelologist More. In his *Psychozoia* More refers to Gabriel and Uriel and their dominion over north and south respectively. In his note he pulls back from this fancy: "As for those terms it was rather chance than choice that cast me upon them. . . . I conceive they be some old Rabbinical inventions or traditions, by the grosse mistake in them. For when as they assign to *Michael* the East, and the West to *Raphael*, they seem never to have dreamed of any East or West but what belonged to their own Horizon, when as, where ever East is, West is also to some Inhabitants, so that both these Angels will have the same province" (*Psychozoia* III.i.n.). Milton, unlike More, is careful to dissociate himself in his verse from discredited traditions.

[38]Robert Hinman claims that Milton is up to something similar in Raphael's extended narration to Adam; I am arguing that such an opposition is foreign to Milton. See *Abraham Cowley's World of Order* (Cambridge: Harvard University Press, 1960), p. 239.

Milton certainly believed in levels of truth, but not in Cowley's sense. The *Christian Doctrine* is reticent on some topics, including angelology, about which *Paradise Lost* is forthcoming.[39] Nevertheless, to say that in the treatise the Protestant poet writes what he believes to be true according to Scripture is to say that the treatise contains for him not all truth, but merely all truth clearly deducible from Scripture and also necessary for salvation, two criteria that do not exhaust verifiable truth. In the decades before *Paradise Lost* Milton had set for himself new standards of poetic truth.

These standards were forged in the heat of polemical controversy, and particularly in reaction to what Milton perceived as the pernicious "poetry" of *Eikon Basilike*. In *The Reason of Church-Government* Milton presents himself as the poet reluctantly writing prose: "I should not chuse this manner of writing wherin knowing my self inferior to my self, led by the genial power of nature to another task, I have the use, as I may account it, but of my left hand" (*CP* 1:808). He sets the "Poet soaring in the high region of his fancies with his garland and singing robes about him" against "me sitting here below in the cool element of prose, a mortall thing among many readers of no Empyreall conceit." Milton hints in *Of Reformation* at the type of poetic composition he could produce if the genre of polemical writing would allow: "if we could but see the shape of our deare Mother *England*, as Poets are wont to give a personal form to what they please, how would she appeare, think ye, but in a mourning weed, with ashes upon her head, and teares abundantly flowing from her eyes" (*CP* 1:585). In *An Apology* he asks "leave to soare a while as the Poets use" (*CP* 1:900). In these works poets are presented as enjoying enviable latitude for allegory and figurative language.

Eikonoklastes marks a turning point in the use of poets and poetry in Milton's prose writings. In this work references to poetry are pejorative; they focus on its mendacious fictionality. After *Eikonoklastes* references to poetry are extremely few and

---

[39]The brief chapter on angels does not address the physiological and metaphysical questions addressed in *Paradise Lost*; it does, as I have indicated elsewhere, address the angels' knowledge.

mostly derogatory (the exception is the *History of Britain*, with its many neutrally historical references to poetry). The catalyst for the change is Milton's outrage at the fictional image of Charles presented as truth in the *Eikon Basilike*.[40] Milton attacks Charles as a "poet": "The Simily wherwith he begins I was about to have found fault with, as in a garb somwhat more Poetical then for a Statist: but meeting with many straines of like dress in other of his Essaies, and hearing him reported a more diligent reader of Poets, then of Politicians, I begun to think that the whole Book might perhaps be intended a peece of Poetrie. The words are good, the fiction smooth and cleanly: there wanted only Rime . . . " (*CP* 3:406). In *Eikonoklastes* Sidney's *Arcadia* becomes "no serious book, but [a] vain amatorious Poem" (*CP* 3:362). Poets now no longer soar with singing robes, but rather "vapor much" (*CP* 3:502). When they are not being trivial they are lying.

From the time of *Eikonoklastes* Milton was done with fiction; his later poems are records of truth delivered directly, not through the mediation of allegories. Milton compares his *Second Defence* to the *Iliad*, the *Odyssey*, and the *Aeneid* because in it he has "celebrated at least one heroic achievement of my countrymen" (*CP* 4:685). More significant is the choice of topics for the late poems: *Paradise Lost*, *Paradise Regained*, and *Samson Agonistes* are all firmly based on scriptural, and therefore true, stories.

In writing *Paradise Lost* with his eye on posterity, Milton was careful to exclude elements that might be falsified by later discoveries in science and philosophy. *Paradise Lost* stands out among seventeenth-century long poems for its attention to the truth of not only its central themes, but also its myriad details. This attention to veracity takes various forms. At times Milton dissociates himself and his Christian epic from the false lore of classical literature. This stance is epitomized in the curt dismissal following his lyrically stunning version of the Vulcan myth:

---

[40]On this topic, see David A. Loewenstein, *Milton and the Drama of History: Historical Vision, Iconoclasm, and the Literary Imagination* (Cambridge: Cambridge University Press, 1990).

> in *Ausonian* land
> Men call'd him *Mulciber*; and how he fell
> From Heav'n, they fabl'd, thrown by angry *Jove*
> Sheer o'er the Crystal Battlements: from Morn
> To Noon he fell, from Noon to dewy Eve,
> A Summer's day; and with the setting Sun
> Dropt from the Zenith like a falling Star,
> On *Lemnos* th'*Ægæn* Isle: thus they relate,
> Erring.
>
> (1.739–47)

At other times Milton dissociates himself from those credulous of the apparitions of folk legend, as when he compares the contracted devils to

> Faery Elves,
> Whose midnight Revels, by a Forest side
> Or Fountain some belated Peasant sees,
> *Or dreams he sees.*
>
> (1.781–84; my emphasis)

The source passage of this simile, *Aeneid* 6.451–54, describes someone looking at what may or may not be the moon through the clouds. In his allusion Milton transfers to folk beliefs about spirits the caution his age urged in the uncritical acceptance of sense perception. Another example of Milton's protection of the truth of his epic is his reference to alchemy:

> nor wonder; if by fire
> Of sooty coal the Empiric Alchemist
> Can turn, or holds it possible to turn
> Metals of drossiest Ore to perfet Gold.
>
> (5.439–42)

Again, Milton grants consent to and then withdraws it from a belief now discredited. The parallel between "Can turn, or holds it possible to turn" and "sees, / Or dreams he sees" is particularly close. Milton disarms objections to the truth of his own narrative by pointing to falsehoods once credulously and universally received.

An attention to the truth, and not the eviscerated poetic truth of Cowley's annotations, permeates *Paradise Lost*. Milton's stance as inspired singer, so insistent in the invocations, involves a degree of veracity that is conventional of prophetic texts more often than of epic ones.[41] Aware as he must have been of the challenge to the Bible posed by the new science, Milton was careful to attend to extrascriptural standards of truth as he filled in the scriptural gaps in *Paradise Lost*. This attention to extrascriptural standards of truth is characteristic of mid-seventeenth-century natural philosophy. Writers as diverse as Hobbes, Browne, and Glanvill busied themselves with sifting the grains of natural and supernatural truth from the chaff of superstition. One of the effects of this new rigor was an erosion of the formerly universal belief in the existence of spirits and their activity on Earth.

Thus there is a simple reason for the materiality of the angels in *Paradise Lost*. Because his epic subject required angels, Milton constructed the only kind of angels that his monist materialism would allow. He places corporeal angels in his true poem because he believes in them.

His belief is implied in the *Christian Doctrine*, even though the chapter on angels (I.ix) is conspicuously silent on their make-

---

[41]See William Kerrigan, *The Prophetic Milton* (Charlottesville: University Press of Virginia, 1974), p. 264. Milton's concern for the literal truth of his poem may explain in part his reticence to have Raphael resolve the dispute between Ptolemy and Copernicus (8.159–68). While Milton is making a point about the irrelevance of astronomy to salvation, surely another reason is that he was undecided about the merits of the Ptolemaic and Copernican systems. Modern readers may not be aware of the tenacity of the ancient system. As late as 1712 Richard Blackmore could leave the question open in his tedious *Creation*. If we are inclined to think that Milton *must* have been a Copernican, we should note Kuhn's observation that in his time no observational test was available to establish heliocentrism conclusively. As astute a layman as Edward, Viscount Conway, could write to his daughter-in-law Anne Conway of his impatience with the Copernican system in 1651: "In my opinion, that [opinion] of Copernicus, for the Earth a heavy dull grosse body to move and the heaven and Starres who are light to stand still is as if a Prince should upon a festivall day appoint all the old and fat men and woemen to dance and all the yonge men and woemen of sixteen and twenty to sit still" (*Conway Letters: The Correspondence of Anne, Viscountess Conway, Henry More, and Their Friends, 1642–1684* [New Haven: Yale University Press, 1930], p. 34). Thus Raphael's hedging: Milton does not want to compromise his true epic with a scientific model that might become obsolete.

up and warns against making doctrinal assertions on their essence. "Those who tried to say more about the nature of angels earned the apostle's rebuke, Col.ii.18: *intruding into those things which he has not seen, rashly puffed up by his fleshly intelligence*" (*CP* 6:315). Speaking with the voice of the exegete here, Milton restricts himself to what is clear from Scripture. But given his unequivocal assertion of angel existence and his monist statements on matter, body, and soul elsewhere in his treatise, he can have believed only in the type of angels that are found in his poem. When Milton writes in *Christian Doctrine* that "Angels are spirits. . . . They are ethereal by nature" (*CP* 6:314), he refers to tenuous matter, not to incorporeal substance.

Milton's God is the apotheosis of the scholastic angel, invisible and essentially unmanifest to our eyes. As the temporary bodies are to Aquinas's angels, so the Son is to Milton's Father: "in him all his Father shone / Substantially express'd, and in his face / Divine compassion visibly appear'd" (*PL* 3.139–41). The Son is a material expression of the Father. His materiality locates him in place. While Milton grants other divine attributes to the Son, he significantly denies him omnipresence (*CP* 6:265). If the Son is material, it is certain that the angels are as well.

The references to angels in Milton's early poetry are few and terse, and they do not indicate any specific angelological stance.[42] Milton's material angels are part and parcel of the materialism that he develops in the 1650s. Milton surely knew that his material angels were unorthodox. He gave their materiality such a prominent place in *Paradise Lost* and ran the risk of alienating orthodox readers because he wished to defend their existence in a world that had grown increasingly skeptical of incorporeal substance. Because the usual view held that angels were partly or entirely composed of incorporeal substance, an attack on that substance amounted to an attack on angels. Sadducism, the Hebrew heresy denying the existence of angels

---

[42]See the hymning angels of the "Nativity Ode" and "At a Solemn Music," the "thousand liveried Angels" who lackey chastity in *Comus*, and the angels' "fiery essence" of "Upon the Circumcision" (l.17).

and spirits, was enough of an issue for Glanvill, the scientifically inclined ally of the Cambridge thinkers, to write his *Saducismus Triumphatus*. Even Hobbes called the Sadducees' spirit skepticism "very neere to direct Atheisme."[43]

Milton offered corporeal angels to a world in which corporeal existence was increasingly seen not as derivative from the spiritual ground of reality, but as the ground of reality itself. He assured his audience that they need not accept a different, incorporeal substance, a substance that Hobbes found self-contradictory, but only a refinement of the substance with which that audience was familiar through its senses. In adopting materialist monism, Milton avoids many of the difficulties and inconsistencies that plagued those poets who attempted to present immaterial beings in narrative action. He need not contradict himself when writing of, for instance, the binding, wounding, imprisoning, or apparition of angels. Spirits exist not in another dimension, but in our own. Even if Milton's version of angel substance did not achieve wide currency, we can recognize the ingenuity of their construction in an age that increasingly weighed the claims of the material. That Milton's solution to the problem of angels did not succeed outside his poem is proved amply by the fact that they were misread as immaterial creatures so soon, so often, and for so long.

[43]*Leviathan*, p. 145 (chap. 8).

~ 6

Sin and Death:
The Substance of Allegory

My argument that Milton's material angels maintain the ontological integrity of *Paradise Lost* raises another vexed issue in the poem's critical history: the allegory of Sin and Death. What are these insubstantial beings, these abstractions, doing in a mimetic epic? The perceived breach of metaphysical decorum is inseparable from a perceived breach of literary decorum: why this extended allegory in an otherwise nonallegorical epic? The questions began in the seventeenth century and continue today. Samuel Johnson, not surprisingly, makes the objection most incisively:

> After the operation of immaterial agents, which cannot be explained, may be considered that of allegorical persons which have no real existence. To exalt causes into agents, to invest abstract ideas with form and animate them with activity, has always been the right of poetry. But such airy beings are, for the most part, suffered only to do their natural office and retire. Thus Fame tells a tale, and Victory hovers over a general or perches on a standard; but Fame and Victory can do no more. To give them any real employment, or ascribe to them any material agency, is to make them allegorical no longer, but *to shock the mind by ascribing effects to non-entity*.[1]

[1]Samuel Johnson, "Life of Milton," in *Johnson's Lives of the English Poets: A Selection*, ed. J. P. Hardy (Oxford: Clarendon Press, 1971), p. 108.

Johnson concludes with characteristic bluntness: "Milton's allegory is undoubtedly faulty." The terms for an answer to Johnson lie in the objection itself. Taking advantage of the fit between allegory and nonentity in the seventeenth century, Milton in a virtuoso performance employs allegory to strengthen rather than violate the ontological coherence of the universe of *Paradise Lost*. The argument in the preceding chapters for the significance of Milton's treatment of substance in *Paradise Lost* would stand even if Johnson were right about Sin and Death. I will suggest in this chapter that even in the allegory, where he seems to play fast and loose with the ontological consistency of his epic, Milton in fact preserves that consistency.

Milton's Augustinian Ontology of Evil

Augustine denies positive ontological status to evil, insisting that evil is not an entity, but privation (*privatio*) of entity. All created things are essentially good, but free creatures can turn away from their own perfections and from God. Evil lies in this free turning, not in the creature's substance. Because evil is the privation, or corruption, of a good nature, it requires the good for its derivative existence. Augustine writes in the *City of God* (XIV, xi) that "evil in truth cannot exist without good, since the natures in which evil exists, in so far as they are natures, are certainly good," and in the *Confessions* (III, vii) that "evil is nothing except the privation of good until that good is gone altogether."[2] What remains after the "good is gone altogether"? The question is the key to the ontology of Sin and Death; the answer is, in a word, nothing: "Thus if things are deprived of all good, they become altogether nothing: accordingly, as long as they are, they are good. Therefore, *wheresoever things are, they are good, and evil*, the origin of which I was seeking, *is not a substance*, because if it were a substance, it would be good"

[2]Here and elsewhere, I translate from the Latin text of the Bibliothèque Augustinienne's *Œuvres de Saint Augustin*; the passages from *De civitate Dei* appear in vol. 35 (Bruges: Desclée de Brouwer, 1959) and the passages from the *Confessiones* in vols. 13 and 14 (Bruges: Desclée de Brouwer, 1962); references to these works will be made by book and chapter number in the text.

(*Confessions* VII, xii; my emphasis). In metaphysical as opposed
to moral terms, evil is nonentity, the negation rather than the
expression of being. In examining Milton's allegory, we will
have reason to remember Augustine's formula in the *City of God*
(XII, iii): "solely good things can somewhere exist, solely evil
things nowhere."[3]

Given his a priori belief in free will, Milton would naturally
be attracted to an argument that finds the origin of evil in the
creature's choice. Furthermore, Milton shares the dual imperative that leads Augustine to his ontology of evil: the fear of
Manicheism on the one hand and of the imputation of evil to
God on the other.[4] For these reasons it is not surprising to hear
Milton echo Augustine in his own *Christian Doctrine* (I, vii):
"Nothing is neither good nor any kind of thing at all. All entity
is good: nonentity, not good [*Ens omne est bonum, non ens non
bonum*]" (*CP* 6:310; *Works* 15:26). The inescapable converse,
true for Milton as for Augustine, is that evil has no ontological
status; it is not an entity but the privation of entity.[5] This much
can be inferred from the collation of the passage just cited with
another from the *Art of Logic* (I, xvii): "*habitus . . . est ens, privatio non ens*" (*Works* 15:148). "*Habitus*" Milton defines as that in
a subject "to which the affirmative by its very nature belongs"
(*CP* 8:267). "*Habitus*," being "*ens*," is therefore "*bonum*"; "*privatio*," being "*non ens*," is therefore "*non bonum*."[6] Metaphysical

[3]The transplantation of this concept from Augustine's Neoplatonic theology to
Aquinas's Aristotelian one indicates its vitality in the Christian tradition; Aquinas speaks of evil as privation in the *Summa theologiae* I, Q.48, art.1.
[4]And if James Holly Hanford's reading of the Commonplace Book is correct,
then Milton consulted the *City of God* in 1657 or 1658, important years for both
the *Christian Doctrine* and *Paradise Lost*; see "The Chronology of Milton's Private
Studies," in *John Milton: Poet and Humanist* (Cleveland: The Press of Western
Reserve University, 1966), p. 101. C. S. Lewis noted the similarity between
Milton's ontology of evil and Augustine's in *A Preface to "Paradise Lost"* (1942;
rpt. London: Oxford University Press, 1961), pp. 66–72; he has been seconded
recently by Peter A. Fiore's *Milton and Augustine: Patterns of Augustinian Thought
in "Paradise Lost"* (University Park: Pennsylvania State University Press, 1981),
pp. 12–22.
[5]For the law of reciprocity assuring this conclusion, see the *Art of Logic* (*CP*
8:297, 312, and 315).
[6]Milton seems to contradict the Augustinian position of the *Christian Doctrine*
when he writes in the *Art of Logic* that "I would also not call sin a privation" (*CP*
8:268). But in his denial that sin is privation, Milton refers to a morally evil

evil for both Augustine and Milton is the loss or privation of entity; it is the measure of the negative distance between created perfection and willed corruption.

Augustine and Milton distinguish between metaphysical evil and moral evil, which, I will demonstrate, are embodied in Sin and Death and Satan, respectively. Metaphysical evil is the negative distance between created perfection and willed corruption; moral evil is the diseased will of the corrupt creature. But, for Augustine and Milton, even moral evil lies ultimately not in action, but in deficiency or privation. Augustine writes in the *City of God* (XII, vii): "Let no one seek, therefore, for an efficient cause of the evil will; for it is not efficient but deficient, because the will is not a doing of something, but a failing to do something." Milton parallels this idea in his discussion of "actual sin" or "the evil action or crime itself" in the *Christian Doctrine* (I, xi): "It is called 'actual' not because sin is really an action, on the contrary, it is a deficiency [*privatio*], but because it usually exists in some action. For every action is intrinsically good; it is only its misdirection or deviation from the set course of law which can properly be called evil. So action is not the material out of which sin is made, but only the *hypokeimenon*, the essence or element in which it exists" (*CP* 6:391). Thus the gulf of nonentity can be seen yawning even behind moral evil.

In the Augustinian conception of evil as the privation of entity lies the ontological rationale for Milton's use of allegory. If Sin and Death embody metaphysical evil, then their "lesser reality" as allegorical characters fits Milton's ontology of evil. The embodiment is illusory and paradoxical, for metaphysical evil does not exist. But to avoid begging the question of the reality of allegorical characters, I turn now to the nature of allegory and its changing status in the seventeenth century.

---

action and not to metaphysical evil. Sumner's translation makes this clearer than Carey's: "I should not say that a sin is a privation" (*Works* 11:149). That Sumner's "a sin" (clearly referring to a morally evil action) is a better translation than Carey's "sin" is discernible from the clause that follows: "because if this or that is a sin or a vice it is not a privation" (*CP* 8:268). It is the "thisness or thatness" of *a* sin that makes it not a privation. In *Christian Doctrine* Milton describes the *action* of a sin not as sin itself but as "the essence or element in which [sin] exists" (*CP* 6:391).

Allegory and Ontology

Coleridge defines personification allegory, the type of allegory with which this chapter is concerned, as the use of "one set of agents and images" to represent "moral qualities or conceptions of the mind that are not in themselves objects of the senses."[7] By the late seventeenth century, after a late flowering in the work of Spenser and his literary heirs, this important literary mode had ceased to answer to the ontological assumptions of the educated audience and had retreated into the strictly circumscribed refuge of Bunyanesque literature. The reasons for allegory's decline are twofold and interrelated. First, by its nature personification allegory involves characters of a different order of reality from those of mimetic narrative. Second, by the light of the seventeenth century's new, and increasingly empirical, standards of truth, which depend on the gradual displacement of realism by nominalism, the different reality of abstractions is demoted to a lesser reality and in some minds to nonreality.

Allegory does not represent real human beings; rather, it personifies the qualities, or abstractions, that inhere in human beings. Angus Fletcher's description of allegorical characters as "daemonic agents" illuminates their relationship to substantial existence. Fletcher suggests a similarity between allegorical agents and the daemons, or intermediate spirits, of Roman religion.[8] These daemons, whose name derives from the term "to divide," share control of men, each directing one function or part of the body.[9] In the same way allegorical agents represent parts of a divided whole. An allegorical character's excessive singleness of purpose parallels the phenomenon of daemonic possession. If an allegorical character were to appear in our midst, we would be struck by his "absolutely one-track

[7]Samuel Taylor Coleridge, *Miscellaneous Criticism*, ed. T. M. Raysor (Cambridge: Harvard University Press, 1936), p. 30.
[8]Angus Fletcher, *Allegory: The Theory of a Symbolic Mode* (Ithaca: Cornell University Press, 1964), pp. 43–46; for another discussion of the affinity between allegory and Roman religion, see C. S. Lewis, *The Allegory of Love: A Study in Medieval Tradition* (London: Oxford University Press, 1936), pp. 48–66.
[9]Fletcher, *Allegory*, pp. 59–60.

mind"; we would perceive that "he did not control his own destiny, but appeared to be controlled by some foreign force, something outside the sphere of his own ego."[10] This single-ness of purpose results from a splintering of personality; an aspect is separated from the whole and embodied. Leaving aside the question of psychotic possession, this description ac-counts for the existence of mimetic and allegorical characters on separate ontological planes.

It is important to note with Fletcher that elaborate physical description does not change an allegorical character into a mi-metic one. Allegorical agents reveal by their actions not inter-nal psychologies but the abstractions (often as complex as psy-chologies in sophisticated allegory) that lie behind them. However much surface detail is added to an allegorical charac-ter like Guyon, he does not become a mimetic one like Eliz-abeth Bennet. Fletcher demonstrates that the "naturalist de-tail" of some allegory does not serve a "journalistic function"; instead it points rhetorically to the daemonic attributes of the character.[11]

While medieval allegorists recognized the difference be-tween the ontological status of persons represented by mimetic characters and the abstractions represented by allegorical char-acters, they nevertheless saw the latter as essentially real. Owen Barfield describes the assumptions behind allegory: "For us, the characters in an allegory are 'personified abstractions', but for the man of the Middle Ages Grammar or Rhetoric, Mercy or 'Daunger', were real to begin with, simply *because* they were 'names'."[12] Barfield here invokes the now familiar connection between allegory and Platonist-Aristotelian realism, which, contrary to modern realism, posits that what we call "abstrac-tions" have real existence.[13] The "ideas" or "universals" of this

[10]Ibid., pp. 40–41.
[11]Ibid., pp. 198–99.
[12]Owen Barfield, *Saving the Appearances: A Study in Idolatry* (New York: Har-court, 1965), p. 86.
[13]See, e.g., Thomas P. Roche, Jr., *The Kindly Flame: A Study of the Third and Fourth Books of Spenser's "Faerie Queene"* (Princeton: Princeton University Press, 1964), p. 4; and Isabel MacCaffrey, *"Paradise Lost" as Myth* (Cambridge: Har-vard University Press, 1959), p. 82.

classical/medieval realism lie behind allegorical agents. It is not surprising that the great age of allegory was a realist age.[14]

Some defining of terms is in order here, because I will be speaking of allegorical agents as representing universals and accidents simultaneously, and some readers might be accustomed to thinking of the former as general and essential and the latter as particular and inessential. In Platonic and Aristotelian terms, accident is a variety of predicate, along with attribute. Any concrete subject has predicates or qualities, which if essential are attributes and, if inessential, accidents. If one were to say that Solomon was a just rational animal and king, one would be naming accidents (just and king) and attributes (rational animal) of the man Solomon. Justice is a universal or idea, but because it is not necessarily predicated of any particular man (as are rationality and animality), it is accidental in whomever it exists. For Plato, the predicates are the unchanging universals, because one can change a subject by changing its predicates, but one cannot change a predicate by changing its subject: thus an unjust John Doe is different from a just John Doe, but the justice of a just Richard Roe is the same justice. The essential rationality and the accidental justice of any particular man participate in the ideas of rationality and justice. Because subjects (the particular) are mutable and predicates (the universals) immutable, Plato granted ontological status to the latter but not to the former. Aristotle diverged by granting ontological status to concrete subject as well as to immaterial predicate.[15]

[14]Despite the perennial challenge to realism from nominalism, represented most visibly by Roscellinus and William of Ockham, nominalism remained a minority reaction to realist orthodoxy. Of course medieval realism was far from univocal, as Meyrick Carré points out in *Realists and Nominalists* (London: Oxford University Press, 1946), an excellent introduction to this topic. It accommodated a variety of positions from Augustine's Neoplatonic extreme realism, through Abelard's and Aquinas's moderate realism, to the very attenuated realism sometimes advanced by the usually nominalist Ockham.

[15]This account is necessarily simplified, especially for Aristotle, who divides predicate into four types (genus, definition, property, and accident), but the necessary simplification does not distort the point in question, since the first three types are divisions of attribute. For Plato on accident, see the *Sophist* 247b. ff., and the *Republic* 5.454; for Aristotle on accident, see *Topics* I.iv–v, and *Metaphysics* VI.iii.

Milton's understanding of accident is in line with the model presented here. In the *Art of Logic* (I, x–xi), he uses the terms "subject" and "adjunct" (*subjectum* and *adjunctum*) for subject and accident and cites Aristotle as his principal authority.[16] Milton gives as examples of adjuncts or accidents such universals as health, strength, beauty, and honor (along with more external accidents such as riches and clothing) (*CP* 8:243). For Milton, as for Plato and Aristotle, accidents are inessential only in the strict logical and metaphysical senses (as in the case of Solomon's justice). Milton explicitly denies that they are necessarily negligible or "fortuitous" qualities: "Whatever happens extrinsically to any subject, whether fortuitously or not, is that subject's adjunct. What are called the goods and evils of the spirit, of the body and of the whole man are adjuncts of the spirit, the body and the man" (*CP* 8:245).

Allegory's vitality owed much to the realist belief in the actual existence of universals outlined above. But the Middle Ages witnessed a progressive moderation of realism, precipitated by the criticism of the nominalist minority, who denied the existence of universals. The universals, from their privileged status in Plato's realm of Ideas (universals exist as separate entities), moved under the influence of Aristotle into things (universals exist, but only within things) and finally retreated into mind (universals exist as modes of thought). One can chart the course of medieval realism by contrasting its early exponent, Augustine, its greatest poet, Dante, and its Renaissance heir, Descartes. While Augustine places the universals in the mind of the biblical God, he otherwise remains entirely consistent with Plato in granting them ontological priority over the concrete subjects in which they manifest themselves.[17] The position given to the universals by Dante is less exalted, as we see in a passage from the *Vita Nuova* (xxv) of particular significance to my argument in its connection of metaphysics and allegory: "It may be that . . . some person, worthy of having every doubt cleared up, could be puzzled at my speaking of Love as if it were a thing in itself, as if it were not only an intellectual sub-

[16]The citation of Aristotle appears in *CP* 8:245.
[17]See *On Free Will* II, xvi, 44.

stance, but also a bodily substance. This in reality is false, for Love *does not exist in itself as a substance, but rather it is an accident in a substance.*"[18] The extreme realists Plato and Augustine would have said that accidents are universals that exist in themselves as well as in particular subjects and moreover that this former existence is more real than the existence of the subjects. In his "Third Meditation" Descartes, employing the scholastic terminology for which Hobbes criticized him, goes further in reducing the ontological pretensions of the universals: "Undoubtedly, the ideas which represent substances to me amount to something more and, so to speak, contain within themselves more objective reality (i.e. participate by representation in a higher degree of being or perfection) than the ideas which merely represent modes or accidents."[19] Descartes makes explicit what seems implicit in Dante. Both of these moderate realists recognize the reality of accidents, which as universals are the stuff of allegorical characterization, but Dante perhaps and Descartes surely assign to them a reality derivative from and lesser than that they acknowledge in substances, whether corporeal or intellectual. For Augustine, the extreme realist, universals have a greater reality than things, for Dante an at least different reality, and for Descartes a lesser reality.

The implications for allegory of this philosophical trend are ominous. If the universals or accidents lose ontological weight, then so do the allegorical agents who represent them. Paraphrasing Descartes, we may say that *characters* representing substantial beings (i.e., mimetic characters) contain more reality than those representing accidents in substances. It is in this sense that I speak of the "lesser reality" of allegorical characters in Milton's century. The term reflects seventeenth-century assumptions on the nature of reality; it is not meant to account in a reductive manner for the experience of allegory in the more thoroughly realist Middle Ages.

Even greater damage to the ontological claims of allegory

18Dante, *La Vita Nuova*, trans. Mark Musa (1957; Bloomington: Indiana University Press, 1962), p. 53; my emphasis.
19Cottingham 2:28.

came at the hands of the nominalists. In his "Objections" to the *Meditations*, the arch-nominalist Hobbes calls Descartes to task for the passage quoted above: "M. Descartes should consider afresh what 'more reality' means. Does reality admit of more or less?"[20] For the nominalist, there are only things, and the layering of reality upon which allegory depends is eliminated.

While the Cambridge Platonists did advocate an extreme realism, theirs was a rearguard action. The mainstream debate in mid-seventeenth-century England was between moderate realism and nominalism; the former lessened the reality of universals and the latter rejected universals altogether. We would expect to find, then, a decline in the status of the literary mode that depends on universals. And, indeed, there is a reaction against allegory in the seventeenth century.[21] Despite the interest in allegory evidenced in his *Wisdom of the Ancients*, Sir Francis Bacon reveals some reservations in his *Advancement of Learning*. Allegory, or "Allusive or Parabollical narration," was formerly necessary "to express any point of reason which was more sharp or subtile than the vulgar . . . ; because men in those times wanted both variety of examples and subtilty of conceit."[22] In Bacon's eyes, this type of allegory at least springs from the limitations, since outgrown, of artist and audience, and not from the nature of unseen reality. He retains the old rhetorical justification for allegory, but without the cosmological and metaphysical sanctions that made it vital.

Appropriately, we find evidence of the decline of allegory in the seventeenth century in its response to the giant of allegory on its threshold, Edmund Spenser. The seventeenth century admires Spenser's descriptive and narrative powers and deprecates his allegory. In his "Preface to *Gondibert*" (1650), William D'Avenant compares the allegory first to feverish dreams and

---

[20]Cottingham 2:130.

[21]For a different perspective on the decline of allegory after Spenser than I offer here, see Michael Murrin's *The Veil of Allegory: Some Notes toward a Theory of Allegorical Rhetoric in the English Renaissance* (Chicago: University of Chicago Press, 1969), pp. 167–98.

[22]*The Works of Francis Bacon*, ed. James Spedding, Robert Leslie Ellis, and Douglas Denon Heath, 14 vols. (London: 1858–74), 3:344.

then to painted scenery that detracts from solid dramatic action. He laments that Spenser's great talents were wasted on allegory instead of "upon matter of a more naturall and therefore of a more usefull kinde."[23] According to Thomas Rymer in 1674, Spenser was misled by the Italian Ariosto; he remarks that "It was the vice of those Times to affect superstitiously the *Allegory*; and nothing would then be current without a mystical meaning. We must blame the Italians for debauching great *Spencer's* judgement."[24] Joseph Addison, in *An Account of the Greatest English Poets* (1694), praises Spenser's descriptions, but feels that the poet's story "amus'd a Barb'rous Age; / . . . uncultivate and rude":

> But now the Mystick Tale, that pleas'd of Yore,
> Can Charm an understanding Age no more;
> The long-spun Allegories fulsom grow,
> While the dull Moral lyes too plain below.[25]

The dichotomy between rude and cultured ages echoes Bacon's; the fact that a mere one hundred years separate Spenser and Addison underlines the seventeenth century's growing confidence in its progress on the road to the possession of a new truth.

Fundamental changes are usually gradual, and the seventeenth century produced allegories. One main current flows from the influence of Spenser, but it dies out with the generation of Spenserians such as the Fletchers and Henry More. A later current is mechanic Puritan allegory, dominated by Bunyan. Yet, however sophisticated the moral psychology of these allegories, they are written by and for a philosophically illiterate segment of the population. These allegories ignore questions of ontology confronted by Milton in his allegory of Sin and Death.

Moreover, evidence of the instability of allegory can be gath-

[23]J. E. Springarn, ed., *Critical Essays of the Seventeenth Century*, 3 vols. (Oxford: Clarendon Press, 1908–9), 2:6.
[24]R. M. Cummings, ed., *Spenser: The Critical Heritage* (New York: Barnes and Noble, 1971), p. 207.
[25]Ibid., p. 224.

ered from allegorists themselves. With surprising frequency in the seventeenth century, poets mix allegorical and mimetic characterization and narration. This error, with which Johnson charged Milton, may almost be called conventional. Giles Fletcher's *Christs Victorie and Triumph* is a curious mixture of the life of Christ and clashes of abstractions in the tradition of Prudentius. Time, Truth, Justice, and Mercy play active roles in Thomas Peyton's *Glasse of Time*. As noted in the last chapter, it is not clear whether these characters are personal beings or personified abstractions. Richard Crashaw's *Sospetto d'Herode*, translated around 1637 from Marino's *Strage degl'Innocenti*, combines classical and Christian mythology (as does Camoens's *Os Lusiadas*).[26] Crashaw mentions Medea and Jezebell in the same breath (st. 43), and the Errinyes are sent to Bethlehem. The Italianate Crashaw is apparently attracted to Marino's late-Renaissance syncretism. To the three classical Errinyes, Marino and Crashaw add a fourth, the allegorical personification Cruelty, who is chosen by the devil for his plot against the Christ child. Marino's and Crashaw's mixture of classical deities, Christian deities, and personification perhaps represents the extreme of the tendency I am examining here. Even the philosophically sophisticated Abraham Cowley finds room for allegory in his unfinished epic *Davideis*. Among Cowley's biblical characters appears Envy, whose description is reminiscent of the iconography dear to the allegorists:

> Her garments were deep stain'd in human gore,
> And torn by her own hands, in which she bore
> A knotted whip, and bowl, that to the brim
> Did with green gall, and juice of wormwood swim.[27]

Aside from the obvious formal differences, this passage would seem to be more at home in Spenserian allegory than in Cow-

---

[26]Richard Crashaw, *Sospetto d'Herode*, in *The Complete Poetry*, ed. George Walton Williams (New York: Norton, 1970), pp. 216–53; in this edition Crashaw's translation appears on pages facing Marino's original.
[27]*Davideis* 1, in *The English Writings of Abraham Cowley: Poems*, ed. A. R. Waller (Cambridge: Cambridge University Press, 1905), p. 246.

ley's mimetic epic. And Cowley's Envy is not one of those characters of whom Johnson approves, who are "suffered only to
do their natural office and retire"; she is given "real employment" by Cowley.[28]

These poems reveal that Milton's mixture of allegorical and
nonallegorical characters, even if not defensible on grounds of
the poet's ontology, would have ample contemporary precedent. More important, they reveal an uncertainty about ontology among the poets. Medieval allegorists, as well as Spenser
and Bunyan, are confident in the reality of the abstractions
they personify and are aware that that reality is different in
kind from material reality. The mixing of categories in much of
seventeenth-century allegory betrays an uncertainty over the
realm of reality occupied by accidents in substances. A few
committed philosophical realists continued to write allegories
(e.g., Henry More and his *Platonick Song of the Soul*, 1647), but
the intellectual environment was no longer as receptive to allegory, which in an earlier age had been, in Lewis's phrase, the
"dominant form."

Milton and Allegory

One can infer Milton's attitude toward the use of allegory
from his poetic practice. We all know that Milton told Dryden
that "Spenser was his original," yet he does not follow Spenser
in choosing the allegorical mode for his epic.[29] Allegorical
characters do appear in his earlier poetry, but sparingly even
there. "Tragoedia," "Elegeia," and "Fama" have circumscribed
roles in the first, second, and fourth elegies respectively. Milton
wonders in "Fair Infant" if his niece was truly "sweet smiling

---

[28]Johnson, "Life of Milton," p. 108.

[29]In his valuable "From Allegory to Dialectic: Imagining Error in Spenser and
Milton," *PMLA* 101 (1986): 9–23, Gordon Teskey addresses this curious fact;
he rehearses the distinction between epic and romance and argues that Milton
disdains the oblique approach to truth that is the hallmark of allegory. Teskey
does not address the allegory of Sin and Death; it will be clear that I disagree
with his statement that there is in *Paradise Lost* "no indication that we should
read [the allegorical tropes] in any sense but the literal" (p. 19).

Youth" or "sage white-robed Truth" (ll. 53–54). A Virgilian mob of personifications crowds the gates of Hell in "In Quintum Novembris" (ll. 139–55); significantly, Milton does not place a similar group at the gates of his epic Hell (Virgil's group is deallegorized and dispersed throughout Books 11 and 12). Nature, Peace, Truth, and Justice appear as mutes in the "Nativity Ode." Even the allegory-charged *Comus* does not rely on personification allegory, although the Elder Brother does discourse on the habits of Wisdom, Solitude, and Contemplation (ll. 375–81).

Of course the best implicit evidence for Milton's increasing dissatisfaction with the allegorical mode, or at least with the mixing of allegorical and mimetic characters, is the metamorphosis of his early plans for his masterpiece. Milton winnows out allegorical personifications in the successive drafts for a drama on the fall in the Trinity manuscript (*CP* 8:554–60). The original draft projects Heavenly Love, Conscience, Death, Faith, Hope, and Charity as speaking characters, and Labor, Sicknesse, Discontent, Ignorance, "with others" as mutes. The second draft adds Justice, Mercie, and Wisdome to the speakers and transforms Fear and Death into mutes. In both drafts the personifications share the stage with humans and angels. In a more articulated third draft, now titled "Paradise Lost," Milton specifies that Justice, Mercie, and Wisdome will debate "what should become of man if he fall," and that Faith, Hope, and Charity will "comfort him and instruct him" (*CP* 8:554–55). In the still more elaborate fourth draft, headed "Adam unparadiz'd," almost all of the personifications disappear. The debate of Justice, Mercie, and Wisdome is gone; instead, Justice and Mercy speak with Adam after his fall (the debate of Justice and Mercy is subsumed in the dialogue of Father and Son in the eventual fulfillment of these early drafts). James Holly Hanford argues that the personifications disappear because "the whole design has moved somewhat away from the Italianate conception" guiding the earlier drafts.[30] There is an

---

[30]James Holly Hanford, "Notes on Milton's *Paradise Lost* and Other Biblical Scenarios," in *CP* 8:587.

element of truth here; Rymer blamed Spenser's allegory on the Italians. But allegorical and mimetic characters were often mixed in English poems of the period. It may be partly true, as Hanford also suggests, that the change results from Milton's "working out" the biblical themes; it is certainly true that, by the time he comes to write his epic, he has worked out a new role for allegory.

One part of allegory's role in the epic has already been established, most notably by Anne Ferry: Milton's allegory expresses fallen epistemology, the perverse refusal of Satan and his devils to acknowledge the unity of a monist universe.[31] As Ferry demonstrates, from the poem's mythic point of view, allegory represents a descent into a sterile and illusory division of inner and outer phenomena, of the spiritual and the physical. Maureen Quilligan's observation that Ferry's "mechanistic definition of allegory" causes her to "miss much of Spenser's power" is accurate,[32] but it does not disqualify Ferry's thesis. As we have seen, Milton's contemporaries shared this definition of allegory and underestimation of Spenser. An intellectual environment fostering a supple and organic response to allegory disappeared along with confidence in the reality of universals, or at least with consensus on their nature. Already present in the seventeenth century is the misunderstanding of and consequent prejudice against allegory that was to culminate in William Hazlitt's famous assurance that if Spenser's readers "do not meddle with the allegory, it will not meddle with them."[33]

My argument on Milton's allegory complements Ferry's. By Milton's time allegory was an ideal vehicle for presenting deficient ontology as well a deficient epistemology. To the extent

---

[31]Anne Ferry, *Milton's Epic Voice: The Narrator in "Paradise Lost"* (Cambridge: Harvard University Press, 1963), pp. 116–46; Ferry's argument builds on earlier work by Arnold Stein, *Answerable Style: Essays on "Paradise Lost"* (Minneapolis: University of Minnesota Press, 1953), pp. 157–58, and MacCaffrey, *"Paradise Lost" as Myth*, p. 197.

[32]Maureen Quilligan, *Milton's Spenser: The Politics of Reading* (Ithaca: Cornell University Press, 1983), p. 92.

[33]William Hazlitt, "On Chaucer and Spenser," excerpted in *The Prince of Poets: Essays on Edmund Spenser*, ed. John R. Elliot (New York: New York University Press, 1968), pp. 24–25.

that Sin and Death are not merely morally evil characters but rather embodiments of metaphysical evil, as I will demonstrate next, they are not additional beings in a monist universe, but the privation of being itself. Milton's genius is to have reserved allegory, the reality of whose characters was more than suspect, for these nonbeings.

Milton's eventual choice of a prophetic and mythic narrative is reflected in the transformation of allegory's role between outline drafts and completed epic. Mediated truth is rejected in favor of direct truth. Even when using allegory, Milton guards the literal veracity of his poem. From the Father to "Parsimonious Emmet" (7.485), substantial beings inhabit the poem. The reality of wisdom or mercy is of a different order. Milton does not wish to compromise the radical claim for the reality of his actors by intermixing with them characters of a "lesser reality." The gulf between substantial and mimetic characters and unreal and allegorical characters is unmediated by real accidents in substances.

The Ontology of Sin and Death

That Milton's readers have not reached a consensus on the ontology of Sin and Death is vividly illustrated by the disagreement between Quilligan and Philip J. Gallagher. Gallagher posits Milton's belief in the literal truth of his narrative and argues that the allegory does not violate ontological consistency for the simple reason that Sin and Death are "consistently real (i.e., physical and historical) throughout Milton's major epic, their allegorical onomastics notwithstanding."[34] Conversely, Quilligan asserts that in Sin and Death Satan "has authored something less than pure *res*. He can't do the real thing."[35] The allegorical episodes are self-consciously fictional "brackets," with which Milton simultaneously reminds the reader of the

[34]Philip J. Gallagher, "'Real or Allegoric': The Ontology of Sin and Death in *Paradise Lost*," *English Literary Renaissance* 6 (1976): 317.
[35]Quilligan, *Milton's Spenser*, p. 126.

fictionality of the entire epic and emphasizes the "intimate truth" of the bracketed material. In a sense they are both half right. Granted the Augustinianism of Milton's ontology of evil, Quilligan's "unreal" characters Sin and Death, whose paradoxical embodiment of metaphysical evil will be explored next, fit without contradiction into Gallagher's "literally true" narrative.

Gallagher's claim that Sin and Death are "real and historical" characters is at variance with the verdict of centuries of readers. Addison speaks for most when he calls Sin and Death "two Actors of a shadowy and fictitious Nature,"[36] as does Joseph Summers when he terms them "real nonentities."[37] Undertaken with an awareness of Milton's ontology of evil, a close examination of the allegory in *Paradise Lost* reveals precisely how and why Addison and Summers are correct.

One important clue to the nature of Sin and Death has not received enough notice. Sin's narration of the fall in the second book differs dramatically from Raphael's in the fifth. In Raphael's long account of Satan's summons to the North, his speech to his followers, and their fall, there is no room for Sin's spectacular cephalogenesis (5.610–710, 743–802). In her own account of the fall, Sin is particular about both place and time scheme; she sprang from Satan's head "In Heav'n, *when* at th'Assembly, and in sight / Of all the Seraphim with thee combin'd / In bold conspiracy against Heav'n's King" (2.749–51; my emphasis). She again points to the time after the horrible incest:

> such joy thou took'st
> With me in secret, that my womb conceiv'd
> A growing burden. *Meanwhile* War arose,
> And fields were fought in Heav'n.
> (2.765–68; my emphasis)

---

[36] Addison, *Spectator*, No. 273, reprinted in *Milton: The Critical Heritage*, ed. John T. Shawcross (London: Routledge and Kegan Paul, 1970), p. 152.
[37] Joseph Summers, *The Muse's Method: An Introduction to "Paradise Lost"* (Cambridge: Harvard University Press, 1962), p. 39. Summers's term does not contradict itself—one definition of entity is "Something that has a real existence; an ENS, as distinguished from a mere function, attribute, relation, etc." (*OED* 3). In the first part of this definition, incidentally, one finds the modern prejudice against the reality of abstraction, which in the seventeenth century militated against allegory.

The monstrous birth and copulation do not occur *after* Satan's tempting speech and *before* the War in Heaven, but *over the same time*. The temporal adverbs make unmistakable that what we have here is an alternative vision of the fall, and not merely an event unfolding within the context of the fall narrated by Raphael. These alternative visions cannot occupy the same ontological space. Sin and Death are not substances; they are "accidents in a substance," and that substance is Satan and his devils.

The character Sin *is* the allegorical embodiment of Satan's turning from God; Death embodies the result of that turning, impairment of the reason and acquired physical grossness. In the *City of God* (XII, vii) Augustine comments that "defection from that which is in the highest degree, to that which is less, this is to begin to have an evil will." Sin and Death are this defection. While Satan is morally evil, Sin and Death are metaphysical evil itself, which is the privation of entity. Their actions, as Sin's narration of the fall suggests, unfold within Satan and other fallen creatures; as such they are unique in the poem's monist universe in which internal condition and external action are not otherwise separated.

Another way of saying all this is that Sin and Death are the measure of the negative ontological distance between Lucifer and Satan. To borrow mathematical terms, they function as negative numbers in a universe created with positives only. We have already seen that Milton connects sin with privation of entity; he does the same with death when discussing the first two of its four degrees in the *Christian Doctrine* (I, xii). The first degree of death entails "the loss of divine protection and favor, which results in the lessening of the majesty of the human countenance, and the degradation of the mind" (*CP* 6:394). Under the rubric of "spiritual death" come "the loss [*privatio*] of that divine grace and innate righteousness by which, in the beginning, man lived with God. . . . The loss [*privatio*] or at least the extensive darkening of that right reason, whose function it was to discern the chief good. . . . Extinction of righteousness and of liberty to do good" (*CP* 6:394–95; *Works* 15:204–6). Death in these senses is an accident in Satan's substance. The darkening of Satan's reason is evident in such moments as his assertion of self-creation and his deluded and sophistical addresses to his followers. His loss of righteousness and ability to do good is pathetically clear in his abortive gestures toward repentance. Zephon bears witness to the loss of majestic countenance in particular and his spiritual decay in general:

> Think not, revolted Spirit, thy shape the same,
> Or undiminisht brightness, to be known
> As when thou stood'st in Heav'n upright and pure;
> That Glory then, when thou no more wast good,
> Departed from thee, and thou resembl'st now
> Thy sin and place of doom obscure and foul.
>   (4.835–40)

The change in "shape" or body entails in a monist universe no less than a change in essence. By the death resulting from sin, Satan is reduced; he suffers a loss of goodness, which is, by definition, being.

In a phenomenon that negatively mirrors Christian liberty, evil kicks creatures free on the ontological ladder. This ladder might be described anachronistically as an up escalator: God makes men and angels perfect in their own ways, and both are offered greater perfection through obedience. Raphael suggests as much to Adam and Eve in his speech on the scale of nature (5.493–503). Abdiel provides a glimpse of a similar improvement for angels; he explains to Satan that God has no thought "To make us less, bent rather to exalt / Our happy state under one Head more near / United" (5.829–31).[38] Through evil, the creature jumps off the escalator and is free to fashion his own, diminished being. This is the ironic truth behind Satan's specious claim of self-creation. Sin and Death, the real nonentities, measure the distance between Lucifer and Satan, as well as that between man "Improv'd by tract of time" (5.498) and the vicious, diseased men populating the dismal chronicle of the epic's final books.

---

[38]For an interesting discussion of this passage, see Albert C. Labriola, "'Thy Humiliation Shall Exalt': The Christology of *Paradise Lost*," *Milton Studies* 15 (1981): 29–42.

That Sin and Death are indeed paradoxical embodiments of privative, metaphysical evil is clear from their ontological distance from the poem's most morally evil substantial character. Peter A. Fiore points out that Satan's *nature* is good, but adds that "This, of course, is not to assert that Satan and the fallen angels are morally good. It simply means that, in an ontological realm, that which exists is good and that which has fallen from existence is evil."[39] Satan is no "Less than Arch-Angel ruin'd" (1.593); his "form had yet not lost / All her Original brightness" (1.591–92). Without the remnants of created perfection, romantic readings of Satan as hero would be not only wrong but inexplicable. Even evil actions, as we have seen, are essentially good actions misdirected, and Satan at times reveals a capacity for good, even if dormant and ineffectual:

> That space the Evil one abstracted stood
> From his own evil, and for the time remain'd
> Stupidly good, of enmity disarm'd
> Of guile, of hate, of envy, of revenge.
> (9.463–66)[40]

As a substantial creature Satan retains shreds of goodness. It is inconceivable, on the other hand, that Sin and Death could be "abstracted from their own evil," for there would be nothing left.

It is not only their difference from the morally evil Satan that identifies Sin and Death as metaphysical evil or nonentity. Their ontological status, or rather the lack thereof, can be inferred from their appearance and their genesis. Sin is given the specious, rhetorical substantiality typical of allegorical characterization. Her body is a collection of emblems, a mismatched assortment of parts created not by God but by a creature's perverse imagination. Her role as mirror for Satan's narcissism (2.764) points to her indeterminate mutability of form and to her insubstantiality as an aspect of Satanic psychology. And if Sin's substantiality is specious, her son's is palpably illusory:

[39]Fiore, *Milton and Augustine*, p. 16.
[40]See also 1.604–9; 2.482–83; 4.42–49, 846–49.

> The other shape,
> If shape it might be call'd that shape had none
> Distinguishable in member, joint, or limb,
> Or substance might be call'd that shadow seem'd,
> For each seem'd either; black it stood as Night,
> Fierce as ten Furies, terrible as Hell,
> And shook a dreadful Dart; what seem'd his head
> The likeness of a Kingly Crown had on.
>
> (2.666–73)

This is not the angels' "soft / And uncompounded . . . Essence pure" (1.424–25). Angels are tenuous substances; Death only "seems" to be a substance, and then only at times.

The manifest insubstantiality of Death has ramifications for Sin. Death would appear to have inherited insubstantiality (and thus nonentity) from Sin. This paradoxical genetic speculation follows from Milton's Augustinian ontology of evil. Milton shares this sentiment from the *Confessions* (VII.xii): "Thus it was revealed and made visible to me that everything you [God] have made is good, and that there are no substances at all that you have not made." When we remember that Milton's angels do not reproduce (one angelological heresy that Milton does not share), we can be sure that to grant Sin and Death independent substantial existence would be to confer divine creativity on Satan. The same dilemma does not arise when we realize that Sin and Death are not substantial creatures, but the measure of deficiency in creatures.

Any argument concerning the ontology of Sin and Death must make sense of the crucial passage on their arrival in paradise:

> Meanwhile in Paradise the hellish pair
> Too soon arriv'd, *Sin* there in power before,
> Once actual, now in body, and to dwell
> Habitual habitant; behind her *Death*
> Close following pace for pace.
>
> (10.585–89)

The description of Sin as "in body" does not point to substantial existence.[41] Sin is potential through human fallibility ("in power"), it is actually committed ("actual"), and it affects the sinner by depriving him or her of grace, righteousness, freedom, beauty, and other perfections ("in body"). Sin and Death are "in body" because they become accidents *in* man's substance after the fall; they have no existence outside the fallen creature, only in his or her turning from God and the resulting spiritual deficiency and physical mortality.

Whatever Milton's metaphysics, Sin and Death appear to be all too unpleasantly real in *Paradise Lost*. In arguing for their nonreality, I mean to argue not that the privative evil that they represent is without effect, but rather that the effects apparently attributable to characters named Sin and Death are in fact attributable to other, "real" agents. The gruesome drama of Book 2 presents in a different metaphysical register the same events that unfold at the end of Book 5. Evidence of Sin and Death's material activity turns out in every case to be suspect. They open the massive gates of Hell for Satan, but Satan is in fact allowed to leave Hell not by them but by the same "will / And high permission of all-ruling Heaven" that allows him to escape the burning lake (1.211–12). The spontaneous self-opening of Heaven's gates (7.205–7) casts further doubt on the apparent material agency of Sin and Death in opening their gates. Sin speaks of the bridge across Chaos as Satan's work, not her own: "O Parent, these are thy magnific deeds, / Thy Trophies, which thou view'st as not thine own, / Thou art thir Author and prime Architect" (10.354–56). And although the bridge seems to be substantial, MacCaffrey observes that "it is impossible to accept the bridge from Hell quite as unreservedly as 'real,' as the cosmography of Book III."[42] Milton seems to ascribe real material agency to Sin and Death when he notes that at their passing "the blasted Stars lookt wan, / And Planets, Planet-strook, real Eclipse / Then suffer'd" (10.412–14). But we learn shortly afterward that the stellar and terrestrial changes that follow man's fall are effected by God and his

[41]For an argument that it does, see Gallagher, "'Real or Allegoric,'" p. 324.
[42]MacCaffrey, "*Paradise Lost*" *as Myth*, p. 199.

angels (10.651–706) and not by Sin and Death, as Quilligan acutely observes.[43] The allegorical characters express rather than cause these changes. As nonentities, Sin and Death cannot create or move anything; at most they measure the degree to which free creatures undo created perfection. Thus Milton does not "give them any real employment, or ascribe to them any material agency," as Johnson complains, and as other poets do with their allegorical characters. Milton clearly divides the derivative and deficient ontological realm of Sin and Death from the main plane of reality in *Paradise Lost*.

Additional Allegory: Chaos and the Limbo of Vanity

I have explained the propriety of Milton's allegorization of Sin and Death in terms of their ontological deficiency. I would like to suggest briefly the ways in which other instances of Milton's allegory confirm my argument. The "horror Plum'd" (4.989) that sits on Satan's crest and the "Victory . . . Eagle-wing'd" (6.762–63) in the Son's chariot are no more than rhetorical flourishes; they have allusive and figurative weight, but they are not characters. The court of Chaos and the Limbo of Vanity are more important exercises in allegory, and both, though in ways different from Sin and Death, are "less real" than other characters and places in the epic.

The character Chaos, inseparable from the realm he personifies, is surrounded by a Hesiodic mythic-allegoric court of Night, Orcus, Ades, Demogorgon, Rumor, Chance, Tumult, Confusion, and Discord (2.959–67). Being material, Chaos is not metaphysical evil. Nor is he even morally evil. We should note that, despite his apparent eagerness to aid Satan, we witness Chaos speaking *only* with Satan. This ineffectual and pliable figure does respond immediately to the word of the Son at creation.[44]

---

[43]Quilligan, *Milton's Spenser*, p. 126.
[44]Regina Schwartz has argued recently that Chaos is hostile to God. Impatient with those who argue from the *Christian Doctrine* for Chaos's neutrality or goodness, Schwartz concludes that "despite [Milton's] doctrine of a good chaos, his

But there is another way in which he is "less real" than creation and creatures. In his nonworld, form and matter are not combined; without stabilizing form, qualities are fluid and "things" cannot sustain themselves: "For hot, cold, moist, and dry, four Champions fierce / Strive here for Maistry, and to battle bring / Thir embryon atoms" (2.898–900). In creation, Milton writes, God adds to prime matter forms, "which, incidentally, are themselves material" (*CP* 6:308). As the state of matter before the addition of forms, Chaos is less real than created substance. Metaphysical evil is the negation of substance; Chaos is the state of matter before substance *as we experience it* comes into being. Thus Milton describes it in terms associated with gestation, as "the *Womb* of nature" in which the elements are "in thir *pregnant* causes mixt" (2.911, 913; my emphasis). Satan, with his characteristic perversity, refers to Chaos as "abortive" (2.441). Chaos is more real than Sin and Death (because it is material), but less real than creation (because it lacks forms). The character and his realm exist on the border between being and not-being. Again, Milton's thought echoes that of Augustine, who describes the first matter in the

---

poem depicts a very different one: a region that is 'waste and wild' and an allegorical figure who claims that 'havoc and spoil and ruin are my gain'" (*Remembering and Repeating: Biblical Creation in "Paradise Lost"* [Cambridge: Cambridge University Press, 1988], p. 10). But in order to arrive at an evil chaos, Schwartz must bracket out not only Milton's prose ("logic has always been a limited guide into the realm of symbols" [p. 33]), but also parts of *Paradise Lost*. If Chaos complains of God's encroachments on his realm in creation, he is no more happy with the stony bridge from Hell to Earth: "on either side / Disparted *Chaos* over-built exclaim'd, / And with rebounding surge the bars assail'd, / That scorned his indignation" (10.415–18). This passage demonstrates the extent to which Chaos's temporary alliance with Satan in Book 2 is based on the Anarch's misunderstanding of evil. As John Rumrich argues in a forthcoming essay, evil in Milton is a principle of inverted order, not of chaotic indeterminacy. Milton successfully walks the fine line between the requirements of theodicy and of narrative motivation when he (1) spends more time on Chaos's reaction to God's creation than on Chaos's reaction to Sin and Death's parodic creation and (2) shows the inherently, if reluctantly, pliant Chaos speaking only with Satan and not with God. Theology tells us that there is no antecedent or background for Satan's first sin, but in narratives we look for motivation. Chaos serves in the text as a mirage of evil; the illusory sense of a fund of evil existing prior to Satan's sin can satisfy our instinctive demand that actions be motivated, a demand frustrated by the mystery of radical evil. But like all mirages, the evil Chaos disappears when we get too close to it.

Confessions (XII, viii) as "almost nothing." Satan calls Chaos "unreal" (10.471), though of course we must take his observations with a grain of salt. In any event, the unformed matter of Chaos represents an order of reality different from creation, and again Milton uses the allegorical mode to signal the difference.

The Limbo of Vanity, significantly, borders on Chaos, and as a "windy Sea of Land" it shares Chaos's confusion of elements (3.440). The keynote to this anti-Catholic set piece is dissolution. Fools float to Limbo, dissolved into "Aereal vapors" (3.445). Limbo attracts those who turn to emptiness rather than to God's perfection, and who are punished not with Hell but with ignominious disintegration (there is an interesting parallel between Limbo and Dante's vestibule of hell):

> All th'unaccomplisht works of Nature's hand,
> Abortive, monstrous, or unkindly mixt,
> Dissolv'd on Earth, fleet hither, and in vain,
> Till final dissolution, wander here.
>
> (3.455–58)

Limbo is a *figurative* counterpart to Chaos, receiving creatures who fall back into nothingness. In its essential figurativeness, Limbo is unique in *Paradise Lost* and does not, after all, require a defense of its allegorical presentation. Unlike Sin and Death and the realm of Chaos, the Limbo of Vanity is not an object of Milton's belief. If this marvelous flight of fancy requires any rationale, it is to be found in the poet's delight in the flight of Ariosto's Astolfo to the moon and in the pamphleteer's savage and polemical wit.

I have outlined a causal relationship between a movement from realism to nominalism and a decline in the status of allegory, and I have argued that Milton's use of allegory reflects this decline. My argument does not depend on viewing Milton as a nominalist, which he emphatically is not. The author of the *Areopagitica* could never assent to Hobbes's proposition that "the first truths were arbitrarily made by those that first of all imposed names upon things."[45] But Milton is interested in the questions of ontology that occupied his contemporaries; his idiosyncratic and consistent monist solution tells us that. It is also certain that he participates in the movement of his century by assigning a smaller and smaller role to allegory. I have proposed that the response of the realist Milton to the decline in the status of universals and the concomitant decline in the status of allegorical characters was to use allegory to present an accident that truly has no ontological weight. Evil is the ultimate accident. While mercy, justice, wisdom, and so on are accidents in particular men, to a Christian realist they are universal entities created by God and essential to creation as a whole. Evil, on the other hand, is radically accidental, essential neither to any creature nor to God's creation. If his contemporaries doubted the reality of the universals represented by allegorical agents, Milton would give them allegorical agents that represented the unreal. They paradoxically embody the nothingness of evil, and not the universals that inhere in creatures.

Thus Milton's allegory of Sin and Death is not haphazard; it corresponds to his Augustinian ontology of evil and comments on the fate of allegory itself. Rejecting the promiscuous use of allegory authorized by contemporary precedent, and with which he himself experimented in the Trinity manuscript, Milton uses allegory in his mimetic epic to point to the ontological deficiency of evil. He reserves allegorical status for the paradoxical embodiments of metaphysical evil, which is the negation rather than the expression of substance. Johnson and the rest were right to recognize ontological and generic inconsistency in *Paradise Lost*. What they did not recognize is that the contrast between the mimetic and allegorical modes is itself consistent with the ontological gulf between the goodness of entity and the nonentity of evil. In the next chapter, I will examine how the devils change as they migrate from one pole toward the other.

[45]*De Corpore: The Elements of Philosophy concerning Body* I, iii, 8, in *The English Works of Thomas Hobbes*, ed. Sir William Molesworth, 11 vols. (London: John Bohn, 1839–45), 1:36.

~ 7

To Shadowy Types from Truth:
Satan's Mechanist Descent

The devils' degrading metamorphosis in Book 10 of *Paradise Lost* is both a concentrated instance of and a figure for Milton's treatment of their ontology. As Satan chose to to appear in a snake, so he is transformed into a snake, "punisht in the shape he sinn'd / According to his doom" (10.516–17). Satan and his followers come to embody their own debased and brutish ontology. But what makes the metamorphosis episode so apt an emblem of Milton's practice is what follows:

> Thus were they plagu'd
> And worn with Famine long, and ceaseless hiss,
> *Till thir lost shape, permitted, they resum'd,*
> Yearly enjoin'd, some say, to undergo
> This annual humbling.
> (10.572–76; my emphasis)

Assumed ontology and true ontology stand in dialectical tension. Milton alternately presents the devils as surrounding themselves with a Cartesian or Hobbesian space, asserting a realm in which God's metaphysics do not apply, and as being forcibly recalled to the monist truth. He at once illustrates that the Cartesian and Hobbesian spaces are prisons and that any vision of reality except his own Christian monism is an illusion. The dialectic from Satan's perspective is similar. Satan asserts ontological error and at the same time realizes the error, as intuition challenges rationalization and sophistry. Henry More writes of "Aereal Daemons," including devils, that *"Platonists, Aristoteleans, Stoicks, Epicureans,* and whatever other sects and humors are on the Earth, may in likelihood be met with there, *so far as that estate will permit*; though they cannot doubt of all things we doubt of here."[1] Satan and his followers can assert false philosophy finally only so far as their essences will permit. To maintain their error, they struggle to doubt things that they cannot truly doubt.

Thus the devils' descent into false ontology and false epistemology to be explored in this chapter is provisional and illusory only. In ontological as well as in martial terms they seek "Divided Empire," but God will "of his Kingdom lose no part / By [their] revolt." Pockets of ontological resistance are reassimilated into the kingdom of Milton's monism.

Heaven's Pavement and Infernal Dregs

Heaven, like everything in Milton's monist universe, is material. The only matter for debate is the degree of its materiality. Heaven and Earth, like angels and men, are ontologically continuous. Heaven's shape is "undetermin'd square or round" (2.1048). Alastair Fowler has pointed out that the "mysterious integration of spirit and matter in man's nature was often symbolized by the squaring of the circle."[2] The indeterminacy of Heaven's geometry emblematizes its simultaneously spiritual and material nature. It is Satan and his cronies who attempt to divide the indivisible, as Sin separates God's "Quadrature" from Satan's "Orbicular World" (10.381).

[1]Henry More, *Immortality of the Soul* (1659), rpt. in *A Collection of Several Philosophical Writings,* 2 vols. (1662; facs. New York: Garland, 1978), p. 180 (III, ix, 2); my emphasis.
[2]*Paradise Lost,* ed. Alastair Fowler (London: Longman, 1971), p. 527 (note for 10.381).

Like all material things, Heaven takes up space. Again, Milton agrees with Hobbes: if something is nowhere it is nothing. Abdiel's night-long flight from Satan's mount to the mount of God underlines the physical vastness of Heaven (6.1–4). The topography of this vast space provides the model for Earth's: "For Earth hath this variety from Heav'n / Of pleasure situate in Hill and Dale" (6.640–41).

Michael Murrin has argued ingeniously that the description of Heaven remains opaque, that its relation to earthly reality is undetermined, because its terms refer to each other and not to earthly reality:

> The system is self-enclosed. Armor may always flash diamonds and gold, the terms may be used consistently, but we have no idea what these terms might mean outside their context. Heavenly terms refer to *each other* and build up a complete world, but one we cannot enter. If other artists created self-contained models, at least they allowed us to understand the vocabulary and did not shut us out. Here it is rather as if we were asked to interpret an unknown language. We have no means of gauging Milton's language, no point of comparison with our experience.[3]

Murrin perceptively analyzes the "otherness" of Heaven. But one need not conclude with Murrin that Milton employs self-canceling images in order to signal that Heaven is different in kind from Earth. The strategy is appropriate for differences in degree as well as kind and can just as well point to a material reality beyond the limitations of our "weaker sight." As men must work their digestions up to an angelic diet, so they must work their senses up to celestial percepts. The material of Heaven may "surmount the reach of human sense" without transcending materiality.

That this is what Milton has in mind is clear from Raphael's description of the devils' ripping open the "soil" of Heaven and seeing underneath

---

[3]Michael Murrin, *The Allegorical Epic: Essays in Its Rise and Decline* (Chicago: University of Chicago Press, 1980), p. 161.

> Th'originals of Nature in thir crude
> Conception; Sulphurous and Nitrous Foam
> They found, they mingl'd, and with subtle Art,
> Concocted and adusted they reduc'd
> To blackest grain, and into store convey'd:
> Part hidden veins digg'd up (*nor hath this Earth
> Entrails unlike*) of Mineral and Stone,
> Whereof to found thir Engines.
>
> (6.511–18; my emphasis)

Here Milton does not "shut us out"; instead he offers a "point of comparison with our experience." Sulphur and nitrogen, earthly and earthy elements, replace amarant, seas of Jasper, and "seeming" Carbuncle. Milton underlines the materiality of Heaven with the aside "nor hath this Earth / Entrails unlike," a variant of a favorite formula, "to compare great things with small." The effect of the figure is here complicated by the disjunction between the experiences of Raphael's audience and Milton's. The figure is normally employed to describe the unknown by reference to the known, and thus Raphael employs it with Adam. The elements beneath Heaven's soil become known to Adam as Raphael describes them, and they are used to point to the nature of the still unknown, or what exists beneath Adam's feet. For the reader the situation is reversed. We have direct experience of Earth's crude elements, but in the terms of the topos they are the unknown to be validated by the known heavenly elements. The apparently casual aside is startling. The crude elements beneath Earth do not shadow the unknown elements of Heaven and make them explicable, rather the very real elements of Heaven make the entrails of Earth explicable.

The materiality of Heaven makes up only one aspect of its monist essence; in spotlighting the "round," one must not forget the "square." The substance of Milton's Heaven is spiritual and animate as well as material. In the ontological continuum, it lies toward the spiritual pole, thus fitting its "more refined, more spirituous, more pure" inhabitants. The matter of Heaven is revealed to be, like the matter of the Son's chariot, "itself

instinct with spirit" (6.752). The animation and spiritual nature
of Heaven's substance is particularly evident at the moment
before creation when the chariots accompanying the Son

> came forth
> Spontaneous, for within them Spirit liv'd,
> Attendant on thir Lord: Heav'n op'n'd wide
> Her ever-during Gates, Harmonious sound
> On golden Hinges moving, to let forth
> The King of Glory.
>
> (7.203–8)

Chariots drive themselves, and gates open themselves. The ma-
terialized spirit or spiritualized matter is ready to spill out into
our universe, the matter of which will be less spiritual, but
spiritual nonetheless.

Milton's Heaven excludes the immaterial at one end of the
conventional ontological spectrum and the inorganic at the
other; the angels' world, like the angels themselves, is material
and organic. As elsewhere in the poem, Milton associates this
ontological continuity with eating:

> Forthwith from dance to sweet repast [the angels] turn
> Desirous; all in Circles as they stood,
> Tables are set, and on a sudden pil'd
> With Angels' Food, and rubied Nectar flows:
> In Pearl, in Diamond, and massy Gold,
> Fruit of delicious vines, the growth of Heav'n.
> On flow'rs repos'd, and with fresh flow'rets crown'd,
> They eat, they drink, and in communion sweet
> Quaff immortality and joy.
>
> (5.630–38)

Milton assimilates the inorganic to the organic here with subtle
skill. If it is hard to sort out the syntax (are "fruit" and "growth"
additional objects of the phrase "piled with" or in apposition to
the objects "food" and "nectar"?), the passage reads very easily
as a list: food, rubied nectar, pearl, diamond, massy gold, fruit,
growth. The move from plant to mineral is mediated nicely by

the term "rubied nectar," but then the orderly descent is complicated by the appearance of "fruit." The interlace continues
with the appearance of "flowers" on the heels of "growth";
coming only 150 lines after the great speech on the one first
matter, where the flower as the summit of the plant gives rise to
the spirits and reason, the reference here suggests the continuity of the mental with the organic and the supposedly inorganic. This reading is confirmed by the next lines; among
the flowers the angels drink "immortality and joy." This passage reveals vividly a poet's response to the problem of articulating monism for a dualist audience.[4]

Milton employs the same delicate interlace to describe the
subcelestial world, which, like its model Heaven, is a great organism, its apparently inert objects springing from "kindly
heat," gestation, and birth. Milton presents the Garden where
"Trees wept odorous Gums and Balm":

> Another side, [lie] umbrageous Grots and Caves
> Of cool recess, o'er which the mantling Vine
> Lays forth her purple Grape, and gently creeps
> Luxuriant; meanwhile murmuring waters fall
> Down the slope hills, disperst, or in a Lake,
> That to the fringed Bank with Myrtle crown'd,
> Her crystal mirror holds, unite thir streams.
> The Birds thir choir apply; airs, vernal airs,
> Breathing the smell of field and grove, attune
> The trembling leaves.
>
> (4.257–66)

Milton borrows from conventional poetic tropes for the weep-
ing trees and murmuring waters, but he complicates and literalizes these figures with the interlace in the passage on the
birds' song. From the birds come airs, which are at once (or
rather in quick succession) songs, their breath, and spring
winds. Their song animates the wind, but at the same time the

---

[4]Milton continues this interweaving in the immediately succeeding lines where
he writes of "Night with Clouds exhal'd / From that high mount of God"
(5.642–43).

wind is animated by the field and grove. The airs that are at
once the breath of birds, their songs, and songs of spring meet
the airs "breathed" by the landscape. The passage highlights
the continuity of the bird with vegetation at the expense of the
distinction between sentient fauna and the merely vegetative
flora.

The longest and most intricate interlace of the sort I have
been describing can be found in Adam and Eve's morning
hymn (5.153–209). This hymn, modeled on Psalm 148, calls
upon all creation, from the angels to the planets to earth and its
inhabitants, to praise the Lord.[5] In expanding upon his source,
Milton introduces language that confers upon objects normally
considered inert the ability to act:

> Thou Sun, of this great World both Eye and Soul,
> Acknowledge him thy Greater, sound his praise.
>
> Ye Mists and Exhalations that now rise
> From Hill or steaming Lake, dusky or grey,
> Till the Sun paint your fleecy skirts with Gold,
> In honor to the World's great Author rise.
>
> His praise ye Winds, that from four Quarters blow,
> Breathe soft or loud; and wave your tops, ye Pines,
> With every Plant, in sign of Worship wave.
> (5.171–72, 185–88, 192–94)

The hymn ends with a passage tying the speakers and the
topography of the garden together in song:

> Witness if I be silent, Morn or Even,
> To Hill, or Valley, Fountain, or fresh shade
> Made vocal by my Song, and taught his praise.
> (202–4)

The landscape here is called upon to echo human song, not
passively, but rather as one voice responding to another. In this

[5]For psalms in Milton, see Mary Ann Radzinowicz, *Milton's Epics and the Book of Psalms* (Princeton: Princeton University Press, 1989).

hymn and elsewhere in the poem Milton turns the pathetic fallacy on its head—it is no longer an illusion to speak of nature sharing thoughts and emotions.

It is one thing to acknowledge that Milton thought of all creation as organic, but it is more difficult for us with our presuppositions to make sense of Milton's writing as if mental activity is distributed throughout organic nature. Hans Jonas has written that "The organic even in its lowest forms prefigures mind, and . . . mind even on its highest reaches remains part of the organic. The latter half of the contention, but not the former, is in tune with modern belief; the former, but not the latter, was in tune with ancient belief." Jonas argues that freedom is the primary attribute distinguishing organism from the inorganic: "One expects to encounter the term [freedom] in the area of mind and will, and not before: but if mind is prefigured in the organic from the beginning, then freedom is. And indeed our contention is that even metabolism, the basic level of all organic existence, exhibits it: that it is itself the first form of freedom."[6] While distinguishing the freedom of simple organisms from conscious human freedom, Jonas insists that it is the ontological foundation of human freedom.

Jonas's conception of organism is not identical with Milton's, but with Jonas Milton ascribes to matter attributes we are used to encountering only when we discuss "mind and will." Freedom is as central to Milton's conception of the one first substance as it is to Jonas's conception of organism. In *Paradise Lost* it is not only sentient creatures who choose their mode of being; Milton's monism extends this choice to matter as well. At creation the spirit of God hovered over the water and

> vital virtue infus'd, and vital warmth
> Throughout the fluid Mass, but downward purg'd
> The black tartareous cold Infernal dregs
> Adverse to life; then founded, then conglob'd
> Like things to like.
>
> (7.236–40)

---

[6]Hans Jonas, *The Phenomenon of Life: Toward a Philosophical Biology* (Chicago: University of Chicago Press, 1966), pp. 1, 3.

Here matter is shaped by the hand of God, but after this creation matter achieves a measure of autonomy. Belial counsels against renewed war against Heaven, because even if

> all Hell should rise
> With blackest Insurrection, to confound
> Heav'n's purest Light, yet our great Enemy
> All incorruptible would on his Throne
> Sit unpolluted, and th'Ethereal mould
> Incapable of stain would soon expel
> Her mischief, and purge off the baser fire
> Victorious.
>
> (2.135–42)

The roles have changed. God is now passive, or rather impassive. It is the stuff or the "Earth" of Heaven, the "Ethereal *mould*," that now acts to expel the stain of the "baser" stuff of Hell. Similarly, after the devils fall from Heaven, "Heav'n rejoic'd, and soon repair'd / Her mural breach, returning whence it roll'd" (6.878–79). When Eve falls, "Earth felt the wound, and Nature from her seat / Sighing through all her Works gave signs of woe, / That all was lost" (9.782–84). The continuity of the chain of being described by Raphael in Book 5 suggests that we take these locutions as more than figurative.

The reactions of the matter of Heaven and Earth are moral and ontological simultaneously; in this they mirror the choices of the poem's rational creatures. Moral choices in *Paradise Lost* have implications for choices about where one wishes to be placed along the continuum of the one first matter. Martin Luther writes that "blasphemy against Christ is immediately followed by a counterfeit reality," and from the time of his sin Satan desperately explores false ontological models in his futile attempt to prevent the consequences of his sin from penetrating his consciousness.[7] In the following sections I will examine the ontological dimensions of the devils' sin.

[7]*Lectures on Isaiah*, in *Luther's Works*, gen. eds. Jaroslav Pelikan and Helmut T. Lehmann, 55 vols. (St. Louis: Concordia; Philadelphia: Fortress, 1955–76), 16:65. I owe this reference to Georgia B. Christopher, *Milton and the Science of the Saints* (Princeton: Princeton University Press, 1982), p. 84.

Infernal Cartesianism

Like Descartes, we will begin with epistemology. His separation of mental and physical events (and then substances) is at
odds with Milton's monism. As we saw in Chapter 1, Cartesian
dualism is more radical and absolute than the familiar Neoplatonic dualism of the Renaissance, in which the outer expresses the inner (see, e.g., Spenser's *Fowre Hymnes*). Descartes
replaces form and matter, spirit and body, with *res cogitans* and
res extensa, a dichotomy analogous to but not identical with the
others. The distinction is made absolute, and the province of
the former is restricted to mind. Descartes argues that one can
"distinguish without difficulty what belongs to itself, i.e. to an
intellectual nature, from what belongs to the body."[8] He divides nature, draining visible phenomena of invisible substance. The attraction of this philosophy for Satan and his followers in Book 1 is obvious. Formerly angels of light, they are
now darkened and disfigured. Satan's first impulse is to deny
the connection of inner and outer, the connection affirmed by
Neoplatonist poets such as Spenser and dismantled by Descartes; Satan claims to retain his "fixt mind," "Though chang'd
in outward luster" (1.97). In Cartesian terms, Satan admits al-
teration in his *res extensa*, but denies it in his *res cogitans*.
Beelzebub ratifies Satan's misperception: "the mind and spirit
remains / Invincible, and vigor soon returns, / Though all our
Glory extinct" (1.139–141). Such distinctions make sense in a
Cartesian universe, but not in a Neoplatonically dualist or Miltonically monist one. From these latter perspectives, the devils
attempt to deny the only logical complement of their grossen-
ing physical nature, the debilitation of spirit. Ironically, the
devils' speeches reveal the disease of mind as well as of body.

Satan later affirms the Cartesian "error" in claiming to have
"A mind not to be chang'd by Place or Time. / *The mind is its own
place*, and in itself / Can make a Heav'n of Hell, a Hell of
Heav'n" (1.253–55; my emphasis). Satan's confidence in the
power of the independent mind is belied by the narrator's

[8]"Synopsis of the Meditations," in Cottingham 2:9.

dwelling on his gross body moments before: Satan flew from the burning Lake "incumbent on the dusky Air / That felt unusual weight" (1.226–27) and landed on "the sole / Of unblest feet" (1.237–38). The manifest deterioration of his physical nature causes Satan to turn to a separable mind or spirit as his essential identity. The solution suggests Descartes: "I knew I was a substance whose whole essence or nature is simply to think, and *which does not require any place*, or depend on any material thing, in order to exist. Accordingly this 'I'—that is, the soul [*l'Ame*] by which I am what I am—is entirely distinct from my body, and indeed is easier to know than the body, and would not fail to be whatever it is, even if the body did not exist" (my emphasis).[9] Descartes argues the irrelevance of body to mind. Cartesian dualism, with its divorce of the "self" from the body, seems for the moment a more serviceable philosophy for Satan's predicament than is Milton's monism, in which "the whole man is the soul, and the soul the man: a body . . . or individual substance, animated, sensitive, and rational" (*CP* 6:318). If Satan were to accept this, he would have to admit his essential, not merely his external, deterioration, as he in fact does later in Book 4.[10]

Satan thus turns to a dualism resembling Descartes's to mitigate his fall, but in reality this "cure" compounds the disease. Trusting in the distinct and inviolate nature of mind, he is ironically trapped in the knot with body. His "dualist descent" has a distinctly Cartesian flavor. By choosing to "imbrute" him-

---

[9]Cottingham 1:127 (*Discourse on the Method* IV).
[10]Belial is the first devil to recognize his metaphysical predicament. He argues that a possible result of continued war might be annihilation:

> that must be our cure,
> To be no more; sad cure; for who would lose,
> Though full of pain, this intellectual being,
> Those thoughts that wander through Eternity,
> To perish rather, swallow'd up and lost
> In the wide womb of uncreated night,
> Devoid of sense and motion?
>
> (2.145–51)

Belial admits that their punishment extends to mind; the "intellectual being" suffers. Moreover, he does not separate mind and body. "Sense and motion" are attributes not of an extraneous shell, but of the "intellectual being" itself.

self in cormorant, tiger, frog, and snake, he enacts a parody of
Cartesian dualism. The relation between Satan and snake fits
Ryle's image for the relationship of *res cogitans* and *res extensa*,
the "ghost in the machine":

> in at his Mouth
> The Devil enter'd, and his brutal sense
> In heart or head, possessing soon inspir'd
> With act intelligential.
>
> (9.187–90)

Perhaps the narrator's indecision as to the manner of Satan's
speaking in the serpent, "with Serpent Tongue / Organic, or
impulse of vocal Air" (9.529–31), is meant to point to the special problem of dualism. The uncertainty as to the manner of
the operation of an artificial Satan/snake dualism might reflect
the mystery of the operation of metaphysical spirit/body dualism.

But to be fair to Descartes, and not to overstate my case,
Satan's Cartesianism is neither coherent nor consistent. It resembles more closely the specter of Cartesianism haunting the
minds of the Cambridge Platonists than it does the thought of
Descartes himself. Satan's dualism is a jerry-built refuge, not a
rigorous intellectual edifice. The God he creates in his addresses
to Eve is reminiscent not of Descartes's rational God but of his
deceiving demon. A God who forbids creatures to eat the fruit
he wants them to eat could, unlike Descartes's, make 2 + 2 at
once 4 and 5. Moreover, despite his insistence on the gulf between mind and body, Descartes suggests a closer union between
them than Satan admits: "Nature also teaches me . . . that I am
not merely present in my body as a sailor is present in a ship, but
that I am very closely joined and, as it were, intermingled with it,
so that I and the body form a unit."[11] Descartes concedes,
moreover, that his philosophy separates an experiential unity.
Satan will feel this also, as much as he tries to ignore it in
emphasizing the separation. He will come to see that he carries

---

[11]Cottingham 2:56 ("Sixth Meditation").

hell in his own mind, and that flight from Pandemonium brings no relief.

Satan's dualism cannot survive its clash with experience. As More says, spirits can hold philosophies only "so far as that estate will permit." Satan in practice cannot separate himself from his "proper shape," his mind from his body. He can assume a beautiful body to deceive Uriel, but his "proper shape" reasserts itself on Mt. Niphates. His dualist disgrace is blasted by the integrity of goodness; as the toad Satan sits by Eve,

> Him thus intent *Ithuriel* with his Spear
> Touch'd lightly; for no falsehood can endure
> Touch of Celestial temper, but returns
> Of force to its own likeness: up he starts
> Discover'd and surpris'd.
>
> (4.810–14)

There is an "own likeness" between interior and exterior, which Satan has tried to escape through dualism. His captors are a philosophically didactic duo. Ithuriel reveals to Satan the unity of his debased spirit and body, and Zephon reminds him of the unitary beauty of goodness. When Satan "Virtue in her shape how lovely, saw, and pin'd / His loss; but chiefly to find here observ'd / His lustre visibly impair'd" (4.848–50), he confronts the error of his dualist challenge to God's monism.

Infernal Hobbesianism

Descartes derives his metaphysics from an epistemology; Hobbes builds an epistemology on a metaphysics. Milton's contemporaries, and particularly the Cambridge Platonists, saw Hobbes's monist metaphysics as founded on one-half of Descartes's increasingly suspect dualism. As the Democritans took, according to Cudworth, the "dead Carcase or Skeleton" of the ancient philosophy,[12] so Hobbes took the dead half of Des-

---

[12]Cudworth, *The True Intellectual System of the Universe* (London, 1678; facs. rpt. Stuttgart-Bad Cannstatt: Friedrich Frommann, 1964), p. 51 (1, xlii).

cartes's radical dualism, and so Satan takes matter in motion for all reality. Why? Primarily because the intermittent reliance on a quasi-Cartesian dualism cannot hide from the devils their internal deterioration. They have become at the fall more grossly corporeal. Physical power they undoubtedly have, and as a result they come to view all power as physical.

Milton emphasizes the intractable bulk of the fallen angels:

> Thus Satan talking to his nearest Mate
> With Head up-lift above the wave, and Eyes
> That sparkling blaz'd, his other Parts besides
> Prone on the Flood, extended long and large
> Lay floating many a rood, in bulk as huge
> As whom the Fables name of monstrous size.
>
> (1.192–97)

Satan enters the poem as "leviathan" (1.201), perhaps in a allusion to Hobbes's masterpiece.[13] The character's immensity weighs down these lines; he is "long and large . . . huge . . . of monstrous size." This passage contrasts sharply with the first description of an unfallen angel, Uriel. Through the eyes of the grossly material Satan we see

> a glorious Angel stand,
> The same whom *John* saw also in the Sun:
> His back was turn'd, but not his brightness hid;
> Of beaming sunny Rays, a golden tiar
> Circl'd his Head, nor less his Locks behind
> Illustrious on his Shoulders fledge with wings
> Lay waving round.
>
> (3.622–28)

The effect is one of light and lightness. The hair plays weightlessly. The body is not opaque; inner purity shines through outward form. A further contrast can be drawn between the flights of Satan (1.221–27) and Uriel (3.555–56).

[13]Samuel Mintz provides examples of the use of "Leviathan" as a name for Hobbes by his contemporaries in *The Hunting of Leviathan: Seventeenth-Century Reactions to the Materialism and Moral Philosophy of Thomas Hobbes* (Cambridge: Cambridge University Press, 1962), pp. 55–57.

Like Anne Conway, Milton considered matter to be congealed spirit, and the effects of advanced congealing are seen in Satan's outward form: "his face / Deep scars of Thunder had intrencht, and care / Sat on his faded cheek" (1.600–602). The entrenchment of scars on Satan's countenance testifies to some loss of the essential ductility of angels; former tenuousness has hardened into rigidity. This congealing reaches within as Satan's heart "hardens" with his moral deterioration (1.572). Satan's literal hardening is the monist complement of the figurative scriptural trope of the hardened heart. Milton characteristically literalizes a spiritual metaphor, according to the monist metaphysics that denies any fundamental separation between spiritual and physical phenomena.

The particularly close relationship between Satan's contraction of gross materiality and his spiritual sin is suggested by a "loaded" term with which Milton describes him at the moment of his fall. Upon witnessing the Son's exaltation, Satan is "*fraught* / With envy against the Son of God" (5.661–62; my emphasis). Again as he approaches Earth (2.1054), we glimpse him carrying a cargo of sin, which weighs down and incorporates the airy lightness of his formerly angelic essence.

The materialization of Milton's devils differs in its essentials from the transformation of fallen angels in the leading literary and artistic tradition, in which Satan and his crew were presented as descending into foul bodies.[14] While this convention reflects Paul's moral dualism, it is essentially figurative and is employed even by those who assert the immateriality of devils. Milton transforms the convention. His devils are not ugly; they are only less beautiful and more material than they once were. The horns and hooves of hoary convention were figurative punishments imposed from without; the bulky materiality of Milton's devils is real and ultimately self-chosen. Milton altered the convention because it did not fit his monism and therefore

[14]For the literary tradition, see John Steadman, "Archangel to Devil: The Background of Satan's Metamorphosis," *Modern Language Quarterly* 21 (1960): 321–35; this article is revised and reprinted in *Milton's Epic Characters: Image and Idol* (Chapel Hill: University of North Carolina Press, 1968), pp. 281–97. For the artistic tradition see Roland Mushat Frye, *Milton's Imagery and the Visual Arts: Iconographic Tradition in the Epic Poems* (Princeton: Princeton University Press, 1978), pp. 43–145.

did not pass the test of literal truth. The devils' migration toward the corporeal pole of the matter-spirit continuum does
meet this test. They are not trapped in an alien substance as in
the tradition of axiological dualism; instead, they modify their
parcel of the one substance—they congeal. In turning from
spirit to matter, they migrate toward the pole at which Hobbes
found all reality.[15]

To express this migration Milton turns in part to the imagery
of disease and leaking that he developed in the antiprelatical
tracts of the early 1640s. In those tracts, as we saw, the violation
of bodily integrity was figured in the leaking of fluid. The zeal
of the bishops issues in wens and tumors; it leaks out and forms
a hardened crust on the outside of the body. After his sin, Satan
also suffers a loss of bodily integrity, when he is wounded in the
War in Heaven (6.327–34). In *Paradise Lost* evil, and thus downward ontological movement, is associated with leaking, excretion, and purging—in other words, with the opposite of assimilation. Goodness and upward ontological movement are associated, we have seen, with digestion. The devils never eat in
Paradise Lost; food, like sexual intercourse, is denied to them.
In *Paradise Regained* the Son tells Satan that "lying is thy suste-
nance, thy food" (*PR* 1.429), and the only meal the devils are
given in *Paradise Lost* is the apples of Sodom:

>   they fondly thinking to allay
> Thir appetite with gust, instead of Fruit
> Chew'd bitter Ashes, which th'offended taste
> With spattering noise rejected: oft they assay'd,
> Hunger and thirst constraining, drugg'd as oft,
> With hatefullest disrelish writh'd thir jaws
> With soot and cinders fill'd.
>
>   (10.564–70)

The digestive and immune systems of Milton's universe act

---

[15]The congealing of Satan's body does not contradict Milton's belief in the
nonentity of evil. The nonentity of evil is not expressed in decreasing
corporeality—spiritualization of substance as we have seen is connected to
moral purity. Instead, the nonentity of evil is expressed in the negative ontological distance between Lucifer and Satan, as suggested in Chapter 6. His
substance becomes less free and active, not less corporeal.

inexorably. Those who obey are sublimed and rarefied. Those who disobey are purged and excreted. Every significant decision is ontological and metabolic as well as moral.

If knowledge is as food, you are what you think. Trapped in the reification of his Hobbesian error, Satan's substance becomes rigid. The voluntary nature of the change reveals itself in this picture of Mammon:

> ev'n in Heav'n his looks and thoughts
> Were always downward bent, admiring more
> The riches of Heav'n's pavement, trodd'n Gold,
> Than aught divine or holy else enjoy'd.
>   (1.680–83)

We glimpse here Mammon choosing the elements of his new being. He looks neither laterally to creatures of his own essence nor upward toward the goal of obedience, ontological ascent. He scours the ground for the more material end of the ontological spectrum.

Mammon betrays his ontological blindness when he suggests that the manufacture of exterior and material splendor will make Hell match Heaven:

> This Desert soil
> Wants not her hidden lustre, Gems and Gold;
> Nor want we skill or art, from whence to raise
> Magnificence; and what can Heav'n show more?
>   (2.270–73)

The answer is "nothing" to those who refuse to acknowledge one of the two modes of prime matter. What "Heaven" can show more, and indeed what Earth can show more, is indicated in the *Christian Doctrine*, as we saw in Chapter 3: "Moreover spirit, being the more excellent substance, virtually, as they say, and eminently contains within itself what is clearly the inferior substance" (*CP* 6:309). Mammon sees only the inferior reflection of a superior mode of the one substance. More and more, the devils choose to inhabit a dead Hobbesian universe.

Significantly, Mammon admires exteriors. Even when looking below the surface, he hunts for a concealed exterior, the "hidden lustre" of precious matter, and not the truly interior "hidden strength" of chastity or any other virtue. Spirit is interior, and body exterior—Milton keeps these categories despite his monism. He writes in *Paradise Lost* of the "paradise within" (12.587). In *Of Education* he writes of languages as dead exteriors; one must study "the solid things in them" (*CP* 2:369). Cudworth, who viewed Hobbes as ignoring the "inside," accused Hobbes's philosophy of hollowness.[16] With this in mind one is struck by Milton's association of the devils with hollowness:

> such murmur fill'd
> Th'Assembly, as when *hollow Rocks retain*
> *The sound of blust'ring winds*, which all night long
> Had rous'd the Sea.
> (2.284–87; my emphasis)

The devils are themselves "hollow rocks," hardened exteriors containing only meaningless and "blust'ring winds." The only time the word "hollow" is used in the epic without referring to the devils is at the creation of light (7.256–58), but the point there is that the "hollow Orb" of Heaven is filled with the voice and prayer of angels. The container is not left empty. One can contrast this passage with one describing the announcement in Hell of the conclusions of the "Stygian Council": "the hollow Abyss / Heard far and wide, and all the host of Hell / With deaf'ning shout, return'd them loud acclaim" (2.518–20). The devils cannot fill this "hollow Abyss," which mirrors the hollowness of each. This hollowness is institutionalized in their earthly triumph:

> By falsities and lies the greatest part
> Of Mankind they corrupted to forsake
> God thir Creator, and th'invisible
> Glory of him that made them, to transform
> Oft to the Image of a Brute, adorn'd

---

[16]For Cudworth on "inside" and "outside," see *True Intellectual System*, p. 831 (V, iii).

> With gay Religions full of Pomp and Gold,
> And Devils to adore for Deities.
>
> (1.367–73)

The devils are adored as hollow idols, exteriors without interiors. Their transformation into statues follows their renunciation of spirit. Milton argued that "strictly speaking the body cannot be killed . . . , since it is in itself lifeless" (*CP* 6:408). The devils choose death in attempting to live only according to the body. Although they do not realize it, in being worshiped as dead and hollow statues, the devils are "punisht in the shape [they] sinn'd" (10.516) as surely as when they are transformed into snakes.

Hell is as close as one gets in Milton's universe to dead, Hobbesian matter. The devils will not receive a respite from pain, but they will conform to the nature of their dead, material world. As Descartes and Hobbes illustrate, when one removes spirit from matter, matter is delivered to mechanism and determinism. While Descartes retains in *res cogitans* a repository of life and freedom, his separation of spirit and body, of the living and the mechanical, violates Milton's monism, and the devils cannot rest in Cartesian dualism. At those times when the devils renounce the spirit and immerse themselves in the material, they renounce Cartesianism for a Hobbesianism that fits into Milton's monism at its lowest verge.

One of the clearest indications of this renunciation is their acceptance of psychic mechanism, and the consequent atrophy of their wills. Satan complains to Beelzebub: "new Laws thou see'st impos'd; / New Laws from him who reigns, new minds may raise / In us who serve" (5.679–81). But the lines point to, among other things,[17] Satan's delivering *himself* up to the laws

---

[17]One of which is Paul's distinction between new law and old law. The exaltation of the Son together with the promise to the angels that the Son will "One of our [the angels'] number thus reduc't become" (5.483) prefigures the new law of the Gospel (see Albert C. Labriola, "'Thy Humiliation Shall Exalt': The Christology of *Paradise Lost*," *Milton Studies* 15 [1981]: 29–42). But Satan treats the new law as old law, as restraint rather than liberation, as legalism rather than salvation; Satan's legalism is only one aspect of his choice of externality. I refer here to the polemical Christian perspective on the Hebrew Bible and the "old law"; for an important corrective see Roger Brooks, *The Spirit of the Ten Commandments: Shattering the Myth of Rabbinic Legalism* (San Francisco: Harper & Row, 1990).

of fatality and mechanism. In this sense, the laws are not imposed upon but embraced by Satan and his devils.

One of the first new laws to exert its force comes from physics, replacing the law of ontological ascent asserted too late by Moloch:

> in our proper motion we ascend
> Up to our native seat: descent and fall
> To us is adverse. . . .
>   . . . Th'ascent is easy then;
> Th'event is fear'd.
>
>   (2.75–82)

The argument is undermined immediately by the reversal of Virgil,[18] and eventually by the revelation that the devils threw themselves down from Heaven (6.864–66). That their fall through space mirrors their moral fall has received much comment; what may need emphasis is that this is the first instance of interstellar gravity in cosmic history. Their formerly "proper motion" belongs to an ontological state they have repudiated. Raphael tells Adam and Eve that they may, if obedient, "wing'd ascend / Ethereal" (5.498–99). Instead, they fall, and Adam must inform Eve, ironically echoing Satan, that Michael is descending to "impose / New Laws to be observ'd" (11.227–28). Gravity will tie them to the soil, as it ties Satan to Hell.[19]

Gravity is only one of the laws governing the relationship of material objects, and Satan at his fall places himself under all of them. Their scope allows us to label Milton's devils as Hobbesian. Again and again, the devils operate under Hobbesian assumptions. In their ontological migration, they exchange their (literary) author's animist materialism for Hobbes's mechanist materialism. Physical cause-and-effect, Hobbes's motion, usurps the place of vitalist freedom.[20]

---

[18]See *Aeneid* 6.126–29: "facilis descensus Averno: / . . . / sed revocare gradum superasque evadere ad auras / hoc opus, hic labor est."

[19]Adam says as well that he expects that the "tidings" will "determine" them (11.226–27).

[20]While the modern law of gravity had yet to be formulated at this time, the term "gravity" was in use by both Aristotelian and anti-Aristotelian natural philosophers (see, e.g., Bacon's *Sylva Sylvarum*, VIII.704). In Milton's time, the debate was between those who searched for a mechanical explanation of grav-

Gravity acts in *Paradise Lost* as a symbol for the element of Hobbes's program most violently antithetical to Milton's thought: determinism. This principle, inseparable from mechanist materialism, informs Satanic philosophy. Hobbes moves with an unblinking consistency from the premise that corporeal bodies are all that exist to the conclusion that all mental actions are determined by physical motions, that they *are* physical motions. The mind is epiphenomenal and therefore must follow the laws of physics and geometry. The devils, too, proceed from materialism to determinism. Determinism emerges as the doctrine on the will that Satan shares with Hobbes, just as a strict empiricism emerges as their shared epistemological doctrine. Satan's word for determinism is fate; locutions such as "since fate inevitable / Subdues us" litter devilish rhetoric (2.197–98), as Dennis Burden reminds us.[21]

Not surprisingly, Satan's determinism is cast in Hobbesian terms. Like many opponents of free will, Hobbes saw randomness as the only alternative to determinism. If choices and events are not determined by inalterable laws, then they can only be irrational and fortuitous. Mammon voices the Hobbesian position in his gloomy assessment of the chance of deposing God:

> him to unthrone we then
> May hope, when everlasting Fate shall yield
> To fickle Chance, and *Chaos* judge the strife.
> (2.231–33)

Chaos is randomness or chance personified. Milton's perspec-

---

ity and those who searched for a nonmechanical one. Henry More ascribed gravity to the action of the "Spirit of Nature," "in execution of an *All-comprehensive and Eternal Counsel* for the *ordering* and the *guiding* of the Motion of the *Matter* in the Universe to what is for the *best*" (*An Antidote against Atheism*, p. 43, in *A Collection of Several Philosophical Writings*, 2 vols. [1662; facs. rpt. New York: Garland, 1978] [II, ii, 7]). In *The Immortality of the Soul* III, xiii, More places his incorporealist explanation of gravity against Hobbes's mechanist one. For Hobbes's explanation of gravity, see *De Corpore* IV, xxx.

[21]Dennis Burden has elaborated the existence of a determinist "Satanic epic" unfolding in counterpoint to the divine epic in *Paradise Lost* in *The Logical Epic* (London: Routledge & Kegan Paul, 1967), pp. 57–75.

tive confronts this one directly; his God, for example, is free, unapproached by "Necessity or Chance" (7.172). Milton's God rules out what for Hobbes are the only human alternatives. And Milton does not restrict the freedom to the theological level; God freely grants freedom to his creatures. If man had been denied true freedom, in God's eyes his will and reason would have been "Made passive both" and have "serv'd necessity, / Not mee" (3.110–11).

The devils serve necessity from the time they sin, as even Beelzebub's passive syntax betrays: "War hath determin'd us" (2.330). Agent becomes object. Beelzebub reveals the choices debated by Moloch, Mammon, and Belial as illusory. For Beelzebub as for Hobbes, "free will" is nothing but "insignificant sounds." Actions are initiated not by choices but by "inclinations," a word with a scarcely submerged physical denotation. The devils after the council in Book 2 disperse, each going where "inclination or sad choice / Leads him perplext" (2.524–25); Death advises his mother Sin to "Go whither Fate and inclination strong / Leads thee" (10.265–66). Again in both instances the agent is the object, and the characters do not choose their place of unrest, but rather *are led*. The use of the singular verb has the effect of combining fate (or necessity), inclination, and choice into one. The word "inclination" with its variations is frequently chosen by Hobbes in his discussions of will or "deliberation," as in this passage: "And though we say in common Discourse, a man had a Will once to do a thing, that neverthelesse he forbore to do; yet that is properly but an *Inclination*, which makes no Action Voluntary; because the action depends not of it, but of the last *Inclination*, or Appetite."[22] For Hobbes, choice or will is the name of the final and prevailing inclination, which is synonymous with physically determined desire and appetite. Miltonic freedom, as his God explains it, is a matter of self-inclining: human will is "to her own inclining left / In even scale" (10.46–47).

The ending of the Stygian council in consensus elicits an outburst from the narrator:

[22]Thomas Hobbes, *Leviathan*, ed. C. B. Macpherson (Harmondsworth: Penguin, 1968), p. 128 (chap. 6); my emphasis.

> O shame to men! Devil with Devil damn'd
> Firm concord holds, men only disagree
> Of Creatures rational, though under hope
> Of heavenly Grace; and God proclaiming peace,
> Yet live in hatred, enmity, and strife
> Among themselves.
>
> (2.496–501)

Of course Milton's political frustration surfaces in these lines. But the peace that follows the council, like the peace urged in it, is artificial. Devil agrees with devil because their choices are determined, or, put more bluntly, because they do not choose at all. If reason is choice, then the parody of reason in the council leads only to a parody of choice. True freedom does not exist in this Hobbesian world. In rigging the council in Hell with the help of Beelzebub, Satan reveals that he desires the obedience disdained by God, that of creatures whose will and reason were "Useless and vain, of freedom both despoil'd" (3.109).

Milton's Devils and Hobbesian Epistemology

The circle closes, and we return to epistemology. Hobbes's denial of the existence of *res cogitans* issued in his denial of innate idea and intuition. When the devils descend into Hobbesian mechanist materialism, they lay aside the epistemological tools incompatible with it. The movement toward a Hobbesian materialist ontology is complemented by a movement toward a radically empiricist epistemology.

In order to assess the epistemological error of the devils, we need an understanding of the manner in which unfallen angels know. Milton accepts with some reservation the orthodox belief that angels know intuitively (I use "intuition" in one of its meanings, i.e., direct apprehension of extrasensory reality). The overwhelming majority of both Catholic and Protestant angelologists follow Augustine and Aquinas on the intuitive as opposed to the discursive nature of the angels' knowledge. An-

gels know directly what we conclude by ratiocination. Milton's
reservation is related to his monism, which causes him to bridle
at the sharp dichotomy of angel and human epistemology. As
usual, he makes the difference one of degree and not of kind.
Raphael tells Adam that "discourse / Is oftest yours, the latter
[intuition] most is ours, / Differing but in degree, of kind the
same" (5.488–90). The categories are not mutually exclusive, as
"oftest" and "most" confirm, and the epistemological ladder is
unbroken. When Raphael explains that reason is the "being" of
the soul, Milton takes us to the limit of rationalism. Milton's
discursive knowledge shares with intuitive knowledge, as material and product, something missing from Hobbesian epistemology, a priori truth.

Milton takes his monism seriously; in order to guarantee
continuity between angels and humans, he consciously limits
the knowledge of the angels. They are not cognizant of all
events in the universe: news of man's fall must travel by mes-
senger from Earth to Heaven (10.18–25); Raphael does not
know the details of Adam's creation because of his absence
from Heaven on an errand (8.229–36). Even apart from these
minor questions of fact, Milton hints at an epistemological
chain in the transmission of abstract truth: the "cherub" Satan
addresses Uriel as an "Interpreter" of God's will (3.654–58).
That Milton is conscious that he has limited the orthodox conception of angel cognition, and that it is more than a matter of
poetic expediency, is clear from *Christian Doctrine*: "The good
angels do not see into all God's thoughts, as the Papists pre-
tend. They know by revelation only those things which God
sees fit to show them, and they know other things by virtue of
their very high intelligence" (*CP* 6:347–48).[23] The uncir-
cumscribed intuition which some find in angels, Milton reserves for God:

> Meanwhile th'Eternal eye, whose sight discerns
> Abstrusest thoughts, from forth his holy Mount

---

[23]Aquinas, for one, proposes a limit on the intuition of angels, arguing that
angels cannot see into each other's thoughts, much less into the thoughts of
God (*Summa theologiae* I, Q.57, art.5).

> And from within the golden Lamps that burn
> Nightly before him, saw without thir light
> Rebellion rising.
>
> (5.711–15)

Here is the epistemological equivalent of the ontological phenomenon examined in Chapter 5: Milton's God assumes the role formerly occupied by scholastic angels, allowing angels to move closer to man.

The fact that God, sitting within the golden Lamps, "saw *without* thir light" differentiates God most emphatically from the devils. The preposition is a pun: God sees without the aid of the lamps the rebellion rising without the circle described by the lamps. The former meaning separates God from the devils, who depend on empirical evidence and thus increasingly on physical illumination of the material objects of their contemplation. The devils' rejection of the higher modes of knowledge is most obvious and most disastrous in their perception of God. While the loyal angels know God's power and glory intuitively, the rebels come to require physical evidence of that power. Abdiel infers that God's "Golden Sceptre" can become an "Iron Rod" (5.886–87). Satan, on the other hand, disingenuously asks what "power of mind" could have foreseen the outcome of the war (1.626). That power is reason.

The devils acknowledge only empirical evidence. Satan overlooks inner virtue, unavailable to the senses: "so much the stronger prov'd / He with his Thunder: and till then who knew / The force of those dire Arms?" (1.92–94). Satan denies both the spiritual force of God, of which external might is only one manifestation, and his own spiritual degeneration. Characteristically, Satan blames his own epistemological error on God, who "still his strength conceal'd / Which tempted our attempt, and wrought our fall" (1.641–42). Abdiel's intuition gives the lie to this argument. God's strength is concealed only in the sense that it is unavailable to the senses, and Satan's charge of concealment is a palpable rationalization. The devils' abdication of intuition moves them on the epistemological scale below not only angels, but humans as well. The most bizarre product of Satan's obstinate empiricism is his claim of self-creation, which has often been contrasted with Adam's liminal intuition of his createdness.

A kinship links empiricism and nominalism. Satan shares both with Hobbes.[24] If *all* knowledge comes through the senses, then abstractions are at most useful fabrications for organizing this knowledge, and the absolutes of the realist become fluid. Hobbes's consistency in drawing implications is disarming: "The first truths were arbitrarily made by those that first of all imposed names upon things, or received them from the imposition of others."[25] The realist Milton sees truth as a priori, as absolute and unchanging. For Milton, truth is not "arbitrary," and only a mangled version can be received "from the imposition of others."[26] The extension of Hobbes's nominalism into ethics makes theodicy meaningless:

> Whatsoever is the object of any mans Appetite or Desire; that is it, which he for his part calleth *Good*: And the object of his Hate, and Aversion, *Evill*; and of his Contempt, *Vile*, and *Inconsiderable*. For these words of Good, Evill, and Contemptible, *are ever used with relation to the person that useth them: There being nothing simply and absolutely so* (my emphasis); nor any common Rule of Good and Evill, to be taken from the nature of the objects themselves.[27]

Satan makes good Hobbesian sense, then, when he says, "all Good to me is lost; / Evil be thou my Good" (4.109–10). The good he has lost is the arbitrarily imposed "good" of God, who first gave names to things. Satan, coming before man, is in a privileged position to give his own names to things. He has no appetite for obedience, which he finds "burdensome" (4.53); he desires rebellion instead. Thus evil does become his good; a statement making no sense for the realist makes sense for the Hobbesian nominalist.

---

[24]Lee Jacobus has argued for a link between Satan's epistemology and Hobbesian empiricism. See *Sudden Apprehension: Aspects of Knowledge in "Paradise Lost"* (The Hague: Mouton, 1976), p. 31.

[25]*De Corpore: The Elements of Philosophy concerning Body* I, iii, 8, in *The English Works of Thomas Hobbes*, ed. Sir William Molesworth, 11 vols. (London: John Bohn, 1839–45), 1:36.

[26]See the *Areopagitica* (CP 2:549).

[27]*Leviathan*, p. 120 (chap. 6).

Nominalism joins empiricism in Satan's Hobbesian rationale for his rebellion. The angels obey God because of his goodness; the devils, like Hobbes, do not recognize any such a priori standard. Hobbes's God is like an earthly sovereign, to be obeyed for his power alone: "The Right of Nature, whereby God reigneth over men, and punisheth those that break his Lawes, is to be derived, not from his Creating them, as if he required obedience, as of Gratitude for his benefits; but from his *Irresistible Power*."[28] Satan deceives himself by underestimating God's physical power, but the "debt immense of endless gratitude" (4.52) does not secure his obedience, as in Hobbes's world it would not. Satan's tribute to God after the fall concerns only his physical strength (1.248–49). While Satan will have moments of remorse and clear perception of God's moral authority, his sin generates a Hobbesian nominalist conception of obedience.

Ultimately, the empiricist and nominalist descent of Satan is limited by the monist truth. Just as the devils do not actually become purely material in a Hobbesian sense through their materialism, so they maintain some vestigial intuition. Intuition emerges most dramatically in Satan's soliloquy to the sun, when he acknowledges his creation, God's goodness, and his own sin (4.40–48). But in order to maintain his chosen debased equilibrium, Satan must deny and forget these recurrences of intuition, which do not fit the circumscribed empiricism that offers him some justification and hope. The light of these vestigial intuitions throws into silhouette the self-deception constantly necessary for Satan, as he spends his energy in bartering rationalism for rationalization.

To be fair to Hobbes, Satan is not a good Hobbesian empiricist. While he relies on sensory evidence, he does so selectively and imperfectly. He is, for example, guilty of the *post hoc ergo propter hoc* fallacy in claiming that his rebellion "shook [God's] throne" (1.105). The shaking of Heaven does follow the rebellion, but is caused not by it but by the Son's chariot (6.833).

---

[28]*Leviathan*, p. 397 (chap. 31).

Satan, moreover, is in the untenable position of an empiricist who does not get his facts straight. The throne is the one locus in Heaven that does not shake.

Despite these qualifications, Milton's devils can be more completely and consistently understood as Hobbesian beings than as Cartesian ones. As if fulfilling the fears of the Cambridge Platonists that Cartesian error is a preliminary step toward deeper Hobbesian error, Milton's devils flirt with dualism but more often expand half of a dualism into a mechanist monism. Milton's ability, moreover, to make the devils into Hobbesian beings derives, ironically, from the monism he shares with Hobbes. For both, matter matters, not only as a trough of analogues for the spirit, but also as the ground of reality. Both therefore do not hesitate to pronounce Hell and its punishments to be material.[29]

A few important differences between Milton and Hobbes on the subject of Hell suggest the poetic justice of Milton's dressing of Hobbesian thought in diabolic clothing. Hobbes does not believe in devils; his Hell is populated exclusively by damned men. Devils are an illusion inspired by dreams and given specious intellectual respectability by Greek philosophy. Satan is merely "any Earthly Enemy of the Church."[30] From Milton's viewpoint, Hobbes leaves an ontological vacuum in the universe, which the poet proceeds to fill. If Hobbes denies the existence of devils, Milton makes devils out of Hobbesian men. Hobbes as it were gives him license to do this, for the damned in his Hell live much as do the men on his Earth. They are physically consumed by flames, and they die (Hobbes does not view the "second death" of Revelation 20:13–14 as metaphorical).[31] Hobbes's view of the damned is, as far as I know, unique: "For the wicked *being left in the estate they were in after Adams sin*, may at the Resurrection *live as they did*, marry, and give in marriage, and *have grosse and corruptible bodies*, as all mankind now have; and consequently may engender perpetually, after

---

[29]For Hobbes on hell, see *Leviathan*, chap. 38.
[30]*Leviathan*, p. 489 (chap. 38).
[31]*Leviathan*, p. 490 (chap. 38); contrast *CP* 6:628.

the Resurrection, as they did before: For there is no place of Scripture to the contrary."[32] Hobbes describes an Arminian's nightmare, a Calvinist world with no elect, tempered only by the absence of immortality. Milton's devils have lives, like Hobbes's men of the famous formula, that are "nasty" and "brutish." They live in a world of dead force and motion, its emptiness Milton's poetic indictment of the philosophy of Hobbes.

[32]*Leviathan*, pp. 647–48 (chap. 44); my emphasis.

~ 8

"After Another Method":
Sacred War as Philosophical Battle

The War in Heaven is the first great testing ground in *Paradise Lost*, ontologically and epistemologically as well as morally.[1] False philosophy is branded by its contribution to the devils' failure in battle, as Milton plays out his intuition, central to *Comus* and *Areopagitica*, that truth is stronger than error. Anne Conway claims that her philosophy is "the strongest to refute *Hobbs* . . . , but after another method."[2] Milton's method is poetry; he takes advantage of his role as poetic maker to give his own monism the victory it would never achieve on the prosaic battleground of seventeenth-century philosophy. Many readers have been puzzled that the conflict between truth and error is a material battle. But against the background of Milton's

---

[1]The War in Heaven has been the focus of considerable critical comment. Valuable book-length treatments are Stella Purce Revard's *The War in Heaven: "Paradise Lost" and the Tradition of Satan's Rebellion* (Ithaca: Cornell University Press, 1980), and James A. Freeman's *Milton and the Martial Muse: "Paradise Lost" and European Traditions of War* (Princeton: Princeton University Press, 1980); see also Michael Lieb's chapter, "Sacred War" in *Poetics of the Holy: A Reading of "Paradise Lost"* (Chapel Hill: University of North Carolina Press, 1981), pp. 246–312. For Milton and the military, see Robert Fallon, *Captain or Colonel: The Soldier in Milton's Life and Art* (Columbia: University of Missouri Press, 1984).

[2]*The Principles of the Most Ancient and Modern Philosophy*, ed. Peter Lopston (The Hague: Martinus Nijhoff, 1982), p. 221. See Chapter 4.

monism, the question of whether the War in Heaven is either spiritual or material becomes nonsense. This mistaken question is the rock on which many interpreters of the war have foundered. Satan, we must recall, is the character in the poem who attempts to separate the material from the spiritual. Those who ask the question are of the devil's party without knowing it; they allow Cartesian and Hobbesian assumptions to impose themselves on a text built upon other assumptions.

The War in Heaven I—"Unequal Work"

The devils, true disciples of Hobbes, view brute physical force as the decisive factor in their war with God and place their trust in armor and weaponry. Satan answers Abdiel's appeal to humility and obedience with an assertion of his own "puissance" (5.864–69). Because Satan recognizes only the material power of God, he responds in kind. The display of physical force is incongruous in a monist Heaven that is fixed more toward the spiritual end of the continuum than is Earth. Michael recognizes this:

> Heav'n the seat of bliss
> Brooks not the works of violence and War.
> Hence then, and evil go with thee along,
> Thy offspring, to the place of evil, Hell.
> (6.273–76)

Grossly physical war, with its "mangling" and "ghastly wounds through Plate and Mail" (6.368), is an ontological violation of Heaven.

The devils' ontological descent, described in Chapter 7, should not be read as merely a metaphor for spiritual condition. Physical condition *is* spiritual condition in a world in which one's closeness to God is measured by one's position on a matter-spirit spectrum. The devils do change physically: once "Spirits of purest light," they are "now gross by sinning grown" (6.660–61). This physical grossness is a serious liability in the

War. And the more they rely on grossly material weapons, the more they themselves suffer. Having rejected the integrity of God's monist universe, they lose the integrity of their bodies. Appropriately, Satan is the first devil wounded:

> Then *Satan* first knew pain,
> And writh'd him to and fro convolv'd; so sore
> The griding sword with discontinuous wound
> Pass'd through him, but th'Ethereal substance clos'd
> Not long divisible, and from the gash
> A stream of Nectarous humor issuing flow'd
> Sanguine, such as Celestial Spirits may bleed,
> And all his Armor stain'd erewhile so bright.
>
> (6.327–34)

The stain, of course, is moral as well as physical. Only Satan attempts to divorce the two. Rabelais's burlesque confirms that the convention of the wounded devil employed by Milton was part of the common currency of European angelology; according to Panurge,

> When one askes the Massoretes and Cabbalists why devils never enter the Earthly Paradise, the only reason they give is that at the gate is a Cherub, holding a naked sword in his hand. But to speak accurately, according to the diabolology of Toledo, I must admit that devils cannot really die by sword-strokes. I maintain, nevertheless, according to the same diabolology, that they can suffer dissolution of continuity. It is as if you were to cut across a flame of burning fire or a thick dark smoke with your cutlass. They shriek most devilishly when they feel this dissolution, which to them is devilish painful.[3]

But if the conception is not original, Milton adds a new context. Physical vulnerability becomes part of the web of irony that entangles Satan. The ontological punishment (as in the tradition) follows a moral crime, but in addition it answers an on-

---

[3]*Gargantua and Pantagruel*, trans. J. M. Cohen (Harmondsworth: Penguin, 1955), p. 352 (Bk. III, chap. xxiii).

tological crime. Satan unintentionally chooses the body that is liable to wounds.

The devils are less gross than fallen humans, as Milton makes clear (6.344–53). But in Milton's universe direction is more important than absolute position. As Raphael suggested, as creatures are good they become more "spiritous," "Till body up to spirit work, in bounds / Proportion'd to each kind" (5.478–79). The lowest bound of angelic incorporealization, we may assume, remains above the density of our bodies. Nevertheless, the devils become physically denser than the angels, who remain "Spirits of purest light." The devils may be immune to "mortal wound" (6.348), but the angels cannot be wounded in any manner, even slight:

> Such high advantages thir innocence
> Gave them above thir foes, not to have sinn'd,
> Not to have disobey'd; in fight they stood
> Unwearied, unobnoxious to be pain'd
> By wound, though from thir place by violence mov'd.
> (6.401–5)

The angels' "innocence" involves ontological as well as moral integrity, just as the devils' guilt entails ontological disintegration. The bodily integrity of the angels expresses in another mode the mental integrity that prevents them from splitting *virtus* and *sapientia*, or strength and wisdom. The loyal angels realize that they owe their strength to God and that true wisdom is obedience to God. The devils, on the other hand, separate *virtus* and *sapientia* and hope at first to prevail by hollow strength. This one-dimensional strength turns out to be weakness.

In the War in Heaven, as elsewhere in the epic, Satan weds Hobbesian empiricism with Hobbesian materialism. He is preoccupied with experimenting with, or "proving," physical forces: "our own right hand / Shall teach us highest deeds, *by proof to try* / Who is our equal" (5.864–66; my emphasis). He ignores intuition and insists here on empirical evidences of

God's power, and he rejoices when he fails to find them. The
first day's battle does not settle the issue against him:

> O now in danger *tri'd*, now known in Arms
> Not to be overpow'r'd, Companions dear,
>
> .   .   .
>
> Who have sustain'd one day in doubtful fight,
> (*And if one day, why not Eternal days?*)
> What Heaven's Lord had powerfullest to send
> Against us from about his Throne, and judg'd
> Sufficient to subdue us to his will,
> *But proves not so*: then fallible, it *seems*,
> Of future we may deem him.
>
> (6.418–29; my emphasis)

His senses convince Satan that God is not omnipotent; God's
raw physical power has been tested and found wanting. With
his time-bound empiricism, Satan projects a limited past experience ("And if one day") into the future ("why not Eternal
days?").

We are now in a position to appreciate the irony of the devils'
consultation after the first day's battle. Satan acknowledges the
disadvantage deriving from their vulnerability to wounds and
pain, but perversely ascribes this to the devils being "less firmly
arm'd" (6.430). His solution ignores the lesson of the first day:

> perhaps more valid Arms
> Weapons more violent, when next we meet,
> May serve to better us, and worse our foes,
> Or equal what between us made the odds,
> In Nature none: if other hidden cause
> Left them Superior, while we can preserve
> Unhurt our minds, and understanding sound,
> Due search and consultation will disclose.
>
> (6.438–45)

This strategy, like all others, will recoil ironically on the rebels.
Book 6 chronicles the devils' vain attempts to find ever-more-

powerful material weapons. This misguided aim follows naturally from their intellectual error. The true solution lies in the "hidden cause," but it is one that Satan's chosen ontology and epistemology will not admit. Having divorced interior from exterior, the devils recognize only a vitiated exterior. The "cause" of the angels' might is "hidden" from the devils because it is not a material cause accessible to empirical analysis: they refuse to see that true strength and wisdom cannot be sundered. This true strength, dependent on wise virtue, is the "hidden cause" of the angels' advantage, as it is the "hidden strength" of the Lady in *Comus*. Obedience protects the angels as chastity protects the Lady.[4]

All life derives from God. In attempting to use force against God, Satan cuts off the source of that force. His error here follows inevitably from his untenable boast of self-creation and his claim that his "puissance is [his] own" (5.864). The problem with this reasoning is obvious when Satan accuses Abdiel of "contradiction" for opposing the rebels who "feel / Vigor Divine within them" (6.157–58). Satan's accusation is itself contradictory, for what else is "Vigor Divine" but life derived from God. Satan wants light without the sun. Satan compounds the contradiction by shrugging off the rebels' vulnerability to wounds, which are "by native vigor heal'd" (6.436). Replacing "Vigor Divine" with "native vigor," Satan drops sophistry for naked error. The illusion of native vigor is to be shattered on the third day of the battle, when the assault of the Son "wither'd all thir strength, / And of thir wonted vigor left them drain'd" (6.850–51).

For the unity of strength and wisdom, Satan substitutes the dichotomy of force and fraud (1.121). Force and fraud inform the European epic tradition; the generic archetypes are en-

---

[4]Our metaphysical language comes laden with dualist associations and denotations, thus making it difficult to distinguish economically between Milton's animate material and Satan's Hobbesian material. When I speak of the devils' reliance on merely material weapons, I do not mean to suggest that the angels' weapons are not material—everything in Milton's universe is material. Instead, I mean to distinguish between matter viewed as inert and the unitary spiritualized matter viewed as alive.

shrined in the *Iliad* and the *Odyssey*. The alternatives show up, interestingly, in *Leviathan*: "The notions of Right and Wrong, Justice and Injustice have [in war] no place. Where there is no common Power, there is no law: where no Law, no Injustice. *Force, and Fraud, are in warre the two Cardinall vertues.*"[5] Unaided force was not enough on the first day of the War, so the devils rack their wits in order to develop the cannon, which is referred to as a piece of fraud. It is a product of debased wisdom, of intelligence not directed toward the glory of God. Significantly for my argument, the "invention" of the cannon is cast in the language of scientific enterprise.[6] The growth of the new science paralleled the growth of the materialism and empiricism championed by Hobbes. The cannon can be called an emblem of Hobbesian force; it allows the devils to put matter in motion, which is the only action that matters for Hobbes. The Hobbesian devils desired "Weapons more violent," and the cannons certainly are that, as they unleash

> chain'd Thunderbolts and Hail
> Of Iron Globes, which on the Victor Host
> Levell'd, with such impetuous fury smote
> That whom they hit, none of thir feet might stand,
> Though standing else as Rocks, but down they fell
> By thousands, Angel on Arch-Angel roll'd.
>
> (6.589–94)

The cannonballs move the angels: Milton thus gives Hobbes (with the devil) his due. The angels are material, and the Hobbesian device, while not wounding them, puts them in motion. In a Hobbesian universe, the war might have ended differently.

Victory for the devils proves illusory and ephemeral. Their thunder and hail reflect God's thunder only feebly. The devils had hoped by their invention to have "disarm'd / The Thunderer of his only dreaded bolt" (6.490–91), but again they take

[5]Thomas Hobbes, *Leviathan*, ed. C. B. Macpherson (Harmondsworth: Penguin, 1968), p. 188 (chap. 13); my emphasis. Hobbes, unlike Satan, is not an advocate of war.
[6]On Satan as technocrat, see Joan Malory Webber, *Milton and His Epic Tradition* (Seattle: University of Washington Press, 1979), pp. 178–80.

the exterior for the whole. They will learn that this thunderbolt is alive as well as material. The devils' thunderbolts are "chained" in a figurative as well as a literal sense: they are chained to dead matter, and their effect is only material. The bane of Hell is its dead materiality, and the devils release on Heaven a foretaste of Hell, with "infernal flame" (483) and "devilish glut" (589).

This matter without spirit is a hollow substance, like the substance of the devils themselves described in the previous chapter, and like Hobbesian matter as seen by the philosopher's adversaries. Throughout the episode of the cannon Milton rings changes on hollowness. The cannons themselves are pictures of hollowness. They are "hollow Engines long and round" (6.484):

> A triple-mounted row of Pillars laid
> On Wheels (for like to Pillars most they seem'd
> Or *hollow'd bodies* made of Oak or Fir
> With branches lopt, in Wood or Mountain fell'd)
> Brass, Iron, Stony mould, had not thir mouths
> With hideous orifice gap't on us wide,
> Portending *hollow truce*.
> (6.572–78; my emphasis)

The hollowness of these weapons reflects the hollowness of their inventors. Raphael describes the approach of Satan's artillery

> in *hollow Cube*
> Training his devilish Enginry, impal'd
> On every side with shadowing Squadrons Deep,
> To hide the fraud.
> (6.552–55; my emphasis)

This description contrasts strikingly with an earlier one of the angels, who "In *Cubic Phalanx* firm advanc'd entire, / Invulnerable, impenetrably arm'd" (6.399–400; my emphasis). The compact body of the "Cubic Phalanx" images the congruity between interior and exterior in the angels, between their wisdom and their strength, and contrasts with the "hollow Cube" of the devils, which reflects their reliance on the external and their emptiness.[7]

The War in Heaven II—"Brutish Contest"

What happens to the bottom line? If the devils' sins have weakened them, how can they survive against the loyal angels for two days? The angels have true strength and not merely physical power; they counter devilish fraud with wisdom. In the Garden of Eden (earlier in the poem and later in real time) the angel Zephon taunts the great Satan: "Thy fear . . . / Will save us trial what the least can do / Single against thee wicked, and thence weak" (4.854–56). Yet the angels do not prevail in Book 6. The primary reason for this anomaly is that Milton reserves the victory for the Son. But in doing so, he places himself in an awkward position: the battle between angels and debilitated rebels must end in a stalemate. The strategy chosen requires of Milton a delicate adjudication of the moral and ontological claims of the angels, and the resulting compromise is a potentially weak link in an unusually well-constructed poem.

Milton's God requires the angels to play the game by the devils' rules. We might have expected the monist angels to overpower the devils with weapons that are simultaneously and inseparably spiritual and material. What need is there for the angels to fight with simply material weapons when they are, after all, as God says to Abdiel, "in word mightier than they in Arms" (6.32)? The military organization of the angels in Heav-

---

[7]In this passage Milton also stresses the integrity of the angels through their maintenance of intuition, the cognitive function discarded by the devils. Zophiel sees through the hollow fraud of the devils even before the cannons are visible: "this day will pour down, / If I conjecture aught, no drizzling show'r, / But rattling storm of Arrows barb'd with fire" (6.544–46). While James Turner, citing Gervase Markham's *Soldiers Grammar* (1627), demonstrates that the devils' hollow formation follows familiar seventeenth-century military practice, he acknowledges that the contrast between the devils' "hollow Cube" and the angels' "Cubic Phalanx" "has of course a moral significance" (*Notes and Queries* n.s. 25 [1978]: 17–18).

en (5.583–94) suggests their orderliness and discipline rather than their martial experience. They stand in readiness for the "good fight of faith" (1 Timothy 6:12) rather than for the "long and tedious havoc" of brute warfare (9.30). In *The Reason of Church-Government* Milton explicates the charge to "war a good warfare" (1 Timothy 1:18): "thou shalt set up Church-discipline, that thou might'st warre a good warfare, bearing thy selfe constantly and faithfully in the Ministery, which in the 1 to the Corinthians is also called a warfare" (*CP* 1:758–59).[8] But Milton does have the angels fight a grossly material battle; God charges them to fight "with Fire and hostile Arms" (6.50), and, as the War begins, the opposing sides employ similar weapons. Abdiel's initial blow upon Satan would be more at home in the *Iliad* than in Heywood's *Hierarchie of the Blessed Angells*, with its spiritual battles. Little separates the two sides at first glance:

> Arms on Armor clashing bray'd
> Horrible discord, and the madding Wheels
> Of brazen Chariots rag'd; dire was the noise
> Of conflict.
>
> (6.209–12)

From swords to mountain brickbats, the angels match the devils weapon for weapon, with the significant exception of the cannon.

Milton hints at the superior, spiritual/material, weapons the angels might have employed. There is, for example, Abdiel's duel with Satan:

> a noble stroke he lifted high,
> Which hung not, but so *swift* with tempest fell
> On the proud Crest of *Satan*, that *no sight*,
> *Nor motion of swift thought*, less could his Shield
> Such ruin intercept.
>
> (6.189–93; my emphasis)

Swiftness is associated in *Paradise Lost* with highly spiritualized essence; it approaches the "immediacy" that marks the "acts of

[8]Milton refers in fact to 2 Corinthians 10:4: "For the weapons of our warfare are not carnal."

God." Raphael emphasizes the inequality of the stroke and the hollowly material shield. Later, Michael suggests a power held in reserve, in telling Satan to return to Hell "Ere this avenging Sword begin thy doom, / Or some more sudden vengeance wing'd from God / Precipitate thee with augmented pain" (6.278–80). The warning points ahead to the War's third day, when that power in the person of the Son will be loosed. The angels, despite their potential, fight with lesser weapons.

The reason for this lies in providence; God "From his stronghold of Heav'n high over-rul'd / And limited thir might" (6.228–29). One aspect of God's limitation of the angels' might is the restraining of their spiritual power. But the equilibrium of the battle is achieved by motion from either end. The angels' spiritual power is limited, and the devils' physical decline is delayed. As God tells the Son:

> to themselves I left them, and thou know'st
> Equal in thir Creation they were form'd
> Save what sin hath impair'd, which yet hath wrought
> Insensibly, for I suspend thir doom.
>
> (6.689–92)

So much for how the battle is equalized. The question that remains is why? One answer is that the War is a test for the loyal angels; their victory is moral, not martial.[9] But there is room for an additional answer. The question we are asking here is put in the poem itself by Abdiel:

> O Heav'n! that such resemblance of the Highest
> Should yet remain, where faith and realty
> Remain not; wherefore should not strength and might
> There fail where Virtue fails, or weakest prove
> Where boldest; though to sight unconquerable?
> His puissance, trusting in th'Almighty's aid,
> I mean to try, whose Reason I have tri'd
> Unsound and false; nor is it aught but just,
> That he who in debate of Truth hath won,
> Should win in Arms, in both disputes alike

9Joseph Summers, *The Muse's Method: An Introduction to "Paradise Lost"* (Cambridge: Harvard University Press, 1962), pp. 125–36.

> Victor; though brutish that contest and foul,
> When Reason hath to deal with force, yet so
> Most reason is that Reason overcome.
>
> (6.114–26)

Reason is a function of the spiritual aspect of the "one first matter," just as the kind of force that Satan employs is a function of the material aspect. The problem behind the War is that Satan does not recognize the claims of reason. His persistent sophistry reveals this. Pledging to add fraud to force, Satan claims that "who overcomes / By force, hath overcome but half his foe" (1.648–49). But before the War, in his debate with Abdiel, Satan has been overcome by reason, itself the power of which fraud is a poor imitation. In Hell Satan argues that "fardest from him [God] is best / Whom reason hath equall'd, force hath made supreme / Above his equals" (1.247–49). In reference to God, the statement is absurd, but if applied to the loyal angels it has a kind of backward logic. The angels have equaled the devils in force, but have been superior to them in *reason*. The devils, at least momentarily convinced by their own sophistry, will not admit to a defeat in reason. Like a stubbornly ignorant man, Satan plays by different rules. God in fact charges the angels "to subdue / By *force*, who reason for thir Law refuse" (6.40–41; my emphasis). The intellectual advantage of Abdiel is invisible to Satan; it is "above the reach of devilish sense."

The participation of the angels in a material battle is an element in a theodicy for the devils. Satan must not only lose, he must also see his error. Abdiel points out to Satan that, despite the experience of his lone dissent the night before, he is not the only loyal angel:

> *but thou seest*
> All are not of thy Train; there be who Faith
> Prefer, and Piety to God, *though then*
> *To thee not visible*, when I alone
> Seem'd in thy World erroneous to dissent
> From all: *my Sect thou seest*, now learn too late
> How few sometimes may know, when thousands err.
>
> (6.142–48; my emphasis)

Abdiel presents Satan with empirical evidence, evidence he can *see*, which is the only kind of evidence he will acknowledge. Instantaneous annihilation by a transcendent God or his infinite army would not have prevented Satan from thinking himself in his last moment the victim of a new set of rules. Rationalizations are being withheld from the arch-Rationalizer. Satan learns that he is not superior even to his fellow angels, much less to God.

In order to prevent Satan's later "what if's," God allows full play to his attempt to grab sovereignty by material force. In the War in Heaven, as in the moment when Satan lifted his head from the burning lake, God "Left him at large to his own dark designs, / That with reiterated crimes he might / Heap on himself damnation" (1.213–15). To allow Satan to pursue these designs to their futile limit, God has the angels fight for two days with the devils' weapons. Abdiel recognizes that the role laid out for the angels involves a lowering of themselves. He obeys God's command to "subdue / By Force" the devils, despite his accurate perception that the contest is "brutish." The angels become brutish temporarily in order to serve God; the devils become brutish permanently by their own evil choice. Satan recognizes a difference, but, as he tells Michael, "The strife which thou call'st evil, . . . wee style / The strife of Glory" (6.289–90).

This difference is implicit in the manner in which either side employs its armor.[10] At the end of the second day's battle, the angels throw off their armor, while the devils are crushed in theirs. The angels' armor had hampered them during the artillery attack; they were bowled over

> The sooner for thir Arms; unarm'd they might
> Have easily as Spirits evaded swift
> By quick contraction or remove; but now
> Foul dissipation follow'd and forc't rout.
>
> (6.595–98)

[10]For a helpful discussion of the purpose of the angels' armor, see Arnold Stein, *Answerable Style* (Minneapolis: University of Minnesota Press, 1953), pp. 33–34.

We are not meant to think that the angels, in throwing away their armor, throw away the armor of 6 Ephesians. Rather, they renounce their reliance on the accouterments of grossly physical warfare. Their "power" comes from a different source. For the angels, the "tinsel trappings" are a hindrance, not an aid, and they realize it.

The devils do not. When crushed by mountains, "Thir armor help'd thir harm, crush't in and bruis'd / Into thir substance pent, which wrought them pain / Implacable" (6.656–58). The devils have made a commitment to physical strength, and now the trappings of physicality recoil on them. Their armor is a shell, and its hollow exteriority symbolizes the devils' hollowness, the empty strength divided from goodness denigrated by Raphael: "For strength from Truth divided and from Just, / Illaudable, naught merits but dispraise / And ignominy" (6.381–83). The devils are ancestors of the Giants derided by Michael (11.689–97).

In the first two days' battle Milton manages to turn a potential conflict to his advantage. He desires to demonstrate the ontological superiority of angel over devil, while reserving victory for the Son. He accomplishes both by having the angels, in obedience to God, fight the devils on their own ontological turf, while at the same time making them impervious to the pain of infernal war and providing glimpses of the spiritual power that has been restrained. Satan has his day in court, as it were, and is found lacking, even with the advantage of the choice of weapons. Despite the final indecisiveness of the battle, he is forced to recognize in its course "how awful goodness is."

Having passed their test, the angels will be granted the martial superiority their goodness earns them after the triumph of the Son on the last day of the War. Gabriel confidently challenges Satan at the end of Book 4:

> *Satan,* I know thy strength, and thou know'st mine,
> Neither our own but giv'n; what folly then
> To boast what Arms can do, since thine no more
> Than Heav'n permits, nor mine, though doubl'd now

To trample thee as mire: for proof look up,
And read thy Lot in yon celestial Sign
Where thou are weigh'd, and shown how light, how weak,
If thou resist.

(4.1006–13)

God has apparently revoked the limitation of the angels' might
and the moratorium on the devils' decline.

The main lesson that Satan learns in the War is that reliance
on brute force divorced from spirit can lead only to chaos.
Satan had boasted to Michael that the rebels would succeed "Or
turn this Heav'n itself into the Hell / Thou fabl'st" (6.291–92),
but this happens to be well beyond his power. He is a destroyer,
not a creator, and the foundation of even Hell is an act of
creation. His temporary legacy is chaotic war, the antithesis of
creation, as "horrid confusion heapt / Upon confusion rose"
(6.668–69). The Cambridge Platonists complained that dead,
spiritless matter would have no organizing principle. The material battle begun by Satan illustrates this point, for Milton
agrees here with Ralph Cudworth and Henry More. With its
aimless and formless shifting, material battle is undecidable; it
mirrors chaos in that both lack forms. In their absence, "nothing" wins by definition. Without the intervention of the Son,
the War would last forever, not in God's joyous eternity but in
the endlessness of Satan's despair. God prevents this, observing
that "War wearied hath perform'd what War can do, / And to
disorder'd rage let loose the reins" (6.695–96). In the War's
third day, Satan's counterpart restores order as he defeats the
devils, an act foreshadowing the ordering of chaos in the seventh book.

The War in Heaven III—God's Thunder

Milton does not need to adjudicate conflicting claims in the
War's third day. The devils are no match for the Son, even after
he limits his own might as the Father limited that of the angels:
"half his strength he put not forth" (6.853). The appearance of

the Son adds resonance to God's earlier measure of Abdiel against the devils, "in word mightier than they in Arms" (6.32). The Son is, in the language of John's first chapter, the "Word of God." Abdiel and his fellows proved not to be physically mightier than the devils; their strength comes from their inclusion in the body of Christ, in the Word. It is a spiritual strength, and one that the Son directs at the devils in the third day's battle.

The Son does speak of his battle with the devils as a physical confrontation when describing the role given to him by the Father:

> Therefore to mee thir doom he hath assign'd;
> That they may have thir wish, to try with mee
> In Battle which the stronger proves, they all,
> Or I alone against them, since by strength
> They measure all, of other excellence
> Not emulous, nor care who them excels;
> Nor other strife with them do I voutsafe.
>   (6.817–23)

The Son will try his strength against that of the devils and not attempt to reason with them, as Abdiel did a book earlier. But this strength combines physical and spiritual force. Here are "more valid arms," arms that not only cause physical pain but also bring final defeat and dissolution.

The first intimation we get of the inseparably spiritual and material nature of the Son's warfare is the description of the chariot:

> forth rush'd with whirl-wind sound
> The Chariot of Paternal Deity,
> Flashing thick flames, Wheel within Wheel, undrawn,
> Itself instinct with Spirit, but convoy'd
> By four Cherubic shapes, four Faces each
> Had wondrous, as with Stars thir bodies all
> And Wings were set with Eyes, with Eyes the Wheels
> Of Beryl, and careering Fires between.
>   (6.749–56)

The chariot mediates the animate and the inanimate and thus becomes a perfect emblem of Milton's monism. This perhaps explains why Milton gives a more prominent place than do other poets to this chariot from Ezekiel. Matter and spirit combine inseparably in the chariot, in which "One spirit . . . rul'd" (6.848). The same is true of the chariot's weapons, which penetrate the devils' shells to sap them of their courage and their resolve. The Son hurls his "ten thousand Thunders" at the devils, "such as in thir Souls infix'd / Plagues; they astonisht all resistance lost, / All courage; down thir idle weapons dropp'd" (6.837–39). The animate thunderbolts contrast sharply with the devils' inert arms; there is a pun on lifeless "idols" in "idle weapons." The thunderbolts leave the devils "Exhausted, spiritless, afflicted, fall'n" (6.852). Thus is restored the congruence of inner and outer condition, the deceptive absence of which Abdiel lamented (6.116–18). The end of the War in Heaven combines physical and spiritual defeat: the devils are forced to the brink of Heaven, and choose to throw themselves into Chaos.

The thunderbolts of the Son are charged with the spiritual strength that God limited in the angels. Earlier, in *The Reason of Church-Government*, Milton had used the image of lightning to describe the spiritual, as opposed to the carnal, weapon of excommunication: "though it touch neither life, nor limme, nor any worldly possession, yet has it such a penetrating force, that swifter then any chimicall sulphur, or that lightning which harms not the skin, and rifles the entrals, it scorches the inmost soul" (*CP* 1:847). The swift "chimicall sulphur" foreshadows the "pernicious fire" of the Son's lightning, which "withers" the strength and "drains" the spirit and vigor of the rebels (6.849–52). The effect of the thunderbolts highlights the pathetic irony of the devils' hope to have, through the manufacture of artillery, "disarm'd / The Thunderer of his only dreaded bolt" (6.490–91). The spiritual nature of the Son's weapons looks forward to the final battle of the Son and Satan, prophesied in Revelation and in Michael's talk with Adam. While the angels fought a nip-and-tuck strategic battle with the devils, the virtue

of Christ's weapons does not depend on strategic position. As
Michael tells Adam:

> Dream not of thir fight,
> As of a Duel, or the local wounds
> Of head or heel: not therefore joins the Son
> Manhood to Godhead, with more strength to foil
> Thy enemy; nor so is overcome
> *Satan*, whose fall from Heav'n, a deadlier bruise,
> Disabl'd not to give thee thy death's wound.
>
> (12.386–92)

The "deadlier Bruise" is the physical/spiritual defeat of Satan
in Heaven. That earlier battle contains the lesson that Michael
here tries to impress upon Adam: physical strength alone is
weakness.

Thus the victory of the Son is a victory of Milton's animist
materialism over his conception of Hobbesian materialism,
which is embodied provisionally in the rebel angels. The devils
foolishly place their faith in false philosophy, in the exclusive
existence of a matter enmeshed in a universal mechanism. The
punishment of this philosophy in Hell is singularly appropriate. As the devils began in a world of the "animate inanimate,"
they end in a world of universal death. Hell is a lifeless waste-
land. While Heaven has its "delicious vines" and "flow'rs"
(5.635–36), Hell has ice and snow, Alps, and "Rocks, Caves,
Lakes, Fens, Bogs, Dens, and shades of Death" (2.621). What
do live in this dark world are perversions of nature; Hell is

> A Universe of death, which God by curse
> Created evil, for evil only good,
> Where all life dies, death lives, and Nature breeds,
> Perverse, all monstrous, all prodigious things,
> Abominable, inutterable.
>
> (2.622–26)

These monstrous creatures embody Satan's distortion of created truth. He has chosen to separate a unity and to assign

primacy to the dead half of the original unity, and his reward is life in a dead, spiritless world.

Their punishment is not only appropriate but also, in the context of the poem, inevitable. There is something of an ontological immune system at work in the poem. The beginning of creation, with the "purging" of the "Infernal dregs / Adverse to life" (7.237–39), reenacts in a different register the purging of the rebels from Heaven. This lifeless matter that must be divided from vital, spiritualized matter is hellish, or "tartareous" and "infernal." Belial acknowledges that a second attempt against Heaven would fail, as the "Ethereal mould" would expel the devils' "baser fire" (2.139–41).[11] Gross hellish material and the spiritualized material that has retained its created perfection separate like oil and water. To return to my first metaphor, the debased material is rejected as an alien substance. There is an echo of the same process in the expulsion of Adam and Eve from the garden; as God tells the Son,

> Those pure immortal Elements that know
> No gross, no unharmonious mixture foul,
> Eject him tainted now, and purge him off
> As a distemper, gross to air as gross.
> (11.50–53)

Abdiel charges that in Satan "faith and *realty* / Remain not" (6.115–16; my emphasis). Satan lacks *reality*. As Merritt Hughes notes, these lines refer in part to Satan's role as "Idol of Majesty Divine" (6.101).[12] He becomes the object of his own error. Having attempted to separate matter from spirit, he rigidifies and becomes more corporeal and less spiritual. In this sense, Satan is less real than he once was. By the process described in the preceding chapters, Satan deprives himself of being by choosing evil. And this is the synthesis of the dialectic of Satanic ontology. Satan chooses debased ontology and as a result approaches Hobbesian being, but cannot finally become a Hobbesian being because he exists *within* Milton's antithetical monism. The result

---

[11]See Chapter 7.
[12]Hughes's note to *PL* 6.115.

is his downward motion within Milton's monism toward the
aspect that Hobbes identified as the whole. His sin is the source
of false philosophy, and his punishment its nightmare realiza-
tion. And finally Milton's monism makes it difficult, and perhaps impossible, to separate the strands of sin and punishment,
since philosophical error and moral error go hand in hand.

In his discussion of Raphael's famous speech on the resemblance of Earth and Heaven (5.571–76), William G. Madsen presents us with a choice of Neoplatonic and typological
readings of the passage and the poem. In the passage Raphael
tells Adam,

> what surmounts the reach
> Of human sense, I shall delineate so,
> By lik'ning spiritual to corporal forms,
> As may express them best, though what if Earth
> Be but the shadow of Heav'n, and things therein
> Each to other like, more than on Earth is thought?

Referring to Raphael's description of Earth as "the shadow of
Heav'n," Madsen writes, "It is my contention that [the Neo-
platonic] interpretation is mistaken, that Milton is using 'shadow' here not in its Platonic or Neoplatonic sense but in its
familiar Christian sense of 'foreshadowing' or 'adumbration,'
and that the symbolism of *Paradise Lost* is typological rather
than Platonic."[13] It is, however, unnecessary to read this and
other passages as *either* typological *or* Neoplatonic; they *are both*
(as long as one does not mean the dualizing Neoplatonism of
More). In insisting on an either/or, Madsen is not thinking
Miltonically, which is to say, monistically.

That this is the case can be gathered from the most overtly
typological statement in the poem. At the end of the epic Michael holds forth to Adam the promise of moral regeneration
through his being "disciplin'd / From shadowy Types to Truth,
from Flesh to Spirit" (12.302–3). The Pauline terms refer in

---

[13]William Madsen, *From Shadowy Types to Truth: Studies in Milton's Symbolism*
(New Haven: Yale University Press, 1968), pp. 88–89.

the first instance to moral and ethical rather than ontological
improvement. But in the background is the parallel promise of
ontological ascent offered to the prelapsarian couple by
Raphael:

> Your bodies may at last turn all to spirit,
> Improv'd by tract of time, and wing'd ascend
> Ethereal, as wee.
>
> (5.497–99)

The parallel is valid because for a monist like Milton carnal-
mindedness is more than metaphor. The moral and epistemological ascent from shadowy types to truth is inseparable from an
ontological ascent from flesh to spirit.

The converse is that moral and epistemological descent leads
from truth to shadowy types, and from spirit to flesh. We have
seen that for Milton the spirit contains the body as an inferior
manifestation of the same substance. The inclusion of flesh in
spirit is reflected in the typological model of the first half of
Michael's promise. The progression from type ("shadowy
types") to antetype ("truth") is not from the false or the alien to
the true, but from imperfect adumbration to the chronologically
posterior but logically and epistemologically prior truth which
contains it. The flesh is the shadow of spirit, a darkened conden-
sation of the one substance. If obedience allows creatures to
improve by tract of time, to pass from flesh to spirit and from
shadowy types to truth, then disobedience does the opposite.
Satan passes from truth to shadowy types, and at the same time
he becomes more shadowy, more corporeal. In the context of
Milton's monism, moral, ontological, and epistemological condi-
tions are inseparable aspects of an indivisible unity.

Epilogue

Historians of ideas have too often shortchanged both poets and philosophers. Despite impatience with disciplinary boundaries in their theoretical statements, Lovejoy and his followers respected those boundaries in practice. The philosophers had original ideas, which they expressed in plain language; the poets took those ideas and clothed them in metaphor and verse. But there is a kind of poetry in the structure and imagery of the *Discourse on the Method* or *Leviathan*, and there is philosophical originality and sophistication in *Paradise Lost*. To point to the literary sophistication of Descartes and Hobbes is not to claim that they are the equals of Dante and Shakespeare. Similarly, to point to Milton's philosophical sophistication is not to suggest that he is as rigorous a thinker as Aquinas or Leibniz. Nevertheless, in writing monism into *Paradise Lost* so consistently and so extensively, Milton enters into dialogue with contemporary philosophers.

This book has demonstrated the place occupied by Milton's animist materialism among many metaphysical models in midcentury, and particularly among the many that offer responses to Descartes and Hobbes.[1] The answers to the questions posed in the Introduction have been implicit in the intervening chapters.

What led Milton to his animist materialism, and how does Milton's materialism relate to contemporary metaphysical models?

The profusion of heterogenous models makes seventeenth-century metaphysics difficult to sort out. Platonism, Aristotelianism, Stoicism, Epicureanism, and Neoplatonism enjoyed enthusiastic and persuasive advocates. At a time notable for the dissonance among emerging models, it is not surprising that Milton, with his characteristic confidence, added his own voice to the cacophony.

Milton had a strong motive for involving himself in the debate over the nature of substance. As the Cambridge Platonists Cudworth and More made clear, the debate had direct implications for belief in freedom of the will. They mobilized to meet the threat of Hobbes and atheistic mechanism and viewed even Descartes with suspicion; despite his affirmation of freedom of the will, Descartes located it in an incorporeal substance so circumscribed that the Platonists feared it would not be an adequate preserve. Cudworth and More, who shared Milton's commitment to defend freedom of the will, chose metaphysical speculation and argument as their main weapons. But each in his own way bears witness to the power of the materialist and mechanist philosophies that he perceives to be threatening human liberty. The very massiveness and obliqueness of Cudworth's response to Hobbes in the *True Intellectual System of the Universe* points to his sense of the extent and depth of the threat posed by Hobbes's version of mechanist materialism. More's exotic contribution to metaphysical debate, extended incorporeal substance, points to his uneasy assimilation of the

---

[1]When Spinoza, for example, writes that the parcels of his one substance, from persons to stones, "are all animate, albeit in different degrees," he sounds remarkably like Milton. See the *Ethics* (II, prop. 13, scholium) in Baruch Spinoza, *The Ethics and Selected Letters*, trans. Samuel Shirley, ed. Seymour Feldman (Indianapolis: Hackett, 1982), p. 72.

Hobbesian dictum that whatever is, is extended. Cudworth and More reaffirmed the existence of incorporeal substance in part as a refuge for freedom of the will, a refuge more secure, because more extensive, than that envisaged by Descartes; for Cudworth and More the action of incorporeal substance lay behind *all* phenomena, not merely mental ones. Milton, in contrast to the Cambridge Platonists, accepted the materiality of all substance, and he viewed that substance as animate; Milton's monism returns to the Hebraic monism that had been obscured by centuries of Platonized Christianity. The metaphysical warrant for freedom of the will is not a separable incorporeal substance, but the universal animation of matter. As demonstrated in Chapter 7, parcels of this matter, in a rudimentary exercise of freedom, separate themselves from each other in *Paradise Lost*.

Anne Conway's animist materialism offers the closest contemporary analogue to Milton's, and her explicit reactions to the philosophies of Descartes, Hobbes, Spinoza, and the Cambridge Platonists provide valuable clues to Milton's implicit reactions. Conway's reservations about Cartesian and Cambridge dualism, and her admission of affinities with Hobbes tempered with criticisms of Hobbes's particular brand of materialism, fit Milton's metaphysics as neatly as they fit her own. Raphael's speeches in Book 5 anatomizing the one first matter, speeches that find their analogues in Conway's *Principles*, set Milton against Descartes and the Platonists as surely as Conway's skeptical and pointed questions concerning the manner in which corporeal and incorporeal substance could be bridged set her apart from the same thinkers. If Conway and Milton both object strenuously to Hobbes's conception of material substance, they endorse Hobbes's sense of the impossibility of maintaining the existence of separate incorporeal substance. Hobbes may have gotten things wrong, he may not have recognized that matter is alive as well as extended, but his assertion of the materiality of all substance makes him the philosopher worth engaging.

Why does Milton feel compelled to introduce philosophy into his poetry?

Inasmuch as an author's presuppositions will make their way into any work, we should expect Milton's first principles to make their way into his poetry. But why does Milton's philosophy enter his poetry, and particularly *Paradise Lost*, so overtly and self-consciously? One could point to the convergence of Milton's egotism and epic convention. Virgil sets out to contain Homer's epics in his own epic; Renaissance epic poets aspire to contain both Homer and Virgil in their poems; and Milton writes an epic that is not only Homeric and Virgilian, but also Lucretian. Having settled on an epic of Genesis, Milton could hardly have failed to include a Lucretian dimension in his poem. For Renaissance thinkers, especially but not exclusively those in the hermetic tradition, Moses is the primal philosopher, poet, and prophet, and Genesis the source of all knowledge, including the cosmological and the metaphysical. As Henry More put it in 1653, "*Moses* seems to have been aforehand, and prevented the subtilest and abstrusest Inventions of the choicest Philosophers that ever appeared after him to this very day."[2] For Milton as for More, the concerns of natural philosophy are inseparable from the concerns of theology, and the question of the nature of substance is central in *Paradise Lost*. Moral health participates in the health of an organic universe. The epic presents the relation of Heaven and Earth primarily through a discourse on digestion; Adam and Eve fall through digesting the knowledge of evil in the apple, and they would have risen by being sublimated in the digestive tract of the world. One cannot understand the economy of Milton's universe, or the effects of obedience and disobedience, without understanding the nature of Milton's things.

Given my argument for Milton's attention to the implications of the philosophical debate of his time, the relative insignifi-

---

[2]Henry More, *Conjectura Cabbalistica, or, A Conjectural Essay of Interpreting the Mind of Moses, in the Three First Chapters of Genesis* (1653), rpt. in *A Collection of Several Philosophical Writings*, 2 vols. (1662; facs. rpt. New York: Garland, 1978), p. 3 (Preface to the Reader). The works in this collection are paginated separately.

cance of metaphysical questions in *Samson Agonistes* and *Paradise Regained* might be more puzzling than their centrality in *Paradise Lost*. The theme of *Samson Agonistes* lends itself to the kind of speculation on the relation of body and spirit familiar from *Paradise Lost*: a divinely chosen hero sins against God, and as a result becomes spiritually bankrupt even while maintaining his physical strength. The treatment of Harapha, "bulk without spirit vast" (1238), resembles the treatment of the rebel angels in the War in Heaven in *Paradise Lost*. In contrast, the Chorus attributes to Samson the kind of spiritual/material strength attributed to the Son in *Paradise Lost*:

> Hee all thir Ammunition
> And feats of War defeats
> With plain Heroic magnitude of mind
> And celestial vigor arm'd,
> Thir Armories and Magazines contemns,
> Renders them useless, while
> With winged expedition
> Swift as the lightning glance he executes
> His errand on the wicked, who surpris'd
> Lose thir defense, distracted and amaz'd.
>   (1277–86)

This passage mirrors closely in language and theme the third day of the War in Heaven. The phrase "celestial vigor" echoes the play on "vigor" that punctuates the descent of the devils in Book 6 of the epic, and the lightning glance and its effect recapitulate the final defeat of the devils.

But parts of *Samson Agonistes* do not fit the picture of the mature Milton's philosophy of substance. Early in the play Samson conditionally endorses the view that the soul is "all in every part" (93), an Augustinian conception depending on the incorporeality of the soul. Shortly thereafter Samson laments in conventional terms the imprisonment of the soul in the body, an imprisonment exacerbated by blindness:

> Thou art become (O worst imprisonment!)
> The Dungeon of thyself; thy Soul
> (Which Men enjoying sight oft without cause complain)

Imprison'd now indeed,
In real darkness of the body dwells,
Shut up from outward light
To incorporate with gloomy night.

(155–61)

In these and other passages Samson speaks as though there is a
dualist gulf between body and soul. In order to explain why
Samson apparently assumes here a relation of spirit and matter
foreign to the older Milton, it is not sufficient to say that the
character does not speak for the author. When characters get
philosophical questions wrong in Milton, as do Comus and the
devils in *Paradise Lost*, they do so either self-consciously in order
to gain an advantage over adversaries, or without self-
consciousness in order to put the best face on things for themselves. Thus, as I argued in Chapter 7, Satan turns intermit-
tently to dualism to deal with an unmistakable worsening of
physical condition.

The ambivalence of *Samson Agonistes* on questions of mind,
body, and substance, so alien to *Paradise Lost*, suggests that Milton began work on the poem in the 1640s, as William Riley
Parker argued on several occasions, and that he resumed work
on the poem after completing *Paradise Lost*.[3] The passage

<hr>

[3] For William Riley Parker's most important statements on this question, see
"The Date of *Samson Agonistes*," *Philological Quarterly* 28 (1949): 145–66; *Milton:
A Biography*, 2 vols. (Oxford: Clarendon Press, 1968), 2:903–17; and "The Date
of *Samson Agonistes* Again," in *Calm of Mind: Tercentenary Essays on "Paradise
Regained" and "Samson Agonistes" in Honor of John S. Diekhoff*, ed. Joseph A.
Wittreich, Jr. (Cleveland: The Press of Case Western Reserve University, 1971),
pp. 163–74. Parker points to the fact that Edward Phillips does not assign
Samson's composition to the same period (late 1660s) as *Paradise Regained*. He
observes that Milton uses "Ashtoroth" as a singular form in *Samson Agonistes* (as
in the "Nativity Ode"), despite explaining in *Paradise Lost* that it is a plural form
for "Ashtoreth" (1.422, 438). He lays out similarities not only between the
prosodic practice of *Samson Agonistes* and Milton's psalm translations of the late
1640s and early 1650s, but also between the note on the verse of *Samson Agonistes* and a letter appended to the Latin "Ode to John Rous" of 1647. In
addition to these technical points, Parker notes Milton's increasing interest in
the Samson story in the late 1640s and early 1650s and argues for early composition on the grounds of the theological content and stance. Parker's arguments, of which I offer only a sample, have met with more resistance than
acceptance, perhaps in part because the new dating would upset so many
interpretive applecarts.

quoted above as reflecting the treatment of metaphysics in the War in Heaven (*SA* 1277–86) exemplifies those prosodic elements more prominent in Milton's later poetry: medial pauses and enjambment. Conversely, the passage reflecting an earlier dualist conception of substance (155–61) exemplifies the greater frequency of end-stops in Milton's earlier poetry. In at least one place thematic and prosodic clues make it possible to discern a late addition to a poem begun early. Samson laments to Manoa,

> O that torment should not be confin'd
> To the body's wounds and sores
> With maladies innumerable
> In heart, head, breast, and reins;
> But must secret passage find
> To th'inmost mind,
> There exercise all his fierce accidents,
> And on her purest spirits prey,
> As on entrails, joints, and limbs,
> With answerable pains, but more intense
> Though void of corporeal sense.
>   (606–16)

Here bodily and spiritual disease are related by analogy and not by identity. The gulf between the two is confirmed by the final lines, in which the "answerable pains" of the mind are "void of corporeal sense." Significantly, rhymes are found at the end of five lines (or six if one hears a rhyme for "sense" in "accidents") out of eleven. Even if one acknowledges the presence of a surprising number of rhymes in *Paradise Lost*, the concentration of rhyme in this passage is more characteristic of Milton's poetry of the 1630s than of the poetry of the 1660s.[4] The rhymes cease, and the percentage of enjambed lines increase, as Samson continues his speech:

> My griefs not only pain me
> As a ling'ring disease,
> But finding no redress, ferment and rage,

[4]See John S. Diekhoff, "Rhyme in *Paradise Lost*," *PMLA* 49 (1934): 539–43.

Nor less than wounds immedicable
Rankle, and fester, and gangrene,
To black mortification.
Thoughts my Tormentors arm'd with deadly stings
Mangle my apprehensive tenderest parts,
Exasperate, exulcerate, and raise
Dire inflammation which no cooling herb
Or med'cinal liquor can assuage,
Nor breath of Vernal Air from snowy *Alp*.

(617–28)

This passage begins by continuing the relation of analogy between mental and physical disease, but in the second half the distinction between the two is blurred. Now the thoughts "mangle . . . apprehensive . . . parts"; they cause ulcers and inflammations. This kind of interpenetration of bodily and spiritual, as related to the juxtaposition by analogy, is more typical of the later Milton. Milton's apparent indecision on metaphysical matters in *Samson Agonistes* concurs with other evidence that Milton began the poem early and reworked it extensively after completing *Paradise Lost*.

If *Samson Agonistes* represents a cross-section or archaeology of Milton's developing philosophy of substance, *Paradise Regained*, Milton's brief epic, seems to represent a fierce and sweeping repudiation of all philosophical speculation. Does *Paradise Regained* signal a retreat from an urbane and learned Christian humanism into a narrow Puritanism? Does Milton at the end of his life turn against the kind of philosophical speculation informing the *Christian Doctrine* and *Paradise Lost*? The Son of God rebukes Satan for his praise of Greek philosophies:

Think not but that I know these things; or think
I know them not; not therefore am I short
Of knowing what I ought: he who receives
Light from above, from the fountain of light,
No other doctrine needs, though granted true;
But these are false, or little else but dreams,
Conjectures, fancies, built on nothing firm.

(PR 4.286–92)

Know God and yourself, Milton seems to say; what is more (including philosophy) is fume. But the rejection of philosophy in *Paradise Regained* is strictly circumscribed. This notorious passage, rather than demonstrating Milton's late aversion to philosophy, places philosophy in the position it always held for Milton and many of his contemporaries, in the service of theology and ethics.

Milton held all his life to the principle articulated in the *Areopagitica*: "To the pure all things are pure [Titus 1:15], not only meats and drinks, but all kinde of knowledge whether of good or evill; the knowledge cannot defile, nor consequently the books, if the will and conscience be not defil'd" (*CP* 2:512). The Christian approaching Greek philosophy with a "spirit and judgment equal or superior" to what he or she finds there (*PR* 4.324) will supply what is deficient and correct the extravagant. The Son of God does in fact specify just what is deficient in Greek philosophy: it is "ignorant" of "how man fell," and it teaches us to seek virtue in ourselves rather than through dependence on grace:

> Alas! what can they teach, and not mislead;
> Ignorant of themselves, of God much more,
> And how the world began, and how man fell
> Degraded by himself, on grace depending?
> Much of the Soul they talk, but all awry,
> And in themselves seek virtue, and to themselves
> All glory arrogate, to God give none,
> Rather accuse him under usual names,
> Fortune and Fate, as one regardless quite
> Of mortal things. Who therefore seeks in these
> True wisdom, finds her not, or by delusion
> Far worse, her false resemblance only meets
> An empty cloud.
>
> (*PR* 4.309–21)

If the Greeks underestimate the hand of God in our actions, they also overestimate the extent to which God, whom they call Fate, manipulates us. They share this perspective with the speculating devils of *Paradise Lost*. Paradoxically, they acknowledge neither the divine gift of freedom of the will, nor the fall through which we have forfeited that gift. Acknowledging neither the effects of the fall nor the necessity of grace in repairing those effects, the Greeks are as regards moral philosophy "in wand'ring mazes lost" (*PL* 2.561). In Milton's eyes, their effort to find virtue in themselves presupposes the kind of freedom that their deifying of fate forecloses, the kind of freedom we can regain only through our reception of grace and acceptance of faith.

The error of philosophy, then, in both *Paradise Lost* and *Paradise Regained*, lies in its claim of autonomy. Secular philosophy divorced from theology and ethics is sinister, and appropriately it is given to the devil. For Milton the worth of a philosophy is measured against the "Light from above" (*PR* 4.289). Milton addresses metaphysical questions in the context of discussions of creation, of the relation of the Son to God, and of the results of creatures' obedience and disobedience. The words of the Son in *Paradise Regained* remind us once again of the centrality for Milton of the cycle of free will—fall—conviction—faith—free will (with grace intervening in each step but the first). If the primary failing of the Greek philosophers is ignorance of the fall, the primary threat of contemporary mechanism is the undermining of free will. The Son of God does not need to be taught the Greek philosophies with their shared errors, nor does he need their help to pass his test in the desert. But Milton finds himself in a different position. He hopes in *Paradise Lost* and the *Christian Doctrine* to be doctrinal to the nation. This in part involves meeting the threat of philosophies that have the potential to divert attention from those ethical truths illuminated by divine light. The Son of God may be proof against the oversights and overreachings of secular philosophy, but Milton's audience might not be. In his promise of mastery over nature, Descartes like Bacon seems either to ignore the effects of the fall or to offer another avenue besides grace to repair the ruins of our first parents; avoiding the fall in his prehistory of the human race in the first part of *Leviathan*, Hobbes points us toward a world in which our instincts are harnessed and balanced rather than reformed. Milton meets the threats posed by these philosophies by constructing an alternative philosophy in verse and prose.

Are poetry and philosophy happily combined or "unhappily perplexed" in "Paradise Lost"?

My fifth chapter offers one answer to this question: Milton is far more scrupulous than his contemporaries in rationalizing the philosophical frame of his epic and in adhering to the frame as his narrative unfolds. Heywood, Beaumont, and Peyton leave more loose ends and present us with more impossible scenes. But Johnson, from whom the question is derived, seems to fault Milton not so much for contradiction as for obtruding metaphysical speculation on his reader in the first place. It is tempting to ask what Johnson, had he lived another ten or fifteen years, might have made of the works of another poet interested in philosophy, William Blake. A reader faced with Blake's elaborate, private mythology finds himself or herself initially without moorings. Having banished conventional categories and demonized conventional gods, Blake is free to create his own world from the bottom up. Milton had no anachronistic Romantic impulse to spin a new mythology out of himself, but the moments when metaphysical speculation is most intrusive in *Paradise Lost,* as in the narrator's discussion of Raphael's digestion or Raphael's revelations about the angels' sexual life, have an effect similar to that of the intrusive mythology of Blake. We learn in these moments that we are not on familiar ground, that an understanding of the world in the poem (and, as far as each poet is concerned, of the world outside the poem) will require an abandonment of comfortable certainties and an imaginative leap. Milton may have been more of Blake's party than Blake himself knew.

If one grants that poets can be philosophers, it would be difficult to think of a philosophy more amenable to happy combination with poetry than Milton's. His animist materialism is particularly suited to a *poet* with metaphysical interests. Against the backdrop of his monist metaphysic, the bodying forth of inner states in concrete forms becomes more than conventional. Repeatedly in *Paradise Lost,* the gap between image and idea narrows, and metaphor verges on metonymy. Milton the poet rises to the challenge of depicting a world that is not divisible into discrete categories of being, but is rather a continuum of the one first matter. His decision to import metaphysical speculations into the epic, far from weighing down his poetry, calls forth the exquisite and subtle interlace of corporeal and "incorporeal," and of animate and "inanimate," in the descriptions of Eden and Heaven. The result, in Milton's terms, is a poetry preeminently simple and sensuous.

According to posthumous tradition, Pascal called Cartesianism "the Romance of Nature, something like the story of Don Quixote."[5] The density of this saying supports the attribution to Pascal. Descartes's dualism, Pascal implies, is as far from reality as Quixote's vision of Spanish society, and is perhaps just as much the result of the intensity of desire—in Descartes's case for a clear and distinct, geometric picture of the world. But this does not exhaust the saying, for Pascal also comments shrewdly on the relation between philosophy and romance, or philosophy and poetry broadly conceived. Philosophers, whatever their truth claims, construct models of the world. Descartes himself points to the role of heuristic fiction in philosophy, although one suspects that he thought he had got beyond them. While Descartes's fiction, in Pascal's view, resembles Quixote's in diverging widely from that which it attempts to interpret, it shares philosophy's general aim to provide likely stories of the way things are. If, because of recent explorations of the frontier between philosophy and literature, we are more ready to acknowledge that philosophical systems are constructions rather than transcriptions of reality, then perhaps we are ready to grapple seriously with Milton's poetic construction of reality in *Paradise Lost*.

[5]"Sayings Attributed to Pascal," in Blaise Pascal, *Pensées*, ed. A. J. Krailsheimer (Harmondsworth: Penguin, 1966), p. 356.

Index

Abelard, Peter, 174 n.
Adamson, J. H., 5
Addison, Joseph, 178, 184
Alchemy, 113–15, 164
Alexander, Sir William, 151
Allegory, 155, 172–77; of Custom
and Error, 93–94; Milton's attitude
toward, 180–93; and nominalism,
172, 174 n., 176–77, 192–93; and
ontology, 169; and realism, 172–
76, 180, 192–93; in seventeenth
century, 177–80, 193; of Sin and
Death, 7, 168–93; of Truth, 94
Allen, Don Cameron, 16 n., 135, 160
n.
Ambrose, Isaac, 158
Angels, 47; and Cambridge Platonists, 139, 141, 146; Conway's,
119; and Descartes, 139; Hobbes's,
128, 139–41, 196, 198; literary,
137–38, 147–57; and metaphysical
beliefs, 137; Milton's, 7, 103, 119,
128, 137–38, 141–48, 153, 157–
61, 165–67, 186, 188; More's, 71–
73, 138–39, 141, 146; scholastic,
142, 145, 147
Ariosto, Ludovico, 178, 192
Aristotelianism, 20, 39 n., 43, 48, 51,
104–5, 112–13, 126, 134, 139, 213
n., 245; and Anne Conway, 120;
and hylomorphism, 22, 99–102,
134

Aristotle, 3, 44, 58–59, 66, 79, 88–
89, 98 n., 99–105, 115–17, 120,
174–75
—Works: De anima, 100; Generation of
Animals, 101–2, 116; Metaphysics, 3,
101–2, 174 n.; Parts of Animals,
102; Topics, 174 n.
Arminianism, 43
Arnauld, Antoine, 23
Atheism and theism, 3, 6, 20–21,
40–41, 43, 57–59, 62–68, 79, 125;
and proofs of God, 22–23, 64
Atomism, 20–25, 30, 31, 42–48, 66,
111–12; and the Cambridge Platonists, 56–59, 63–64, 74 n.
Aubrey, John, 8
Augustine, 7, 191–92, 216, 248; and
evil as privation, 169–71, 185, 188;
and realism, 174 n., 175–76
Austen, Jane, 173

Babb, Lawrence, 104 n., 135
Bacon, Sir Francis, 2–3 nn., 25, 28,
32, 48, 111–14, 120, 253; and alle-
gory, 177–78; and Milton, 114–15,
117, 135
—Works: Advancement of Learning,
113, 177; Novum Organum, 113;
Sylva Sylvarum, 88–89, 213 n.; De
Viis Mortis, 112–13; Wisdom of the
Ancients, 177
Barfield, Owen, 173

Bayle, Pierre, 14
Beaumont, Joseph, 7, 151 n., 157, 254
Benlowes, Edward, 7, 152–53
Blackmore, Sir Richard, 165 n.
Blake, William, 254
Blumenberg, Hans, 59 n.
Boehme, Jacob, 5, 153
Boethius, 62
Bostocke, R., 105
Boyle, Robert, 31, 56, 108, 126
Bramhall, Bishop John, 37 n., 40, 52, 97
Brooks, Roger, 212 n.
Browne, Sir Thomas, 165
Brush, Craig B., 44 n.
Bullinger, Heinrich, 129 n.
Bunyan, John, 172, 178, 180
Burden, Dennis, 160 n., 214
Burns, Norman, 129
Burton, Robert, 148
Bush, Douglas, 151 n.

Cabbalism, 114–15, 118, 123
Calvin, John, 37 n., 129
Cambridge Platonists, 6, 9 n., 21–22, 50–78, 81, 83; and atomism, 56–59, 63–64, 74 n.; and Conway, 123–24; and Descartes, 52 n., 59–60, 63–68, 74–76, 205, 221, 245; and Hobbes, 51, 53, 59–63, 74–75, 206, 221, 237, 245–46; and Milton, 6, 108–9, 117, 132–35. *See also* Angels; Cudworth, Ralph; Dualism; Free will and determinism; Mechanism, opposition to; More, Henry; Substance, incorporeal
Camoens, Luiz de, 179
Carey, John, 95 n., 171 n.
Carré, Meyrick, 174 n.
Cassirer, Ernst, 65 n.
Causes, final, 20, 31, 66–67, 126
Cervantes Saavedra, Miguel de, 255
Charles I (king of England), 163
Charleton, Walter, 9, 31, 41, 43, 46–48, 59, 130
Christopher, Georgia B., 202 n.
Chrysostom, John, 84
Coker, Matthew (faith healer), 71
Coleridge, Samuel Taylor, 16, 172

Conway, Anne (third Viscountess Conway and Killultagh), 6–7, 70–71, 111, 120, 148, 165 n., 223; and Cambridge Platonists, 123–24, 246; and Cudworth, 117, 125; and Descartes, 119, 123–26, 130–33, 246; and Hobbes, 119, 123–24, 130–32, 246; and Milton, 117–33, 208, 246; and More, 117–19, 121. *See also* Free will and determinism; Mechanism, opposition to; Monism
Conway, Edward (second Viscount Conway and Killultagh), 165 n.
Copernican cosmology, 165 n.
Cowley, Abraham, 7, 160–62, 165, 179–80
Crashaw, Richard, 179
Cudworth, Ralph, 6, 8, 9 n., 51–68, 76–77, 98, 108, 237; and Conway, 117–25; and Descartes, 51–52, 59, 63–67, 245–46; and Hobbes, 51–52, 59–63, 245–46; and "plastic nature," 54, 68–69
—*Works: Treatise concerning Eternal and Immutable Morality,* 52, 57 n., 62–63; *True Intellectual System,* 53, 55, 57–68, 71 n., 76, 132, 206, 211

Damrosch, Leopold, 37 n.
Dante Alighieri, 16, 175–76, 192, 244
Darsy, H., 64 n.
D'Avenant, Sir William, 177–78
Debus, Allen G., 105 n., 114–15 nn.
Democritus and Democritan physics, 57–59, 118–19, 206
Descartes, René, 3, 6–7, 9–11, 15, 17–18, 21–29, 41, 44–46, 48–51, 57 n., 59–60, 63–68, 70, 74–76, 98, 100 n., 114, 117, 139, 175–77, 244, 253, 255; and Conway, 119, 123–26, 130–33; and Hobbes, 30–35, 176–177, 206–7; and Milton, 80–81, 86, 101, 125–26, 136, 142, 245–46; and Milton's devils, 194, 203–6, 212, 221, 224. *See also* Cambridge Platonists; Dualism; Free will and determinism; Mechanism; Substance, incorporeal
—*Works:* "Comments on a Certain

Descartes, René (*cont.*)
Broadsheet," 24, 29 n.; *Description of the Human Body,* 26–27; *Discourse on the Method,* 15, 26, 28–30, 204; *Meditations on First Philosophy,* 3 n., 22, 24, 30, 67 n., 203, 205; *Passions of the Soul,* 26–27; *Principles of Philosophy,* 24 n., 25, 28–29, 66, 67 n.; "Replies to Objections to the *Meditations,*" 31, 67; *Treatise on Man,* 26; the *World,* 15, 25, 28–29
Devils, Milton's, 194–243; and Hobbesian empiricism, 216–21, 226–29; and hollowness, 210–12, 230–31, 236; materialization of, 208–16, 224–31; and nominalism, 219–20
Digby, Sir Kenelm, 9, 30, 98–99 n., 139
Digestion as monist metaphor, 102–6, 121, 141–42, 153, 199, 209–10, 247
Dijksterhuis, E. J., 4 n.
Disease imagery, 85–88, 209, 250–51
Dryden, John, 180
Dualism: Cambridge Platonist, 60, 63, 69–76; Cartesian, 22–30, 63, 131, 133–34, 203–6; Charleton's, 47–48; ethical, 69–71; Milton's early, 79–83; Pauline, 70, 82–87, 208; Platonist, 74, 79–87, 91, 144, 242
du Bartas, Guillaume de Salluste, 146–51, 155–56, 159
Duns Scotus (Joannes D. S.), 5
Dury, John, 9–10

Eckhart, Meister, 5
Eikon Basilike, 109, 162–63
Empiricism. *See* Devils, Milton's; Hobbes, Thomas
Empson, William, 112 n.
Epicurus and Epicureanism, 20–21, 25, 42–43, 47, 57, 63, 245
Euripides, 101
Eusebius, 5

Fallon, Robert Thomas, 223 n.
Fallon, Stephen M., 43 n., 89 n., 123 n.

Ferry, Anne, 182
Ficino, Marsilio, 71
Fiore, Peter A., 170 n., 187
Fisch, Harold, 13 n.
Fletcher, Angus, 172–73
Fletcher, Giles, 7, 150–51, 156 n., 159, 178–79
Fletcher, Phineas, 7, 150–51, 155, 178
Fludd, Robert, 4–5, 114–15
Force and fraud, 228–29
Forms, substantial, 20, 58 n.
Fowler, Alastair, 157–58, 195
Freeman, James A., 223 n.
Free will and determinism, 3–4, 6, 18–21, 42–43, 212–16; Cambridge Platonists on, 51–54, 245–46; Conway on, 117, 131–32; Descartes on, 24, 108; Epicurus on, 42–43; Gassendi on, 43; Hobbes on, 36–39, 96–97, 108, 127, 214–15; Milton on, 79, 96–99, 117, 127, 131–32, 214–16; Milton's matter and, 201–2. *See also* Mechanism
Frye, Roland Mushat, 208 n.

Gabbey, Alan, 65 n., 108 n.
Gabirol, ibn (Avicebron), 122
Galen and Galenism, 86, 102, 104–5, 112, 134
Galilei, Galileo, 8, 21 n., 29, 31 n., 32, 72 n.
Gallagher, Philip J., 183–84, 189 n.
Gassendi, Pierre, 6, 9, 21, 23, 25, 28, 30 n., 31, 41–48, 51, 59, 63–64, 81, 86, 104, 126, 130
Gelbart, N. R., 46 n.
Genesis, 15, 28–30, 48, 247
Glanvill, Joseph, 72, 117, 122, 165
—Works: *Lux Orientalis,* 58 n., 61 n., 70–71 nn.; *Saducismus Triumphatus,* 54–55, 134, 167; *Vanity of Dogmatizing,* 53, 56, 64 n., 72 n., 133
Glisson, Francis, 113 n.
Gravity, 213–14
Gregory of Nyssa, 5

Hall, Thomas S., 113 n.
Hanford, James Holly, 8 n., 170 n., 181–82

Harrison, Charles T., 31 n.
Hartlib, Samuel, 9–10
Harvey, William, 111, 115–17, 120
Hazlitt, William, 182
Hell, Hobbes's and Milton's, 221–22
Helmont, Francis Mercury van, 117–18, 123
Helmont, Jean-Baptiste van, 46
Hermeticism, 114, 116 n., 247
Heywood, Thomas, 7, 148, 151, 156–57, 232, 254
Hill, Christopher, 5, 9 n.
Hinman, Robert, 161 n.
History of ideas, 11–16, 244
Hobbes, Thomas, 2 n., 3–4, 6–9, 11, 13 n., 14, 17–18, 23–25, 28, 36–41, 43–49, 51, 59–63, 66–69, 74–75, 78, 117, 165, 167, 244; and Conway, 119, 122–24; and Descartes, 30–35, 176–77, 206–7; and empiricism, 33–35, 216–21, 226–29; and Milton, 80–81, 96–98, 107–10, 127–34, 136, 245–46; and Milton's devils, 194, 206–22, 224–27, 241–42; and nominalism, 177, 192–93, 219–20. *See also* Angels; Cambridge Platonists; Devils, Milton's; Free will and determinism; Hell, Hobbes's and Milton's; Materialism; Mechanism; Soul, corporeality of; Substance, incorporeal
—*Works: An Answer to a Book . . . Called the "Catching of the Leviathan,"* 39–40; *De Cive,* 32 n.; *Considerations upon the Reputation of . . . Thomas Hobbes,* 32; *De Corpore,* 31 n., 32, 41, 51, 192–93, 214 n., 219; *Elements of Law,* 32 n.; *An Historical Narrative concerning Heresy,* 33 n.; *De Homine,* 34; *Leviathan,* 32–40, 60 n., 62, 74, 87, 109, 128–29, 139–41, 167, 215, 219–22, 229, 253; "Objections to Descartes's Meditations," 31, 60; *Questions concerning Liberty, Necessity, and Chance,* 52
Hollowness. *See* Devils, Milton's
Homer, 161, 163, 229, 232, 247
Hughes, Merritt Y., 241

Hunter, Michael, 16 n., 19–20, 46 n.
Hunter, William, 4–5, 99 n., 116 n.
Hylozoism, 43–45, 68

Immortality, 6, 19–20, 24, 123. *See also* Soul, incorporeality of
Innate ideas, 24, 61–63
Intellectual history, 16–17
Ixion, myth of, 93–94

Jacobus, Lee, 219 n.
James, William, 61–62
Johnson, Samuel, 2 n., 8, 17, 137–38, 142–43, 155–57, 254; and Milton's allegory, 168–69, 179–80, 190, 193
Johnston, David, 32 n.
Jonas, Hans, 201
Joy, Lynn Sumida, 42 n.

Kargon, Robert, 21 n., 24–25, 29 n., 43 n., 46 n., 112 n.
Kelley, Maurice, 129 n.
Kerrigan, William, 6 n., 82–83, 112 n., 165 n.
Koyré, Alexander, 75 n.
Kuhn, Thomas, 165 n.

Labriola, Albert C., 186 n., 212 n.
LaCapra, Dominick, 17
Lamprecht, Sterling P., 30–31 nn., 65–66 nn., 139 n.
Lawrence, Henry, 158
Leibniz, Gottfried Wilhelm, 3–4 n., 10 n., 11, 46 n., 108, 126, 244; and Conway, 118–19, 123
Leucippus, 58–59
Lewis, C. S., 157–58, 170 n., 172 n., 180
Lieb, Michael, 223 n.
Limbo of Vanity, 190, 192
Livy: story of Menenius Agrippa, 86–87
Locke, John, 11, 14, 61 n., 108–9
Loeb, Louis E., 3 n.
Loewenstein, David, 89 n., 163 n.
Lopston, Peter, 118 n., 122 n.
Lovejoy, A. O., 11–14, 244
Lucretius, 15, 247
Luther, Martin, 37 n., 202

MacCaffrey, Isabel, 173 n., 182 n., 189

MacKinnon, Florence Isabel, 61 n., 67–68 nn., 75–77 nn.

Madsen, William G., 242

Malebranche, Nicholas, 133

Mandelbaum, Maurice, 5 n., 11 n.

Marino, Giambattista, 179

Markham, Gervase, 231 n.

Materialism, 3, 74; Epicurus's, 20–21; Gassendi's flirtation with, 45; Hobbes's mechanist, 31–35, 63, 127–30, 134, 206–22. *See also* Milton: animist materialism; Milton: poetry and materialism; Monism; Soul, corporeality of

Materiality as criterion of reality, 77–78, 134, 166–67

Mechanism, 3–4, 6, 20, 22–23, 25–31, 45–49, 56, 63–68; and Descartes, 24–30, 33, 48–49, 65, 123–26; and Hobbes, 31–36, 41, 124, 131

Mechanism, opposition to: Cambridge Platonists', 51, 54–56, 61–69; Conway's, 122–26, 131; Milton's, 79, 107–10, 126, 240–42, 253

Merchant, Carolyn, 118 n., 123 n.

Mersenne, Marin, 10, 23, 29–31

Metaphysics, status of, 2–7

Milton, Elizabeth Minshull, 8, 127

Milton, John: allegory, 93–94, 168–73, 180–93; animist materialism, 1, 5–7, 10, 18, 78–111, 114–15, 119–36, 142–46, 153, 165–66, 186, 195–206, 208–12, 220–21, 223–26, 238–43, 244–46; and Aristotle, 88–89, 99–105, 115–17, 134; awareness of contemporary philosophy, 8–11, 41; and Bacon, 114, 135; and Cambridge Platonists, 6, 108–9, 117, 132–35; and Cudworth, 132; and Descartes, 80–81, 86, 101, 125–26, 136, 142, 194, 203–6, 212, 221, 245–46, 249; disease imagery, 85–88, 209, 250–51; divided audience in divorce tracts, 90–92; evil, Augustinian conception of, 170–71, 184, 187–88, 209

n.; God, 122, 128–29, 202, 217–18; and history of ideas, 12; and Hobbes, 80–81, 96–98, 107–10, 127–34, 136, 194, 206–22, 224–31; insides and outsides, 210–12; knowledge, intuitive and discursive, 216–19; material Heaven, 195–99, 202, 223–24; metaphysical obstetrics, 95, 121–22; and More, 4, 127–28, 132–35; mortalism, 80, 129–30; and new philosophy, 135; poetry and materialism, 195–201, 254–55; politics, 109–10, 127; sex, 90–95, 160; truth, conception of, 160–66, 183. *See also* Angels; Devils, Milton's; Digestion as monist metaphor; Free will and determinism; Hell, Hobbes's and Milton's; Mechanism, opposition to; Monism; Ontological mobility and moral value; Soul, corporeality of; Spirits, corporeal; War in Heaven
—*Characters:* Abdiel, 186, 196, 218, 224, 228, 232–35, 238, 241; Adam, 1–2, 81, 102–6, 143, 146 n., 186, 197, 201, 213, 217, 240; Beelzebub, 203, 212, 215–16; Belial, 143, 204 n., 214–15; Chaos, 190–92; Comus, 82, 249; Elder Brother, 82, 181; Eve, 146 n., 159, 186, 201–2, 213; Gabriel, 142, 236–37; God (Father), 166, 202, 217–18, 231, 233–35, 241; Harapha, 248; Ithuriel, 206; the Lady, 82, 228; Mammon, 210–11, 214–15; Michael, 146 n., 224–25, 233, 235, 239–40, 242–43; Moloch, 213, 215; Mulciber, 164; Raphael, 1–2, 81, 102–6, 110, 119, 141–46, 153, 161 n., 165 n., 184–86, 197, 202, 213, 217, 226, 236, 242–43; Samson, 248–51; Satan (*PL*), 142–43, 146 n., 159, 171, 185–88, 191–92, 194–222, 224–42; Satan (*PR*), 251–52; Sin and Death, 171, 183–90, 192; the Son (*PL*), 166, 231, 233, 236–40; the Son (*PR*), 251–52, 253; Uriel, 142, 206–7, 217; Zephon, 186, 206, 231; Zophiel, 231 n.

Milton, John (*cont.*)
—*Poetry:* Arcades, 80; "At a Solemn
Music," 166 n.; *Comus,* 81–83, 96–
97, 166 n., 181, 223, 228; Elegies
1, 2, and 4, 180; Elegy 3, 80; "Epi-
taph on the Marchioness of
Winchester," 80; "Fair Infant,"
180–81; "Il Penseroso," 80; "In
Obitum Praesulis Eliensis," 80; "In
Quintum Novembris," 181;
"Nativity Ode," 80, 166 n., 181;
"On Time," 80; *Paradise Lost,* 1, 2–
3, 7, 8 n., 16, 21, 80–81, 93 n.,
96–97, 102–7, 114–15, 119, 121,
125–26, 135, 141–46, 163–66,
181, 184–221, 223–43, 248, 249;
Paradise Regained, 94 n., 97, 135,
163, 209, 248, 251–53; "The Passion," 94 n., 148 n.; *Samson Agonistes,* 163, 248–51; "Sonnet XIV,"
95; "Upon the Circumcision," 166
n.
—*Prose: Apology against . . . Smectym-
nuus,* 3, 85, 88, 162; *Areopagitica,*
86, 97, 98 n., 105, 122, 192, 219
n., 223, 252; *Art of Logic,* 126, 170
nn., 175; *Christian Doctrine,* 2 n., 3,
5, 8 n., 16, 19, 80, 94, 96, 98–102,
104, 121, 125–26, 129, 138 n.,
142, 144, 162, 165–66, 170–71,
185, 191, 204, 210, 217; Commonplace Book, 8 n., 84, 170 n.;
Defence of the People of England,
109; divorce tracts, 90–95;
Eikonoklastes, 109, 162–63; *History
of Britain,* 163; *Likeliest Means to Remove Hirelings,* 2, 85 n.; *Of Education,* 88, 135, 211; *Of Reformation,*
83–84, 86–88, 162; Prolusions,
135; *Readie and Easie Way,* 109–10;
Reason of Church-Government, 2, 84–
85, 90 n., 162, 232, 239; *Second Defence,* 96, 163; Trinity manuscript,
181, 193
Mind-body problem, 3, 17, 22–28,
68–77, 98–107, 114, 119–23, 133
Mintz, Samuel I., 13 n., 31 nn., 52
n., 207 n.
Monism, 60; Conway's, 118–24, 246;
Hebraic, 82–83, 246; More's ap-

proximation of, 74–78. *See also* Digestion as monist metaphor;
Materialism: Hobbes's mechanist;
Milton: animist materialism; War
in Heaven
More, Henry, 4, 6–7, 9 n., 10, 13 n.,
51, 53–54, 56–57, 60–78, 98, 108,
115 n., 121, 139, 144, 237, 242;
and allegory, 178, 180; and angels,
148, 152–53, 158, 161; and Conway, 117–19, 121; and Descartes,
51, 64–70, 74, 76, 245; extended
corporeal substance, 74–77; and
Hobbes, 50–51, 60–66, 68, 74, 78,
214 n., 245–46; and Milton, 4,
127–28, 132–35; "spirit of nature," 54, 68–69; "vehicles," 71–
74, 141. *See also* Cambridge Platonists; Monism
—*Works: Antidote against Atheism,* 56,
60–61, 63, 73 n., 127 n., 134, 214
n.; *Conjectura Cabbalistica,* 57, 58 n.,
64, 69, 247; *Divine Dialogues,* 65;
*Explanation of the Grand Mystery of
Godliness,* 138–39; *Immortality of the
Soul,* 53–61, 64–66, 71–75, 133,
141, 146 n., 195, 214 n.; *Platonick
Song of the Soul,* 51, 62, 70, 78, 108
n., 152–53, 161; *True Notion of a
Spirit,* 57 n., 67–68, 73–77
Mortalism, 80, 129–30. *See also* Soul,
corporeality of
Moses, 57–58, 64, 247
Murrin, Michael, 177 n., 196

Neoplatonism, 45, 70, 72, 74, 79–83,
108, 115, 123, 144, 170, 203–6,
242–43, 245
Newcastle Circle, 46
Nicholas of Cusa, 5
Nicolson, Marjorie, 4, 13 n., 30 n.,
65 n., 71 n., 117 n., 135, 158
Nominalism. *See* Allegory; Devils,
Milton's; Hobbes, Thomas

O'Keefe, Timothy, 84 n.,
Oldenburg, Henry, 10
Ontological mobility and moral value, 70–73, 77, 83, 90–91, 102–6,
119–22, 132, 194–222. *See also* De-

Ontological mobility (*cont.*)
vils, Milton's; Digestion as monist metaphor; War in Heaven
Origen, 5
Overton, Richard, 13 n.

Pagel, Walter, 71 n.
Paget, Nathan, 9, 41
Paracelsus, 46, 111–12, 154
Parker, William Riley, 11, 86 n., 97, 249
Pascal, Blaise, 125, 255
Passmore, John, 51 n., 68 n.
Patrides, C. A., 50 n., 60 n., 70 nn.
Paul, Saint, 82–86, 88, 208, 212 n. *See also* dualism
Perception, 34, 61–63
Percy, Henry (ninth earl of Northumberland), 21
Peyton, Thomas, 7, 151 n., 157, 159 n., 179, 254
Phillips, Edward, 86 n., 249 n.
Plato, 58–59, 60 n., 64, 70, 79–86, 88–89, 115, 118–19; and realism, 174–76
—Works: *Phaedo*, 81–82, 84 n.; *Phaedrus*, 80, 82–84, 86; *Republic*, 80, 174 n.; *Sophist*, 174 n.
Platonism, 22, 43, 69, 74, 96, 105, 132, 155, 157–58, 245. *See also* Dualism
Plotinus, 4, 80
Pompanazzi, Pietro, 161
Pope, Alexander, 4, 13–14
Popkin, Richard, 10 n.
Pordage, Samuel, 152–54
Protagoras, 58
Prudentius, 179
Psellus, Michael, 145 n., 155
Pseudo-Dionysius, 5, 148
Ptolemaic cosmology, 165 n.
Pythagoras, 57, 64

Quilligan, Maureen, 182–84, 190

Rabelais, François, 225
Rattansi, P. M., 46 n., 79 n.
Ray, John, 66 n.
Redondi, Pietro, 21 n.

Rees, Graham, 112–13 nn., 114
Regius, Henricus (follower of Descartes), 29
Revard, Stella Purce, 223 n.
Robins, Harry F., 5
Robinson, John A. T., 82 n.
Roche, Thomas P., Jr., 173
Rorty, Richard, 16
Roscellinus (medieval nominalist), 174 n.
Rosenfeld, Leonora C., 26 n.
Rossi, Paolo, 113 n.
Rumrich, John Peter, 5, 102 n., 112 n., 122 n., 191 n.
Rust, George, 58 n., 69, 70 n., 72, 117
Ryle, Gilbert, 205
Rymer, Thomas, 178, 182

Sadducees, 139, 166–67
Salkeld, John, 147
Samuel, Irene, 91
Sarasohn, Lisa, 43 n., 44 n.
Saurat, Denis, 4, 114 n.
Saveson, J. E., 52 n.
Schaffer, Simon, 39, 56 n.
Schmitt, Charles B., 20 n.
Schneewind, J. B., 16
Schurman, Mlle de (acquaintance of Descartes), 29
Schwartz, Regina, 190–91 n.
Scotus Erigena, 5
Shaftesbury, third earl of (Anthony Ashley Cooper), 54 n.
Shakespeare, William, 244
Shapin, Steven, 39, 56 n.
Shawcross, John T., 84 n., 184 n.
Shin, Kyungwon, 54 n.
Sidney, Sir Philip, 24 n., 163
Simonides, 14
Skinner, Quentin, 16
Smith, John (Cambridge Platonist), 52–53, 69–70
Soul, corporeality of: Bacon on, 112–14; Charleton on, 46–48; Gassendi on, 44–46; Harvey on, 115–17; Hobbes on, 33–36, 48, 129–30; Milton on, 44, 47, 100–107. *See also* Materialism; Mortalism; Spirits, corporeal

Soul, Incorporeality of, 3, 42, 64; Bacon on, 114; Cambridge Platonists on, 51; Charleton on, 46–48; Gassendi on, 45–46

Spedding, James, edition of Bacon, 89 n., 112–13 nn., 177 n.

Spenser, Edmund, 62, 70, 172–73, 203; and allegory, 177–80, 182

Spinoza, Baruch, 3, 6, 10, 40, 46 n., 108, 124, 245 n., 246

Spirits, corporeal, 27–28, 65–66, 72–74; Bacon on, 111–14; Conway on, 120–21; du Bartas on, 150; Phineas Fletcher on, 150; Milton on, 86, 96, 101–6, 120, 133–34. *See also* Soul, corporeality of

Sprat, Thomas, 14

Statius, 161

Steadman, John, 208 n.

Stein, Arnold, 182 n., 235 n.

Stoics and Stoicism, 5, 43, 45, 245

Substance, incorporeal, 3; Cambridge Platonists on, 50–59, 67–69, 74–77, 132–34, 152–53, 246; Descartes's *res cogitans*, 22–27; Gassendi on, 43, 45; Hobbes's attacks on, 33–34, 39, 128–29, 139

Summers, Joseph, 184, 233 n.

Sumner, Bishop Charles, 171 n.

Swift, Jonathan, 4

Sylvester, Joshua. *See* du Bartas, Guillaume de Salluste

Tasso, Torquato, 147, 148 n.

Taylor, Charles, 17–18

Taylor, George Coffin, 147 n.

Teskey, Gordon, 180 n.

Thomas Aquinas, 7, 22 n., 99–100, 170, 244; on angels, 141–42, 147–50, 154, 156–57, 161, 216, 217 n.; and realism, 174 n.

Thomason, Catherine (friend of Milton), 95

Tulloch, John, 65 n.

Turner, James G., 89–90 nn., 93 n., 231 n.

Typology, 242–43

Vesalius, Andreas, 104 n.

Vida, Marco Giralamo, 147–48

Virgil, 161, 163–64, 181, 213, 247

Vitalism, 6, 111–36. *See also* Conway, Anne; Milton: animist materialism

Waldensians, 85 n.

Ward, Richard, 53 n., 75 n.

War in Heaven, 184–85, 223–42, 248, 250; angels' invulnerability, 228, 234; devils' vulnerability, 226–28; Son's monist weapons, 238–40; as theodicy for devils, 234–37

Webber, Joan Malory, 229 n.

Webster, John, 57 n.

Werblowsky, R. J. Zwi, 70 n., 114–15 nn.

West, Robert H., 13 n., 144–45 nn., 147 n., 157–60

Westfall, Richard S., 16 n.

Whichcote, Benjamin (Cambridge Platonist), 60, 70–71, 117

White, Thomas, 139

Willey, Basil, 55 n.

William of Ockham, 174 n.

Williamson, George, 13 n., 134 n.

Woodhouse, A.S.P., 5, 127 n.

Worthington, John, 52 n., 117

Yolton, John W., 34 n., 63 n., 109 n.

Library of Congress Cataloging-in-Publication Data

Fallon, Stephen M. (1954–)
    Milton among the philosophers : poetry and materialism in
seventeenth-century England / Stephen M. Fallon.
      p. cm.
    Includes index.
    ISBN 0-8014-2495-X (alk. paper)
    1. Milton, John, 1608–1674—Philosophy. 2. Philosophy,
English—17th century. 3. Materialism in literature. 4. Philosophy
in literature. I. Title
PR3592.P5F35 1991
821'.4—dc20

                                            90–55729

CPSIA information can be obtained at www.ICGtesting.com
Printed in the USA
BVOW05s0736111114

374549BV00001B/2/A